Special educational needs

Special educational needs

R. Gulliford

Senior Lecturer in Education, University of Birmingham

Routledge & Kegan Paul   London

First published 1971
by Routledge & Kegan Paul Ltd
Broadway House,
68-74 Carter Lane,
London, EC4V 5EL
Printed in Great Britain by
Northumberland Press Limited
Gateshead
Set in 10/11 Juliana
© R. Gulliford 1971
No part of this book may be reproduced in
any form without permission from the
publisher, except for the quotation of
brief passages in criticism

ISBN 0 7100 7011 x (C)
0 7100 7012 8 (P)

Contents

Preface

The aim of this book is to provide teachers, and especially those taking initial, in-service and further courses of training, with a foundation of information and ideas about children with special educational needs. The personal disabilities and environmental circumstances which create special needs vary from severe ones requiring specialized teaching to mild and more frequent ones which are provided for in ordinary schools. Teachers need to be able to recognize these needs, to be aware of what can be done in ordinary schools and to know something of the work of special schools and services. It has not been the intention to describe in detail the special methods of teaching such groups of children as the visually handicapped and the hearing impaired since there are standard books available. Rather, the intention has been to provide an account which could be read as a preparation for visits and alongside lectures; which could be a starting point for more thorough study of particular handicaps through the reading lists provided. Since, however, slow learners, maladjusted and language retarded children are so frequent, their educational needs have been discussed in more detail.

I am grateful to many colleagues in special and remedial education who have read parts of this book, corrected errors and supplied helpful information.

R. Gulliford

one

Special educational needs

John is an averagely intelligent boy of twelve who has so far failed to learn to read. He co-operates well and tries desperately hard to learn. He enjoys school, especially practical activities (he is good at swimming), and takes great interest in lessons but is frustrated by his inability to write about what he knows. He has hesitant speech and finds difficulty in expressing himself. He would not really be suitably placed in a special school for educationally subnormal children yet his extreme educational failure creates a special need which is as urgent as that of children with more obvious disabilities.

Peter had a limp and one arm and hand were so weak that he made little use of them. He had a mild spastic condition which was not sufficient to require special schooling. He got on fairly well at school except that he was slow in any kind of written work and became anxious when he was not keeping up with the others. He tried to hurry and then presented poor work. Unfortunately, he was teased by other children in the playground although he tried to join in games. Fortunately, it was possible to arrange for him to go to a secondary school with a good remedial department where care was taken to allow for and help with his difficulties. He is now doing well academically and socially.

Six-year-old Joanne is quite intelligent and can do good work which her teacher makes a point of praising and encouraging. But she is a great problem because of violent moods and outbursts of aggression towards other children, sometimes towards the teacher. These occur especially when other children do something well and are praised. She has an inexhaustible need for approval, recognition and affection and limited control over her impulses. Home discipline is strict. The parents are well meaning but misguided and severe physical punishment is an accepted thing at home; it exacerbates the behaviour tendencies which it is intended to cure. This vicious circle was broken into when her parents were persuaded to adopt more positive methods of discipline and care. Joanne is now progressing more or less normally and her behaviour causes little difficulty.

This book is about children like these whose learning and adjustment are hampered by personal disabilities or environmental handicaps, often occurring together and almost inevitably having effects which spread to other aspects of their development and progress. It is part of the normal experience of teaching to meet and have to provide for such children since the majority of children with some degree of disability are catered for in ordinary classes in ordinary schools. Some require and receive special help by placement in a special class, by remedial teaching, or by the work of speech therapists, child guidance, and medical or social services. A few children with moderate or severe disabilities require special education and personal care throughout childhood and adolescence, usually with the need for continuing supervision into young adulthood.

There have always been schools and teachers taking particular trouble over children with educational, behavioural and social problems, but the concept of special education as extending into ordinary schools has only recently been more clearly and confidently expressed. The reasons for this are partly historical. In the early days of universal education, the main problem was to provide some kind of teaching for the large mass of the child population. From 1890 onwards, the needs of children with marked disabilities began to be recognized and the first special schools and classes were organized. It is not surprising that the first needs to be distinguished were those of children with obvious disabilities – the blind and the deaf – in 1893. In 1899 an Education Act was passed permitting provision for physically and mentally defective children. In the Education Act of 1921, five categories were recognized (the blind, deaf, epileptic, physically and mentally handicapped). These early enactments emphasized defect as a basis for requiring special schooling and it was also significant that 'defective' children were the subject of separate Acts or separate sections of Acts (Pritchard, 1963).

The Education Act of 1944, however, brought handicapped children within the general provisions; special educational treatment was made part of the general duty of local education authorities to ensure that children were educated in accordance with their age, ability and aptitude. The section of the Act which required education authorities to provide primary and secondary schools also required them to provide for pupils who suffer from any disability of mind or body in special schools *or otherwise*.

This legislation reflected the growing attitude that handicapped children were not to be regarded as a race apart and recognized the need to bring special schools into closer relationship with the rest of education. Moreover, in the subsequent Regulations which defined different kinds of handicap, the categories of educationally subnormal and maladjustment clearly referred to needs for special educational treatment which ranged from the most severe ones (requiring special schooling) to the less severe which could be provided for in ordinary schools. In both cases, the number of children involved is so great that it is not conceivable that special schooling should be provided for them all. Moreover, the categories were defined in *educational* terms – the need for some form of special educational treatment – rather than in terms of *defect*.

The categories defined in the Handicapped Pupils' and School Health Service Regulations 1945 were: blind, partially sighted, deaf, partially deaf (changed to partially hearing in 1962), educationally subnormal, physically handicapped, delicate, diabetic (combined with delicate in 1953), epileptic, maladjusted and speech defective. This list included some new ones – the maladjusted and the speech defective; delicate children were distinguished from the physically handicapped; the partially sighted from the blind and the partially hearing from the deaf.

Experience and research in the last twenty-five years have brought about further developments in our thinking about the nature of educational handicaps and how these should be provided for in education. In the first place, we have moved a long way from simple ideas about a few major *defects* – blindness, deafness, physical and mental defect. We think rather of *special educational needs* which may arise from personal disabilities or environmental circumstances and often from a combination of the two – and that in any case the degree of need is always relative to the contribution of both factors. In addition to the major sensory, physical and mental disabilities, we have become increasingly aware of other disabilities and circumstances which seriously affect school progress – emotional difficulties, specific learning difficulties, and cultural and social disadvantages. We have become increasingly aware of the frequency with which a marked need for special educational help is the result of a combination of several disabilities, and, indeed, that a major requirement in the future is specialized provision for children who are multi-handicapped.

It is also realized that distinctions between different kinds of special need are not clear dividing lines – while we require in practice to categorize needs we cannot inflexibly categorize children. Thus in 1945 a distinction between ordinary backward children and mentally defective children was avoided by creating the broad category of educationally subnormal, which technically included a large number of backward children in ordinary schools as well as the very backward children who needed to go to special schools or classes. We have just decided to remove another of these arbitrary divisions – between severely subnormal children who were considered 'unsuitable for education' and those subnormal children who could benefit from special education. In the field of sensory handicaps, the needs of partially sighted and partially hearing children were distinguished from those of the blind and the deaf by separate categorization in 1945. This having been accomplished, many consider it sufficient now to have categories of *visually handicapped* and *hearing impaired*; while the needs of children with different degrees of visual and hearing handicaps will still be met, some practical difficulties of making distinctions will be avoided.

Moreover, it is increasingly recognized that many of the special needs of children with one kind of major handicap are very similar to those of children with other handicaps. Thus the need for special teaching for children with mental limitations, specific learning difficulties, language and speech retardation, social and emotional handicaps occur in varying degrees in *all* handicapped groups and provide common elements in all forms of special teaching. It is also obvious that many of the problems of organization and provision are similar in all kinds of special need – diagnosis and assessment, parent guidance and practical help, pre-school education, further education and after-care. The recognition of these areas of overlap in the characteristics of children and of their needs for special services and teaching has even led to some suggestions that it is not necessary to set up categories – that it is sufficient that local education authorities should have the duty of educating all children according to their age, ability and aptitude. Many, however, consider that some broad categories are an advantage in delineating the variety of special needs for which different kinds of provision need to be organized.

We are no longer inclined to define special need in terms of particular disability but to view it in terms of the total handicap. In fact, it is helpful to make a distinction between disability and handicap. *Disability* is the kind and degree of impairment which results in some loss of capacity or function. Thus, sensory and physical defects, low innate potentialities for developing intelligence and neurological impairments can be assessed or measured for degree of impairment of function. The extent to which the impaired function becomes a *handicap* depends on many other factors. First, its importance for ordinary living and learning. Some disabilities are not much of a handicap. Defective colour vision is a serious handicap for only certain kinds of job; in school it is so little of a handicap that many children go through school unaware of it; this, however, would not be true of the disabilities of low intelligence or hearing loss. The extent to which a disability becomes a handicap depends on the society and culture we are in – to be mildly mentally retarded in a simple, illiterate society is much less of a handicap than in a modern, complex, literate one – hence our increased concern and provision for the educationally subnormal. Certain disabilities are liable to have more handicapping consequences than others. Profound deafness is in some ways a more serious handicap than blindness, since it impedes the acquisition of language and therefore affects the development of thinking as well as social communication.

This comparison also suggests that the handicap is relative to the ease with which the disability can be circumvented or compensated for. Many disabilities are no longer the educational handicap they used to be, as a result of improved medical treatment. No invention has found a completely satisfactory way round the language and communication problems of the profoundly deaf, though recently improved electronic aids have assisted with the painstaking methods of teaching. Various means have been developed, however, to improve the blind person's mobility, and the question is sometimes discussed how far the special education of some normal blind children could be organized in ordinary schools. Following this theme, we can note that some physical disabilities need be little of a handicap if the environment is organized appropriately. Thus more chairbound physically handicapped children could be educated in ordinary schools if lifts, ramps and other modifications to the buildings were made and so long as there were appropriate attitudes on the part of staff and children.

Many school factors play a large part in the degree of educational handicap arising from a disability. A child with a low level of intelligence can be unhappily handicapped in a school with predominantly bright children or where the attitudes and expectations of staff are geared to high achievements. In another school, the attitudes, methods and organization might be such that the child could be easily assimilated. His disability would not be so much a handicap. Lack of real understanding of the disability (resulting in too little, or even too much, attention) can affect the degree of handicap.

Home factors also play an important part. It is a not infrequent observation that a child with quite a severe disability gets such a quality of help, support and encouragement from home that he is able to adjust satisfactorily to normal schooling. Conversely, a mildly disabled child with unhelpful home circumstances may need to be placed in a special school. The family's effect on the degree of handicap is, of course, itself affected by the attitudes of society towards handicapped children as expressed in the attitudes of immediate neighbours or the mass media, and, most critically, in the community's readiness to provide such things as assessment, treatment, education and many other forms of help.

The provision of services to ensure early and continuing treatment and education have great significance for minimizing many handicaps. The provision of early auditory training for the deaf child is crucial. Medical treatment, physiotherapy, parent counselling and pre-school education are essential for many physically handicapped children. Recognition and treatment of emotional and learning difficulties early in the school years may prevent serious educational and social handicaps in adolescence and adult life.

Last and most important is the child himself. How educationally or socially handicapped he is by his disability depends on his intelligence, his personality, the way he is developing (especially his attitude to himself and to his disabilities and his relationships with other people), and whether he has several disabilities. While we can make some generalizations about the special needs of children with particular kinds of disability, we cannot rely exclusively on these generalizations. Whenever decisions have to be made about teaching, treatment, educational placement or employment, we have to assess individual needs and potentialities.

To summarize: we have moved forward from the position of identifying defects of mind and body as a basis for education in *special schools* to the recognition of special needs for education and personal care resulting from a complex of personal and environmental factors and that these needs may be met in a special school, in special classes or units in ordinary schools or be the subject of some extra attention and care within the ordinary work of schools. The concept of special need is broader than previous ideas associated with handicapped children and special schooling. Recognition of a relatively large number of children showing some degree of emotional unsettlement, educational retardation and social disadvantage, means that measures for providing special help in ordinary schools must receive more attention in terms of organization, methods of teaching and the training of teachers. It is no longer possible to make a sharp division between special and ordinary schools; this is another line of demarcation which is disappearing.

Organizing education for children with special needs

During the last twenty-five years, there has been considerable growth in the amount and variety of resources for educating children with special needs. Special schools are provided for a greater variety of handicaps; some schools provide selective secondary education and others cater for children with additional handicaps. Teaching has been expanded in hospital schools and home teaching has become an established service. Special classes and units and other means of giving special teaching in ordinary schools have developed and it is recognized that this is a field in which more needs to be done. Remedial teaching and advisory services have grown up as a means of helping children who have difficulties in learning. Other peripatetic teachers (such as those for the deaf) are probably just the beginning of a new development to support the work of ordinary schools. Services for teaching English to non-English-speaking pupils have developed quickly in areas where they are needed. In addition to special and remedial education, the term 'compensatory education' has received some currency to refer to a variety of modifications of education required for children whose social and cultural background limits their capacity for and response to education.

This variety of resources has grown up in response to a variety of needs, and it is important to attempt some clarification of the different purposes they serve – even though the needs often overlap.

Special education offers a continuous form of special teaching for children who need either special environment, special medical treatment, special methods of teaching or a special curriculum. For some handicapped children, it is needed over most of their school life; for others a return to ordinary schooling becomes possible at some stage, and for others still (such as some ill or physically handicapped children) special education may be required during the period of months or years when their illness is being treated.

Remedial education tends to be part-time, relatively short-term and limited to specific objectives such as remedying failures or difficulty in learning certain school subjects, especially in basic educational skills. It is teaching which is additional to normal schooling rather than an alternative form of education.

Compensatory education embraces a great variety of modifications of curriculum, methods of teaching, educational-social work required by pupils whose development has been retarded by cultural and social limitations. Thus, younger children need emphasis on language and other aspects of readiness for schooling; older pupils need a purposeful, well motivated school experience. In some areas, the whole work of the school may be described as compensatory; in others, only a few pupils may need compensatory procedures, e.g. liaison between school and home and with social work services, and close attention to individual physical and psychological needs.

These terms are not mutually exclusive. Some children in special education also need elements of a remedial and compensatory approach. Some children receiving remedial education would be better served by special education either in a special school or in special classes. Distinguishing the terms in theory, however, helps to distinguish aims and requirements in practice. Although the term 'remedial' is commonly applied to work with slow learners in second-ary schools, it would be unfortunate if the association of 'remedial' with 'basic subjects' led to a restricted view of the task. Some slow learners in secondary schools require 'special' education and some need 'compensatory' education.

Organizing special education

The first and overriding aim of any form of organization is that child-ren should receive the special treatment and education that they need in order to ensure their optimum development and to minimize their handicaps. Ways are increasingly sought of achieving this aim while avoiding the disadvantages of separation from normal children and separation for lengthy periods from the family. Clearly it is diffi-cult, both economically and efficiently, to provide seriously handi-capped children with the expert teaching or specialized treatment they need without gathering them together in one place. In the case of less common handicaps (e.g. blindness) or, in thinly populated areas for other handicaps, residential schooling is often necessary. Even so, there is an increasing trend for weekly boarding and for using part-time attendance at local normal schools for pupils who are ready for it. There is also discussion of the idea that some special day schools might be organized for a range of handicapped children who might otherwise have needed residential placement – but the teaching of the different groups would have to be very well organized to achieve the aim stated at the beginning of this paragraph.

A report, *Living with Handicap* (National Bureau for Co-operation in Child Care, 1970), points out that there are at least thirteen different ways of providing for handicapped children. While some children require full-time day or residential schooling, there are various modi-fications between this and full integration in ordinary schools: (1) Full-time residential special schools. (2) Hospital schools. (3) Resi-dential special schools with provision on a five-day-week-basis. (4) Resi-dential special schools serving as a base from which pupils attend appropriate ordinary schools in the neighbourhood, full-time or part-time. (5) Residential hostels providing tutorial help for pupils attend-ing normal schools full-time. (6) Multi-purpose hostels providing for a variety of handicapped pupils and also providing short-stay facilities for children in care, holiday facilities for handicapped children and relief in family crises. (7) Day special schools. (8) Day special schools allowing some pupils to attend neighbouring ordinary schools part-time. (9) Special classes in ordinary schools and special units attached to ordinary schools. (10) Peripatetic teaching, e.g. remedial teachers and peripatetic teachers of the deaf. (11) Resource centres in ordinary schools, i.e. bases for materials, equipment, remedial and other specialist teachers. (12) Full integration in ordinary schools. (13) Home teaching.

Residential education has some very pronounced advantages as well as some disadvantages. A boarding school permits a more intensive approach to a child's needs through the creation of an environment and school community which is educative and therapeutic without interruption and discontinuity. Clearly this is an advantage for many maladjusted children whose home environments are emotionally and/or culturally impoverished. The corresponding disadvantages could be in some cases that the child is being educated out of the context of his home and neighbourhood. This is a factor which has to be considered in decisions about placement. Many schools for maladjusted children rightly insist on social work with the home continuing while the child is away, and in other schools weekly boarding enables the child to maintain contacts with his family at weekends. There is also the danger that the residential school may be remote from normal life so that the social understanding and social competence skills required by so many children are not acquired and exercised. Residential schools are aware of this and plan accordingly; it is perhaps an advantage when a school is placed on the edge of a town rather than in a remote country mansion.

Residential education is undesirable for young children; it ought to be avoidable except as a last resort with junior-age children, and with adolescents we should perhaps use it only if parents wish it or if there is no practicable way of satisfactorily providing treatment and care in the community (e.g. multi-handicaps), or if boarding education is an important element in the prescription (as with many maladjusted children). In spite of these qualifications, it should be said that the boarding education provided in the British system of special education is a great asset permitting the rehabilitation of many children who would otherwise founder.

Apart from hostels for maladjusted children and residential accommodation provided in secondary and special schools in thinly populated areas, there has not been much experiment in the use of hostels. Hostels have been strongly advocated as a means of avoiding hospital living for the severely subnormal, and several are now operating.

Special school or ordinary school?

It is frequently stated that wherever possible handicapped children should be educated in ordinary schools. No one disagrees with this assertion. The question is, what is meant by 'wherever possible'? This calls for a careful assessment of the child's needs and of certain essential requirements in the ordinary school – the knowledge, attitudes and teaching skills of the staff and the atmosphere and organization of the school.

Special schooling is most obviously required when there is a need for special treatment (physiotherapy, nursing care), special equipment or modified buildings, specialized methods of teaching (teaching for the deaf; braille; special methods for the intellectually handicapped) or the creation of a particular kind of learning environment (for the maladjusted and some kinds of learning disability). It is an advantage of the special school that it facilitates the concentration of equipment and resources. It also facilitates the economical use of medical, psychological and other specialists, such as speech therapists, visiting regularly. This also avoids children's lengthy visits to clinics, and promotes co-operation and understanding between teachers and specialists – the latter, for example, are able to appreciate the educational handicap of the child's condition and its treatment rather than merely the disability.

There are, however, less obvious but more important aspects of special schooling which could well be the ones to suffer from a casual assumption that ordinary schooling is an easy alternative. First, special schooling is able to provide continuity of education and understanding of the child (in some cases starting in the pre-school period). There can be clearly defined aims and a well-planned progression of education in all its aspects including preparation for and supervision of transition to working life. The staff of a special school acquire an intimate knowledge of the problems and methods in their field, a close knowledge of pupils and their families, and not least of the benefits is that new teachers in a special school receive an *ad hoc* but effective in-service training.

These values can of course be maintained in a system of special classes or units in ordinary schools but must be planned and worked for. For example, there must be sufficient special classes to span the age range so that children progress from stage to stage and so that any class does not have too wide an age range. There must be someone who can give the leadership and co-ordination which the headteacher does in a special school. Specially trained teachers are needed – one cannot appoint a teacher inexperienced in special work as one can in a special school, where he would get the help and guidance of colleagues. There would be a greater need for inspectors and advisers in special education who can supervise the work of special classes, encourage educational developments and, by occasional staff conferences, promote the exchange of ideas and experience which occurs easily in a special school. The processes of selection, admission and psycho-educational assessment of pupils need to be carefully organized.

It is often a disadvantage that special schooling separates children from their fellows, missing the stimulation, interests and social learning from mixing with others. Travelling away from their own neighbourhood reduces the opportunities of making friends locally and the length and inconvenience of travelling time is not to be ignored. These disadvantages are compensated for if children can get the special help they need and would not otherwise get. It must be recognized that special schooling is a relief from the strain of trying to keep up and match up; it can be a relief from always feeling or being made to feel different.

For the average or bright child, disadvantage may occur academically at the secondary stage because of the relatively small numbers and limited staff resources. Selective secondary education is available for handicapped children, though this usually means boarding education. For others, many schools are arranging part-time attendance at local secondary schools and an increasing number of schools enter children for external examinations. A survey by Martin (1969) of examination work in schools for physically handicapped, delicate and partially sighted children reported 45 per cent of schools entering some pupils for examinations, and the number is growing.

With all these qualifications there is no doubt that some children now in special schools could be catered for in ordinary schools if special classes were well organized for them. In a few areas, special classes for backward children have been organized instead of, or as a supplement to, special schools, but in most places the backward children are simply catered for in the C stream or the 'remedial' department with an approach which often falls short of what is required. Partially sighted children, owing to their small numbers, have sometimes been accommodated in special classes, often suffering from too wide an age range and lack of direction. There are fifteen classes at present. The development of partially hearing units is an example of successful provision for handicapped children in ordinary schools. They were started in 1947 and increased rapidly after 1960 so that in 1968 there were 215 units with 1,498 children. A survey of these units provides one of the few accounts of the problems of special class organization and many of the comments would have application for other groups of handicapped children (see p. 147). According to the Health of the School Child 1966-8, there were also 12 classes for delicate children, 159 for maladjusted and 35 for physically handicapped.

The issue of special schools or special classes is often discussed on an either-or basis which is quite clearly unrealistic. Both are needed. As has been said already, more children could be educated in ordinary schools if special classes were well organized, staffed with specially trained teachers and well-supported by health, psychological and advisory services. This would still leave many children whose handicaps are so severe that intensive special education would be needed. This applies to many children with severe disabilities but it is the severity of total educational and social *handicap* (following our earlier discussion) which is the right way to think about it. The increasing number of children with additional disabilities and those whom we can categorize as multi-handicapped suggests no decrease in the number of children requiring special schooling – rather some reorientation of the special school's role as is happening in schools for the physically handicapped. Similarly the function of schools for educationally subnormal children needs reconsideration, possibly by concentrating on intellectual handicap so that children whose serious educational retardation is environmentally induced should be educated in special classes in ordinary schools.

Remedial teaching

Remedial teaching organized in various ways has a potentially important role. There has been quite a rapid expansion of remedial teaching services since the late 1940s when public concern grew about the large number of backward readers in schools. Some remedial teachers work in schools with groups and individuals who need extra help, especially early in the junior school. In a few cases they work in centres which children attend several times a week. More frequently they are peripatetic teachers visiting a number of schools to teach groups and in some well organized services giving advice on materials and methods, undertaking surveys and other services. Their work should be closely integrated with the school psychological services. Sometimes they work in and from child guidance centres.

As Sampson (1968 b) points out in reporting the result of a survey of remedial teaching, the original aim of remedial teaching was to remedy educational retardation, i.e. children who were failing educationally but normal in ability. It soon became apparent that remedial teachers could not concentrate on 'under-functioning' children and, as Sampson's survey shows, remedial teachers have been trying to help schools cope with children who are backward because of social and cultural limitations, lowish ability and emotional difficulties. Some of these children need special *education* rather than remedial teaching. The remedy for junior school children who are slow to acquire basic educational skills is not twice-weekly sessions with a remedial teacher but the provision of good teaching, smaller classes, an active child-centred approach emphasizing language development and experience. Remedial teaching has sometimes been used as a palliative, whereas more radical remedies are needed. This is not to say that remedial teaching, especially when it includes an advisory element, does not provide a very useful service. But the training and experience of remedial teachers should perhaps be focused increasingly on the children who have specific and severe learning disabilities – children for whom something more than good teaching seems to be needed.

Comprehensive services for children with special needs

Though the teacher is naturally inclined to focus on the child at school age, the community as a whole should, and is gradually trying to, plan for the *prevention* of disabilities and other circumstances which give rise to special needs, for their *identification* at the earliest possible time and for thorough *diagnosis and assessment* of medical, educational and social needs. A wide variety of services is needed to provide continuing assessment and treatment, support and help to the family and of course a range of facilities to provide education. As the child's school life draws to a close, other services relating to employment, social work and further education should dovetail into the work of the school.

Prevention has many aspects. More is continually being discovered about the transmission of inherited defects so that genetic counselling should be available to prospective parents who are known to be at risk of having a defective child. Medically, improvements have been made in pre-natal care, at birth and in the immediate period after birth, and efforts are continually being made to identify and overcome some of the hazards of this most vulnerable period in life. The preventive role of medical care extends into the early recognition and treatment of disabilities discussed in the next section. Early treatment may not only minimize the handicap but may prevent secondary physical and psychological ones.

An important aspect of this is the provision of guidance, information and practical help to parents especially when serious disabilities are diagnosed. The attitudes set up at this early stage, the effectiveness of the parents' contribution to nurturing the child's development and the family's adjustment to the presence of a handicapped child can make a considerable difference to the child's future progress and personality. Many studies give an insight into these needs: Tizard and Grad (1961) with the mentally handicapped; Hare (1966) with spina bifida children; Langdon (1968) with the blind; S. Hewett (1970) with the cerebral palsied. Parents are in an unfamiliar situation. To start the deaf child on the long road to communication, the visually handicapped child to exploring and understanding his environment, the mentally handicapped to acquiring language and personal competence requires advice, information and demonstration from those who are experienced and skilled. Parents want to help. Most of them also want to know something of the way ahead – will he go to school? Will he be able to work? Definite answers cannot always be given but the route can be indicated and the parents' role in the present can be explained. All this requires not one discussion but many, with the possibility continually open to parents of coming back to the source of information and guidance. This is an aspect of prevention and care which has been left too much to chance. A more co-ordinated system of guidance and counselling is needed (Carnegie, 1964).

A similar need is recognized in the field of social work. Since the Children and Young Persons Act 1963, Children's Departments have been trying to swing the emphasis towards prevention rather than coping with family crises; the new Children's Act 1969 takes this a step further. In this preventive work, education and social work must work ever more closely together as more trained personnel become available.

Education itself has important preventive aspects. Education for parenthood, family and social living should be an element in the secondary curriculum and an important one for those whose own background creates the likelihood of perpetuating the inadequacies and maladjustments which have hampered their own personal development. In the pre-school years, nursery education provides a significant means of influencing parents as well as a means of drawing attention to and helping to remedy deviations from normal development. But there is a great area for experiment in reaching a greater number of parents and especially for getting through to the non-coping families whose mothers cannot organize themselves to take advantage of nursery schools and play groups and whose inadequate living conditions and poor methods of child care go virtually unrelieved.

At the age of five, when the majority of children come for the first time under organized and continuous observation, preventive aspects of education are accepted routinely as part of the normal work of infant schools, though some perform this role more readily and actively than others. There is a great need to consider what more can be done at this critical stage of readiness for learning to compensate for inequalities of experience and nurture or to make an early start on alleviating the effects of minor disabilities.

The pupil-centred attitudes and home-school links of the infant school are spreading upwards through junior and secondary schools but, not being such an intrinsic feature of the approach, need to be organized.

Much depends too on awareness and observation by teachers who recognize early the signs of emotional, social and learning difficulties. All too often teachers of older pupils are trying to cope with problems which might have been reduced or avoided by earlier preventive action.

The first responsibility for the *identification* of children likely to have special needs is a medical one. In recent years, most local health authorities have kept an 'observation' register of babies born 'at risk' of handicapping conditions; unfavourable family history (e.g. deafness); adverse pre-natal factors (e.g. rubella – german measles – contracted during the first three months of pregnancy); abnormality of the birth process; prematurity, low birth weight or poor condition in the post-natal period. These children have been followed up by health visitors, paediatricians and infant welfare doctors to ensure that disabilities are detected early and treatment instituted. This procedure has not been without its problems, since even if as many as 40 per cent of babies are placed on the register, less than 60 per cent of handicapped children will be identified. It is important therefore that all young children should be screened for disabilities and difficulties in development. Two examples of this are screening for phenylketonuria which occurs only about once in every 10,000 births; screening for hearing impairment can begin at about nine months of age. Procedures have been devised for screening vision. Health services are taking these responsibilities seriously and progress is being made towards efficient and early identification.

Moderate degrees of disability may however be overlooked in the pre-school period and emotional and educational handicaps may not be distinguishable until children have been at school for a while. The first point underlines the importance of the medical examination at school entry and the second point stresses the importance of teachers' observations and judgments about pupils.

It is sometimes assumed that the doctors' role is to examine only for physical defects affecting vision, hearing and movement, heart and lungs and to assess general physical condition. But school doctors are increasingly alerted to developmental and minor neurological factors which may have significance for children's learning and behaviour. In some places, parents' questionnaires provide information which have this wider relevance. Teachers can also provide observations which are of the utmost value and they should not hesitate to draw attention to features of a child's behaviour, learning or health which concern them. Assessment is a co-operative activity and it should not be assumed that the doctor is doing the whole of the job.

After pupils have been in school for several terms, it is possible to

distinguish those with difficulties in learning who need some form
of special help. The National Child Development Study of nearly
11,000 seven-year-olds (Pringle *et al.*, 1966) attempted to assess the
extent of this need in infant classes. Headteachers were asked, 'Apart
from anything which the class teacher may be able to do in the
normal way, is the child receiving any help within the school because of mental or educational backwardness?' Five per cent of the
children were having such help (7 per cent boys; 4 per cent girls) and
it was thought that a further 8 per cent who were not having help
would benefit. The headteachers were further asked, 'Do you consider, irrespective of the facilities in your area, that the child would
benefit *now* from attendance at a special school?' It was thought
that 2 per cent would benefit (2·6 per cent of boys; 1·4 per cent of
girls). For a further 1·8 per cent headteachers were uncertain; 0·4 per
cent of the sample were already in special schools.

These figures suggest that headteachers do not have difficulty at
the end of the infant school in identifying children who need some
form of special educational help. The 2 per cent judged to be in need
of special schooling should be referred for assessment so that, if the
need is confirmed, an early start in special education can be made.
This does not always happen, children continuing to be referred at
later ages and even after eleven years.

It would be an advantage if there were a more systematic procedure
for identifying children needing special help, partly to ensure that
early help is given and partly to provide information about the extent
of special need. Remedial and school psychological services often undertake 'screening' procedures in the first and second years in the
junior school in order to identify backward children. Screening could
also be undertaken at the infant school stage drawing upon teachers'
observations and supplemented by performance on a number of critical tasks – reading, writing, drawing, etc. It would be an added advantage if such a procedure drew attention to children with other special
difficulties – persisting speech difficulties, emotional and behavioural
problems and specific learning difficulties (see de Hirsch, p. 92).

An attempt to ensure early identification of difficulties in the infant school would need to be followed by careful observation and
assessment of progress later. Hopes of progress might not be realized;
the existence of real difficulties might not become apparent until later.
So the more usual surveys in the junior school would still be needed
and after transfer to secondary schools, a determined attack on remaining educational difficulties is essential. Unfortunately, in present
circumstances the number of children still needing special help at this
age continues to be quite high. Although national standards of attainment have risen, there are still about 10 per cent of ten-to-twelve-year-
old pupils with reading ages below eight years and in some areas of

course the proportion is much higher. There are also the children who are suffering the effects of environmental handicaps which are liable to produce backwardness and unhappiness, if not outright troublesome behaviour. If early remedial and compensatory efforts are to be made on their behalf, there is need for good communication between primary and secondary schools and for some arrangements whereby difficulties in learning and personal adjustment are noticed and helped.

Assessment should follow the identification of disability and should be continuous so that reassessment occurs at intervals and at any time during childhood, especially at critical points such as school entry, making decisions about school placement and at school leaving. Three main elements should be included: *medical*, with whatever specialist examinations are needed to assess the disability and to look for additional ones; *psychological* and *educational*, to assess the child's developmental and educational needs; *social*, to assess the needs of the family and environmental factors in the child's development. It is inefficient if a child's condition is assessed and treated by sophisticated medical procedures but his developmental and educational needs are only vaguely assessed and the parent's needs for advice and help are imperfectly recognized and provided for. A multidisciplinary approach is needed to the total handicap. There has been considerable discussion in recent years about the means of organizing this. In addition to shortages of personnel with specialized skills, assessment services are of several different kinds and work in different places with resulting difficulties of communication. To remedy this, assessment centres of various kinds have been proposed in which the three main elements are represented and able to draw upon a variety of other special skills and diagnostic services. Such assessment centres or teams are likely to be of various kinds. Some will need to be highly specialized and regionally placed so that they can draw upon a variety of hospital services. Some may be less specialized and more local in character. Some may be organized as diagnostic or observation units in which children can be observed over a period and their response to education and care included in the assessment. Good communication with health, education and social services departments, general practitioners and schools is essential and co-ordination of the efforts of different workers must be achieved.

Meanwhile, there is a wide range of services which can be called in to co-operate with schools in the care of children with special needs.

The *School Health Service* which was established in 1907 to provide medical inspection soon extended its functions to the provision of clinics and treatment. Nowadays, while medical inspections of all school entrants continue to be an important function, more thorough examination of selected groups of pupils has tended to take the place of later examinations, the children being selected on the basis of questionnaires to parents or teachers and in response to special requests from teachers and health visitors. The role of the teacher in bringing to the notice of doctors children who cause them some concern is therefore an important one and is often a first step to obtaining the help of other services. Through local authority health services and the National Health Service the school medical service is able to draw upon a wide range of specialist examinations. The school doctor and particularly the school nurse are often able to help with social problems through their previous knowledge of families or the area.

The *Child Guidance Clinic* provides for the examination and treatment of children who are having pronounced difficulties in their development. The basic team includes a psychiatrist who is a doctor with training in child psychiatry, a psychiatric social worker whose training in social work includes an emphasis on mental health problems, and an educational psychologist who in addition to his psychological training has experience as a teacher. In addition the team may include a psychotherapist who is concerned mainly with treatment by play therapy or other means and a remedial teacher involved mainly in various kinds of educational treatment. Paediatricians, speech therapists and other workers may contribute to the clinic work but, in any case, referral for a wide range of specialist examinations occurs – hearing, vision; paediatric and neurological examinations.

The usual practice in clinics is to make a thorough study of the problem referred: the psychologist assessing the child's abilities, disabilities, attainments and personality; the social worker focusing on the child's development, the family, and the child's present situation in it; the psychiatrist looking at both medical and psychological aspects of the child and family. The diversity of information is thoroughly discussed at a case conference with a view to treatment within the clinic, advice to the school, and requests for the help of other medical or social agencies.

In most places, educational psychologists also work within a school psychological service assessing educational problems, helping to identify children who need special education, and advising teachers. In most places also a *remedial teaching service* functions as part of the service. Remedial teachers may give remedial teaching to groups and individuals, provide advice on organization, methods and materials as well as initiate new educational approaches. Through their close contact with schools and the use of surveys and screening procedures they help to identify and arrange treatment for children who need it. Any teacher who feels a lack of knowledge about suitable methods and materials for a backward class or child should seek contact with remedial teachers or with the educational psychologist. Services often have a central display of materials and organize courses on remedial methods.

Speech therapists are not, as is sometimes supposed, concerned only with correcting defective articulation. They are also concerned with helping children who have difficulties and disorders in the development of language and speech and their work requires an ability to assess the child's development as a person in the family and as a learner in school. They like to work in close collaboration with psychologists, doctors and, not least, teachers. The shortage of speech therapists means that they have had increasingly to work through advice to teachers, conserving their time for the more difficult problems of children with the most marked language disorders.

Collaboration between *social work* and education is essential if the needs described in this book are to be satisfactorily catered for. There are many hopeful signs of progress : schools are increasingly looking for ways of improving co-operation; the Local Authority Social Services Act 1970 should lead to better co-ordination of social work. This act combines local authority social work services, referred to below, into a social services department which should in time result in a more coherent and co-ordinated pattern of service.

At present, there are several channels between home and school. Apart from any work undertaken by the school staff, the *Education Welfare Officer* has traditionally been a source of information about and contact with individual homes. His work varies according to local requirements and has been limited by the fact that he is not a trained social worker. Whatever the pattern in the future, it is to be hoped that social workers will be available to be as closely linked as they have been with the schools.

Children's Departments were set up in 1948 to care for children who have for some reason to be cared for away from their own parents or relatives. Since 1963 Children's Departments have been given the duty of preventive work to reduce the need for children to come into care or to be brought before the courts so that in practice many kinds of adverse family circumstance affecting the children can lead to help from the Children's Officer. The Children's and Young Persons Act 1969 carries this preventive function a stage further (p. 132).

Several other services may be appropriate for cases where particular problems occur in a family. *Mental Welfare Officers* keep in touch with families where a member has recently had a mental illness or in which there is a mentally handicapped person. *Probation Officers* are social workers attached to the courts and in addition to working with children on probation they may be supervising the rehabilitation of ex-prisoners, helping prisoners' families or helping couples with matrimonial problems. In many areas, there is fruitful co-operation between local *police* and schools and in efforts such as Police Juvenile Liaison Schemes to help reduce delinquency.

NSPCC inspectors work closely with Children's Departments. Their special experience of families where there is neglect or cruelty can usefully be drawn on when such cases occur in school and also for more general preventative work. In some areas, there are *Family Service Units* working with the families in greatest need.

There is a variety of other services which may need to be known about – the Department of Health and Social Security for its financial assistance where a parent is unable to work; Citizen's Advice Bureaux, Councils of Social Service, Council for Community Relations, Liaison Officers for various immigrant groups, community service volunteers of various kinds, local churches, WRVS and many other sources locally for obtaining material assistance, holidays and clothing for children and families.

Co-operation between education and social work does not depend only on knowledge of the functions of different kinds of social worker. It also requires some understanding of the differences in aims and methods of approach in social work. Whereas the experience and training of the teacher may lead him to believe that some useful advice or firm talk is the answer, the social worker sees the problem as first understanding the family situation and making a relationship through which advice and help can be given. Depending on the problem, the social worker modifies attitudes, increases understanding and helps the family to help themselves. The social worker also views the family as a whole rather than simply the child and this often results in teachers and social workers having rather different ideas about the family and what can be done.

This chapter has referred to a great variety of services for children with special needs and their families. As will be seen in the following chapters, provision does not always match the need. In particular, more attention now needs to be given to the ways in which special help can be organized in ordinary schools, to the furthering of co-operation with parents and in the co-ordination of various kinds of medical, psychological, social and educational help.

Further reading

CENTRAL ADVISORY COUNCIL FOR EDUCATION (1967), *Children and their Primary Schools* (The Plowden Report), Chs. 5, 6, 7, 21 and Appendix 10.
CLEGG, A. AND MEGSON, B. (1968), *Children in Distress*, Harmondsworth: Penguin.

DEPARTMENT OF EDUCATION AND SCIENCE (1969), *The Health of the School Child,* Report of the Chief School Medical Officer of the Department of Education and Science 1966-8, London: H.M.S.O.

GULLIFORD, R. (1969), *Backwardness and Educational Failure,* National Foundation for Educational Research.

JACKSON, S. (1969), *Special Education in England and Wales,* Oxford University Press.

KERSHAW, J. D. (1961), *Handicapped Children,* London: Heinemann.

SCHOOLS COUNCIL WORKING PAPER 27 (1969), *Cross'd with Adversity,* London: Evans Methuen Educational.

SHERIDAN, M. D. (1965), *The Handicapped Child and his Home,* National Children's Home.

WEBB, L. (1967), *Children with Special Needs in the Infant School,* Gerrards Cross: Colin Smythe.

WORKING PARTY ON HANDICAPPED CHILDREN (1970), *Living with Handicap,* National Bureau for Co-operation in Child Care.

two

Special kinds
of teaching

A great variety of impediments to learning are discussed in the following chapter. Are there any characteristics which are common to the teaching required? From one point of view, the differences are so great – for example, between teaching a class of blind children and a class of backward children from poor environments – that the question may seem rather absurd. From another point of view, it could be said that their main common requirement is good teaching; which is certainly true. But just as one could describe and distinguish the characteristics of good infant teaching and those of good sixth-form teaching, it should be possible to attempt to describe the elements common to teaching children with special educational needs.

The aims of special teaching are basically the same as for any kind of education; but there is a difference in the order of priorities. In the education of ordinary children whose development is within the normal range, it is appropriate that educational progress should be the teacher's main aim – which should not mean that other aspects of personal development are neglected. In the education of children with special needs, the first priority is to promote the optimum development of the child's capacities and personality. Disabilities and environmental handicaps bring about uneven development and it is essential to do everything possible to compensate for the direct effects of the handicap and also to avoid side-effects such as emotional unsettlement, immaturity or social isolation. Much more than in ordinary teaching, the special teacher has to be observant of children's development and accept the responsibility for guiding it.

This priority has many practical consequences. The teacher requires an intimate knowledge and understanding of the individual child – his strengths and weaknesses in mental abilities, his different levels of emotional, social and physical maturity, the particular effects on him of the handicap, the influence of home and family. The teacher requires a knowledge of the stages and processes of development so that he can recognize and provide for needs which are much at variance with the child's actual age. He must in short be at least as much interested in children and how they develop as in what he wishes to teach. Indeed he must be prepared to select and modify what and how he teaches to meet the needs he recognizes in his pupils. It follows that he does not judge the success of his work *only* in terms of improved academic attainments. He can feel a sense of achievement from even small signs that the child is beginning to realize his potentialities, overcome his disabilities, be ready for learning or group participation and displaying more confidence and competence as a person. It also follows that he puts more stress on teacher-pupil relationships; he will be more involved in the lives of his pupils – often indeed compensating for the inadequacies of home relationships or correcting the balance when over-expectation, over-protection or rejection are adversely affecting the child's growth.

This emphasis on all-round growth does not, however, mean relegating academic attainments and the acquisition of knowledge to a poor second place. Though second in the order of priorities they require equal attention. The fact that a variety of circumstances – sensory and mental deficits, ill health, absence, environmental circumstances – are liable to cause educational retardation indicates the importance of ensuring the best conditions for efficient learning. Some of the conditions are:

The need to be clear about educational objectives With some children, the goals are the same as those for ordinary children of the same level of ability, and little modification of curriculum, though probably of method, is required. With some whose ability to learn is limited the aims and content of the curriculum need to be formulated in terms of pupils' present needs for development and their future needs after leaving school. A third group of children who, as far as can be predicted, are unlikely to be independent and capable of open employment need an emphasis on social competence and a preparation for 'planned dependence' (see Gardner (1969) for a discussion of this concept).

The effects of the handicap on learning capacity This should be known so that appropriate expectations can be set and modifications of method made. For example, the intellectually handicapped child is liable to be weak in selecting what is important and relevant to attend to in learning and in generalization and transfer. The environmentally handicapped child may be weak not so much in learning potentiality as in knowing how to set about learning and in responding to the normal motives for learning. The consequences of visual and hearing impairments for experience and modes of learning have to be fully understood.

Appraisal of learning abilities and disabilities The notion that a child's capacity to learn is adequately indicated by his level of intelligence as assessed informally by the teacher or measured by an intelligence test is now seen to require considerable qualification. Level of intelligence has to be considered in relation to other factors – sensory and physical disabilities, the child's personality, the degree of home interest and encouragement. Moreover, learning depends on a wide range of mental functions: perceptual and perceptual-motor processes; language; conceptual and reasoning development; and each of these can be sub-divided into component functions. The task of special teaching is increasingly seen to require a diagnostic assessment of these functions, especially in cases of severe retardation and learning difficulty. The nature of assessment is discussed further on p. 30.

Planning sequences of learning It is a feature of special teaching that the teaching of critical skills should be well planned and systematically carried out. This is true of teaching language to deaf children, of reading and number in the educationally subnormal, of social competence skills with subnormal pupils. It is also true of methods designed to remedy specific weaknesses in perceptual and other functions revealed by diagnostic assessment. However, a systematic approach is often thought to conflict with other values that teachers rightly hold dear – the values of incidental learning experiences, of enjoyable spontaneous opportunities for learning, of highly motivating activities, of 'whole' experiences rather than isolated learning of specific skills. There need be no conflict. Rather the equal dangers of an overemphasis on either a formal, structured or an informal, unstructured approach should be recognized. The systematic teaching of language in a deaf school does not preclude – indeed it draws life from, the visit to a town – from talking about personal experiences and from a lively school environment. A well organized scheme of teaching reading does not conflict with a varied activity method in an infant school. The crucial point is that the structure of the method, the sequence of learning, should be clearly in the teacher's mind.

The importance of motivation Good motivation is desirable in any form of teaching but is essential for children with special needs. The need raises many issues: content and methods of teaching, teacher-pupil relationships; school-home co-operation; personality development, especially the question of pupils' attitudes towards themselves – their self-concepts.

Assessment of progress Checking that learning is proceeding adequately is even more important than with ordinary children. The basis for this assessment is the teacher's knowledge of the normal progression in learning such skills as language, reading, writing, primary mathematics and social competence. Assessment is facilitated if the school has developed sequences of materials and activities which, apart from their teaching purposes, also indicate the progress being made. Methods of recording progress can be related to these. Additional checks can be obtained by using attainment tests where suitable ones are available.

A third aim which is to the fore in the thinking of teachers in special education is the need to ensure that children are being educated so that they have the best preparation for successful adjustment to living and working in the community after they have left school. While this is not forgotten with ordinary children, this aim reflects a particular urgency for many handicapped children : the child with low intelligence is likely to have greater difficulty in managing the problems of living in modern society; sensory and physical disabilities create problems of communication and mobility. This again prompts consideration of the relative importance of academic goals and those of personal and social growth. While adequate educational achievement is a distinct advantage in relation to possible jobs and even more for functioning in a literate society, experience and research show that personality and social adjustment are *relatively* more important. A young person with good personal attributes and an ability to get on with other people is more likely to be successful than one with good academic attainment but inadequacies of personality. In practice, of course, it is desirable to achieve both.

This social aim has significance for the curriculum whether conceived as what is learnt systematically through schemes of work or incidentally as opportunities arise. Handicaps tend to limit, sometimes severely so, the child's experience and awareness of his social environment. Much knowledge and experience which comes incidentally to average children through their own activities or those of their families cannot be taken for granted in children with special needs, and it is necessary to consider how visits, journeys, audio-visual aids, social and environmental studies can assist both academic progress and the social aim of education. A social bias in the curriculum provides a rational alternative to the proverbial 'watered-down' academic curriculum.

For some young children and older multiply handicapped children, there is a job to be done in enabling the child to look after himself in toileting, dressing and feeding. In ordinary education, it is only nursery and infant teachers for whom this is an element in their work. In many branches of special education, the teaching of social competence skills – self-help, occupation, socialization and communication – is a major task prior to or alongside academic or pre-academic learning. As with all children, there is a need to develop the capacity to occupy themselves independently through interests and leisure activities and with adolescents special attention is needed for preparation for school leaving and post-school living.

Planning curricula for children with special needs

Each kind of special teaching has its own specialized methods and techniques for teaching children with particular handicaps. With the educationally subnormal, the failure to learn basic educational skills looms large; with deaf pupils, the teaching of language and communication is a central concern; with maladjusted children, it is the treatment of emotional and behavioural problems. As we have seen, teachers are also concerned with broader issues of personal growth and social adjustment and are aware of the many kinds of learning and experience needed by their pupils. There is plenty of inspired experiment in different methods and many worthwhile activities are introduced to provide a broadly based education. It is seldom, however, that the curriculum as a whole becomes the subject of scrutiny and discussion.

An examination of the aims of special education and how these are translated into schemes of work could be a fruitful exercise for staff as a whole to undertake. It is perhaps most likely to have value where the kind of education requires a different kind of emphasis from that of the normal academic curriculum of a primary or secondary school. For example, backward children in secondary schools need work which has been well thought out in terms of its purposes and pupils' needs and capacities; the education of the severely subnormal will require an even more radical departure from the traditional conception of the curriculum.

Taylor (1970) has provided an outline of the steps required in formulating a curriculum plan. The first step is to decide on the general aims of education for the pupils in question. In many special teaching situations, *social* education is considered an important goal. Is this sufficient? Some would suggest that apart from aiming to promote social competence and adjustment, many aspects of special education aim at promoting *personal* development. Others might wish to specify other broad aims. The discussion of general aims among a group of teachers is itself a useful activity. Someone is sure to suggest as aims 'confidence', 'feelings of success', 'happiness' – and while everyone will agree that these are desirable aims, there is the question of how useful they are as starting points for specifying curriculum content.

The next step is to analyse the aims into *general objectives* which indicate the behaviour, skills and attitudes which are to be sought. Thus, the *personal* aim might be itemized as promoting: (1) mental abilities; (2) language skills; (3) emotional maturity; (4) social maturity; (5) fine and gross motor skills; (6) moral concepts. There are obviously other objectives which could be specified or the list could be stated quite differently. As an example of a breakdown of the *social* aim, the ten general objectives or life-functions of the Illinois Curriculum Guide can be instanced: citizenship, communication, home and family, leisure time, management of materials and money, occupational adequacy, physical and mental health, safety, social adjustment and travel. Again, other objectives could be stated according to the needs of the particular pupils.

The next step is to translate each of these general objectives into a set of *specific* objectives. Clearly these will be different for different handicaps and different ages of pupil. Thus with slow learners of primary age the *general* objective of improving mental abilities might be analysed into the following *specific* objectives: (1) auditory and visual perceptual skills; (2) hand-eye co-ordination skills; (3) perceiving and verbalizing similarities and differences; (4) sorting and classifying; (5) concepts of seriation and conservation; (6) ability to engage in constructive, experimental and imaginative play; and so on. With adolescent physically handicapped children, the *general* objective of *emotional* maturity could be analysed into: (1) ability to express feelings verbally and non-verbally; (2) positive attitude to self, balancing personal potentialities and limitations; (3) developing realistic ambitions; (4) achieving a balance between desire for independence and need for some dependence; (5) beginning to develop a 'philosophy' of life, i.e. feelings, beliefs, attitudes or guiding principles; (6) awareness of others, readiness to sympathize with or be of service to others. For practical purposes, the next stage of itemizing the learning, experience and activity required for achieving each specific objective is the important one. Thus in the examples just given, the objectives indicated for improving mental abilities would consist of sequences of teaching steps and materials for promoting the desired skills. The specific objectives of emotional maturity would require more general specifications: the use of creative and personal expression; creating opportunities for achievement and personal satisfaction; for meeting other adolescents; experience of the community and places of work; visits to school of previous leavers; and so on.

Even if the procedure is taken only as far as the statement of specific objectives together with some account of how they are to be achieved, the exercise will have been worthwhile since it is apt to bring to notice purposes which have not been consciously formulated or which receive insufficient attention. A further step, however, is expressing the specific objectives in terms of topics and activities. The result is apt to be rather overwhelming; there are so many things one could do if there were time, material and staff resources. But it is better perhaps to have to face the choices consciously at this stage than make it in default. Moreover, one of the values of a curriculum plan is that the content can be spread out over the school years, an important feature being the inclusion of topics at the primary stage which make a preparation for more extensive treatment at the secondary stage.

Taking a number of general objectives within the general aim of *social education*, the list of topics and activities in the Appendix were itemized as an indication of possible content of social education for backward secondary age pupils. In a setting where specialist teachers would be contributing to the teaching, the outline would suggest content that could be separately dealt with or by means of team teaching. It obviously suggests projects or, to use the American term, units of experience. Other sources of ideas about social education are given in School Councils Working Paper 11: *Society and the Young School Leaver*, and Working Paper 17: *Community Service and the Curriculum*. The former refers to the tendency for humanities courses to be the least successful in schools and suggests that a frequent cause of failure 'seems to be that the course is often based on the traditional belief that there is a body of content for each separate subject which every school leaver should know' – rather than based on the needs and interests of the youngsters. In a special school or class the needs and interests of pupils tend to stay very much in mind but there is still value in a systematic attempt to plan the curriculum.

Co-operation with parents

A feature common to all kinds of special teaching is the need for the closest co-operation between home and school. The basis of this is the same as in any school: (1) good personal relationships between parents and teachers; (2) understanding by the parents of the aims and methods of the school; (3) opportunities for parents to make a positive contribution to the school's work; (4) ensuring a two-way channel of communication about the child. In the case of children with disabilities, parents' awareness of a problem usually increases opportunities for home-school contacts though parents' emotional involvement often calls for greater skill and insight on the part of the school.

Parents of children with obvious disabilities have usually been concerned about their child's progress from an early age and the school is often dealing not only with the reactions of parents to the current situation but with attitudes and anxieties built up over the years. The majority of parents are keen to know what they can do but since education is often equated in their minds with school learning it is not always easy for them to appreciate that the best help they can give is often indirect – providing experiences, creating conditions for confident personal development, giving encouragement and help without causing stress and anxiety. There are of course those parents and family situations which need continuous support and help from the school and some where the help of experienced social workers is required.

Opinions differ about the best ways of promoting home-school co-operation. Formal events such as open-days and PTAs have some part to play but these are unlikely to be the best means of contacting parents of the least successful pupils. Creating a feeling that the staff is approachable and willing to talk with parents at school is one way but some parents are unlikely to take advantage of that opportunity. Some special schools and remedial departments have found that visiting parents at home has been very much welcomed (Herbert and Clack, 1970). Some of the parents most in need of someone to talk to who does not represent 'officialdom' are unlikely to visit school even though the school proclaims an 'open-door' policy. Several studies show that such parents are much more interested in their children's schooling and welfare than is often thought but they need help from the school about how to show their interest. A number of secondary schools have given one teacher the task of being a home-liaison teacher and a number of courses are now available for training teacher-social workers and counsellors. Such developments are sometimes viewed suspiciously as something new. They are a development rather than an innovation. There have always been teachers, remedial teachers, house tutors and headteachers who have functioned as counsellors. What creates the need for a separate person is the increase in the size of schools, the increase in the number of problems in some schools, the need for more co-ordination of social work efforts and the increased awareness that education cannot sufficiently achieve its aims for all pupils unless additional help is available for children with educational failures and social adversities.

Having one member of staff with special responsibility in this area does not absolve others of responsibility. Counselling and social work cannot be the function of one person. This is very obvious in the case of parents of handicapped children. They may receive different kinds of help from the medical consultant, the school medical officer, the general practitioner, the health visitor, social workers, the school, other parents of handicapped children, neighbours and friends. Counselling is as wide as the community and expressed in its attitudes and provision of help. Similarly in ordinary schools, the extent to which the school is part of the community and understood by it is as important as the means organized for communicating with parents.

Assessment and educational diagnosis

A final requirement of special teaching is assessment of the individual learner. This requires assessment of his general development as a person, of his abilities and present levels of attainment and, in cases where learning is very retarded or difficult, a more detailed examination of strength and weaknesses. In some situations, the results of psychological and other examinations are available but, whether these are available or not, the observations of the teacher are basic to assessment. These observations can be related to the knowledge of what is normal for the child's age or stage of development and are also considered along with other information about the child's home circumstances, medical record and previous school history. In some schools, the observations of several people who know the child are discussed at a case conference and conclusions reached about the different kinds of experience and teaching required. Peter (1965) calls this prescriptive teaching in which all information is utilized for 'devising teaching procedures to yield desirable changes in the child's academic progress, emotional condition and social adjustment'.

Assessment by informal observations

The majority of teachers have to rely on their own observations of pupils' capacities and needs, supplemented on occasion by educational and other tests and by the assistance of an educational psychologist. Ideally all the children whose learning is 'at risk' should have a psycho-educational examination in order to assess their assets and liabilities in learning.

Observation is, of course, more than noticing. It requires a framework of ideas which directs the observer's attention and enables him to interpret what he sees. It requires a knowledge of the normal sequences of development and of the nature of processes of learning and adjustment. A further condition of good observation is that there should be a sufficient range of observations in different situations on which to make judgments.

The following outline cannot be more than a starting point.

PHYSICAL GROWTH AND DEVELOPMENT

In some cases, there is a general physical immaturity; in others, some awkwardness and inco-ordination is apparent. Large motor skills (walking, running, playing games) and manipulation (using play materials, apparatus, tools) are important for many school activities but are also important for the child's view of himself and his capacities and for his ability to participate in activities with other children.

Some children with learning difficulties have an imperfect awareness of the body, its parts, movements and positions. This affects the basic awareness of Self (the body image) and there is a failure to develop a stable system of reference for understanding spatial relationships (left, right, up, down, near, far, and so on) (Kephart, 1960).

Physical development has to be assessed in relation to the child's previous experience. Some improve rapidly with increased physical activity; others continue to have difficulties. Apart from the normal experiences provided through physical education, dance and manipulative experiences in class, some children need more specific training. Kephart suggests methods of assessing and training basic motor skills and there are numerous books and articles on physical education and movement with handicapped children.

PERCEPTUAL DEVELOPMENT

The information received through the senses has to be organized and interpreted. Visual and auditory perception are the most important – interpreting pictures, shapes and letters visually; interpreting sounds, spoken words, tunes auditorily. Tactile and kinaesthetic perception are probably more important than we realize and, of course, are particularly relied on by visually- and hearing-impaired children. The impressions from different senses have to be integrated and the order or sequence of information preserved.

There are many opportunities for observing the development of perceptual abilities in the use of apparatus, pictures, charts, models and in learning to read.

PERCEPTUAL MOTOR SKILLS

Many tasks require co-ordination of hand and eye (as in dressing, drawing, writing, construction, practical and creative activities) and co-ordination of hearing and movement (speaking, phonic work, moving to music). Failure in such skills can undermine other learning and results in the child avoiding certain activities.

ATTENTION

The ability to attend to relevant stimuli is obviously basic to learning. Some children are over-active and distractible; some are slow and lethargic or tend to perseverate (to continue some action or mental activity beyond the point needed). This level of attention can be distinguished from the concentration which depends on interest and motivation.

These motor, perceptual-motor and attentional processes are basic to the development of higher thought processes and of readiness for educational skills. Much of nursery-infant experience is concerned with developing them but older children who are slow learners or failing educationally require continued help in these areas.

COGNITIVE DEVELOPMENT

On the basis of his perceptual organization of experience, the child is able to organize his thinking. He groups and categorizes his experience by noting similarities and differences, understands relationships between things and learns to reason about events and situations, making judgments and solving problems. He is increasingly able to use language to refer to things, concepts and relationships, to guide his learning and to state what he understands.

There is, of course, ample opportunity for observing the child's thinking in learning, in his play, through his drawings and paintings and his interests. It is important, however, to ensure that observations are made over a wide range. Judgments based on academic learning only or on external appearances such as personality or superficial reflections of home background are liable to error.

LANGUAGE

Observations of the range and understanding of vocabulary need to be supplemented by observations of effectiveness in expressing and comprehending ideas and meanings. The question is whether language is available for helping learning as well as for social communication.

The operation of all these mental processes is influenced by emotional and social factors:

EMOTIONAL DEVELOPMENT

Is the child emotionally settled and confident for his age? Does he show signs of seeking security, attention, affection and approval? Is he able to express and control his emotions? Can he respond to the normal motivations for learning? Has he adequate self-concepts and reasonable expectations of himself in achievement and behaviour?

SOCIAL DEVELOPMENT

Does he relate to adults and other children? Does he want to participate with others and is he accepted by them?

SOCIAL COMPETENCE

Bearing age and general development in mind, is he acquiring independence in basic living skills and in moving around the environment?

These aspects of development are important in themselves but also because they are interacting and interrelated. A lag in one area has consequences for others. The isolated child misses the experience with others which stimulates communication, interests, knowledge, practice of physical skills, the expression and control of emotions. Emotional unsettlement is liable to interfere with friendships and group acceptance and the same is true of other difficulties – the less intelligent child has less to offer to the group; the perceptually disorganized child may fail to grasp the pattern of the game in the playground or the activity in PE; the physically 'clumsy' child may withdraw from activities requiring physical skills.

Some aids to assessment

Each of the above headings is, of course, a subject in itself and observation will be as rich and meaningful as experience and knowledge make it. A number of sources can be referred to for greater detail. For development up to and including the five-year level, Sheridan's *The Developmental Progress of Infants and Young Children* itemizes behaviour in four groups : posture and large movements; vision and fine movements; hearing and speech; social behaviour and play. The schedule, like many others, draws upon the work of Gesell (1954) whose books provide descriptions of typical achievements at different age levels in motor, adaptive, personal-social and language development. The Vineland Social Maturity Scale assesses self-help, locomotion, occupation, self-direction, socialization and communication covering the whole age range to adulthood but there are too few items at many age levels. The Progress Assessment Charts (Gunzburg, 1963), itemize behaviour in the categories self-help, communication, socialization and occupation. The Primary Form covers mentally handicapped children; Form 1 is for use with IQs below about 55; and Form 2 is for use with young people in the IQ range 55 to 80+. These serve for assessing pupils' needs for planning, teaching and recording progress. The Manchester Scales of Social Adaptation (Lunzer) for children up to fifteen years assess social knowledge and social functioning in play, moving about the environment, having responsibilities.

Whether or not these scales are used, a perusal of them is useful in the preparation of the school's own charts and records of progress.

A method of evaluating emotional and social adjustment during the school years is the *Bristol Social Adjustment Guide* (Stott, 1966). Many schools have found these useful if only to increase awareness and understanding of behavioural difficulties (see p. 47). The *Children's Behaviour Questionnaires* (Rutter, 1967) have two forms, consisting of twenty-six questions, one form for completion by parents and one by teachers. It is useful between the ages of seven and thirteen for 'screening' groups of children for emotional difficulties and could be used therefore as a basis for planning preventive measures.

The assessment of learning abilities

This assessment of personal-social development is needed because response to education involves the whole personality and adjustment of the learner. It is, then, necessary to assess the abilities and processes most closely involved in learning – perception, thinking and language.

An individual test of intelligence (such as the New Revised Stanford Binet Scale or the Wechsler Scales) is a collection of tasks sampling a range of these abilities. The resulting score (IQ or standardized score) tells us how the child compares with other children of the same age and thus indicates whether expectations for learning may be about the same, higher or lower than those for average children. In making this inference, we have to take into account the possible limiting effects of sensory, physical or multiple disabilities. We also have to remember that the IQ is a measure of present mental functioning and may change after special teaching, therapy or improvement in the environment. A further qualification is that though low IQ suggests certain kinds of learning may be difficult, it does not mean that they cannot be learnt. They may take longer to learn and the learning may need to be carefully graded and well-motivated.

Many tests can be used over the whole range of handicapped children. However, physically handicapped children whose hands are affected may not be able to use tests requiring the manipulation of materials. Performance and non-language tests may be required for children with severe speech and hearing impairments; the Williams version of the Binet Scale is used for visually handicapped children. The interpretation of testing, however, requires even greater care than usual. Tests standardized on ordinary children assume normal experience and handicapped children may have had restrictions imposed by their disability or by their environment. It is still useful to have this comparison with normal standards so long as the score is not assumed to be 'accurate' and unchangeable – and so long as decisions take much other information into account. It is, for example, important to take account of areas of specific weakness due to the disability or to additional deficits.

The IQ does not, however, tell us whether the child does better in some kinds of thinking than in others though the record of the test itself can be studied to find out particular strengths and weaknesses. The Wechsler Scales are so arranged that a Verbal Quotient and a Performance Quotient are obtained and scores on different kinds of sub-tests (e.g. recalling digits, seeing similarities between words, putting pictures in sequence) can be examined for diagnostic clues. For example, a child sometimes does very well on verbal reasoning tasks but has marked difficulty in making up a jigsaw or copying a design in coloured bricks. Such observations can be explored further in order to find out what conclusions can be drawn for teaching.

A number of commonly used tests assess rather different abilities. Thus the Raven's Matrices is a non-verbal test using patterns. The English Picture Vocabulary Test requires the selection of one out of four pictures in response to a given word and contrasts with the Crichton Vocabulary Scale which requires oral definitions of words. If the results from several tests are available it is worth noting any marked differences, comparing them with observations of the child and considering whether they have teaching implications.

Some psychologists are now using the Reynell Developmental Language Scale for children up to five years which assesses expressive and comprehension aspects of language.

The need for tests which assess specific functions rather than global intelligence has been strongly felt for a long time. As we have seen, an IQ is useful as an indication of pupils' capacity but gives little help for planning teaching. It was with this need in mind that Kirk developed the Illinois Test of Psycholinguistic Abilities. This has sub-tests designed to assess (1) three *processes*: decoding (or reception), association, encoding (expression); (2) several sensory *channels* (decoding of visual and auditory symbols; expression through speech and gesture); (3) two *levels* – the 'thinking' level and the level of automatic verbal behaviour and the sequencing of visual and auditory information. The resulting profile indicates which processes need remediation and which can profitably be utilized in learning.

Several tests assess perceptual processes. The Frostig Developmental Test of Visual Perception has sub-tests for eye-motor co-ordination, figure ground perception, perceptual constancy, perception of position in space and spatial relations. The Wepman Test (1958) assesses discrimination of speech sounds; other tests of perceptual functions are described by Tansley (1967). Kephart (1960) has described a survey of motor and perceptual-motor abilities which he considers basic to the child's awareness of his body and its movements in space and through that of the child's awareness of left and right, direction and orientation. The Bender Visual-Motor Gestalt Test (1938) requires the copying of ten patterns and reveals weaknesses in reproducing spatial relationships.

There is a wide range of tests and methods of assessment; these are very thoroughly discussed in relation to handicapped children in a handbook edited by Mittler (1970). A psychologist drawing upon these can often point to areas of strength and weakness which have implications for methods of teaching, but such an assessment should not be regarded as the final word. Teaching itself is a form of continuing assessment in which impressions are confirmed or modified and pupils' response to particular methods and experiences are assessed.

Tests of word recognition, reading accuracy, speed and comprehension, spelling and diagnostic tests are essential in the teacher's repertoire. They are discussed in detail in Jackson's A *Teacher's Guide to Tests*.

Further reading

ASSOCIATION FOR SPECIAL EDUCATION, *What is Special Education?* Proceedings of International Conference 1966, Association for Special Education.
CRAFT, M., *et al.* (eds.) (1967), *Linking Home and School*, London: Longmans.
GESELL, A. (1964), *The First Five Years of Life*, London: Methuen.
GOLDSTEIN, H., AND SEIGLE, D. (1958), *The Illinois Curriculum Guide*, Urbana, Illinois: Institute for Exceptional Children.
GOODACRE, E. (1970), *School and Home*, National Foundation for Educational Research.
GULLIFORD, R. (1965), 'Planning their future', *Special Education*, 54, i, 4-7.
JACKSON, S. (1968), *A Teacher's Guide to Tests*, London: Longmans.
PETERS, L. J. (1965), *Prescriptive Teaching*, New York: McGraw-Hill.
SCHOOLS COUNCIL WORKING PAPER 11 (1967), *Society and the Young School Leaver*.
SCHOOLS COUNCIL WORKING PAPER 17 (1968), *Community Service and the Curriculum*.
SHERIDAN, M. D. (1960), *The Developmental Progress of Infants and Young Children*, London: HMSO.
TAYLOR, P. H. (1960), *Curriculum Planning for Compensatory Education – A Suggested Procedure*, Schools Council.

three

Emotional difficulties

Emotional upsets and occasional difficulties in adjustment are inevitable in the process of growing towards maturity. It would be an
unusual child indeed who in the pre-school stage did not show some
tendencies to excessive emotional reactions and behaviour. Within
limits these are the manifestations of a healthy degree of self-
assertiveness and the emergence of valuable human drives through
the expression and organization of which an individual personality
develops. These are normally managed within the family discipline
in such a way that the child is helped to achieve reasonable con-
formity to the requirements of his environment *and* to harmonize
his inner urges in such a way that he feels a sense of identity and
personal worth, a sense of security which enables him to tolerate
the insecurities of new experience and of new steps towards independence and social co-operation. Much the same can be said of adolescence for the new drives and environmental demands at that time
bring about a re-patterning of personality with inevitable dishar-
monies and stresses in feeling and behaviour. Clearly the range of
normality is wide.

Some degree of unsettlement is also likely at crisis points in childhood and adolescence. Many five-year-olds show signs of this in the
first few weeks of schooling, however well it is managed – excessive
tiredness, temper, weepiness, regressive behaviour such as thumb-
sucking or bed-wetting. Later in school life the transition to a different teacher or school or difficulties in learning particular subjects
can cause temporary upsets. And there are the inevitable hazards
of illness, hospitalization, and bereavements which require processes
of readjustment.

But *emotional handicap or maladjustment* is of a different order of seriousness. The Underwood Report (1955) on the education of maladjusted children said: 'It is characteristic of maladjusted children that they are insecure and unhappy and they fail in their personal relationships. Receiving is difficult for them as well as giving and they appear unable to respond to simple measures of love, comfort and reassurance. At the same time they are not readily capable of improvement by ordinary school discipline.'

The Report grouped symptoms under six headings:

(1) Nervous or emotional disorders – fears, anxieties, withdrawal and timidity.
(2) Habit disorders – enuresis, nail-biting, feeding disorders.
(3) Behaviour disorders – temper tantrums, stealing, cruelty, aggression.
(4) Organic disorders – mainly those with a neurological dysfunction as the basis and often showing as marked overactivity, distractibility or impulsiveness.
(5) Psychotic behaviour in which disruption of normal development takes place at all levels.
(6) Educational and vocational difficulties.

This classification gives little help in understanding the nature of or evaluating the seriousness of disturbance. Symptoms have first to be considered in relation to the child's *age*. Very dependent behaviour (such as wanting to be taken to school) would be unusual in a ten-year-old. Tempers and other strong reactions are not unexpected in pre-school children but would be regarded more seriously in a junior. Periods of moodiness and depression are not uncommon in adolescents though they might be taken more seriously in a junior. In making such judgments the child's general *development* and the presence of particular disabilities have to be taken into account. Some allowance could be made for dependent behaviour in a retarded child or for strong reactions to difficulty and frustration in a child with physical or sensory disability. The child's *social and cultural background* also needs to be considered. A marked inability to concentrate and settle to tasks in a child from a 'good' home might point to some emotional unsettlement whereas in a child from a 'poor' home it might reflect lack of experience of satisfying activity. Likewise aggressiveness and petty delinquency might be interpreted differently. (At the same time, it is important to avoid stereotyped thinking about what can be expected of children from different backgrounds.)

In evaluating behaviour, it is desirable to enquire whether the child shows other signs of emotional disturbance. The National Child Development Study (Pringle *et al.*, 1966) found that 11 per cent of children continue to be wet at night after the age of five, 11 per cent of seven-year-olds bite their nails and 11 per cent are 'irritable, quick to fly off the handle'. Clearly such frequently occurring behaviour needs to be considered in relation to the child's development as a whole and whether there are other signs of difficulty. It is also useful to enquire in what situations and at what times symptoms occur, and how frequently. Are timidity, uncommunicativeness or awkward behaviour found both at home and school, in certain situations or with certain teachers or people more than with others? How persistent and long-standing are the child's difficulties?

In general, the more seriously unsettled child is likely to have difficulty in relating to others either as a result of withdrawal or awkward, hostile behaviour. He lacks emotional resilience, over-reacting to difficulties, criticism or failure and shows an immature response to requirements and situations which the normal child takes in his stride. Anxiety and tension are liable to show in inability to concentrate, restlessness, apprehensiveness and reaction to slight changes in the environment. A marked discrepancy between actual school achievement and impressions of what could be achieved is commonly the case and sometimes disturbance has more marked effects on thinking and learning. An unrealistic view of things is not uncommon with compensatory fantasies and aspirations. Low self-esteem may be evident in poor motivation or be expressed verbally in self-depreciation.

The prevalence of maladjustment

The different criteria for assessing the seriousness of emotionally disturbed behaviour make it difficult to find out how many children may be regarded as maladjusted and in need of special help. What is clear, however, is that the number of children whose emotional and personal development is not proceeding normally is much higher than many would suppose.

Surveys undertaken in three areas for the Underwood Committee produced figures varying from 5·4 to 11·8 per cent for the proportion of children needing special help as maladjusted children, and, in addition, their figures indicate others who need some modification of the home or school situation. A survey of 11,000 seven-year-olds (Pringle et al., 1966) using the Bristol Social Adjustment Guides found that 13 per cent showed behaviour indicative of maladjustment though the authors were careful to point out that this simply shows the proportion with high symptom scores on the assessment. The Isle of Wight survey (Yule and Rutter, 1968) sought reliable information from surveys of 2,193 children in the nine- to twelve-year-old age group in order to establish the need for special services. From screening procedures, 286 children were selected for intensive psychological and psychiatric assessment. Their estimate was that 5·7 per cent showed a psychiatric disorder. Of these about 36 per cent showed neurotic disorders, 36 per cent conduct disorders and 23 per cent were a mixed group. While there was only a slightly smaller number of boys than girls with neurotic disorder, the proportion of boys to girls with conduct disorder was nearly 4 : 1. The social class distribution was similar to that of the general population.

An important finding was that nearly a quarter of the children in the maladjusted group were more than twenty-eight months retarded in reading. Moreover, more than a third of the children with conduct disorders were at least twenty-eight months retarded, whereas the neurotic group showed reading retardation only a little more frequently than the general population.

Special provision for maladjusted children

The conclusion from these and other studies is that a considerable proportion of children are likely to need some special help at some point in childhood on account of difficulties in emotional development and social adjustment. The number involved is greater than could be provided for by special services such as child guidance clinics and special schools and classes, even if there were enough personnel and resources to expand them. Much must depend on preventive work by advice and support to parents, by greater co-operation and liaison between schools and homes and between education and social work. Since schools carry the main responsibility for helping children, more effort needs to be given to helping teachers understand and help unsettled children, and more attention needs to be given in research and practice to identifying what methods of organization, discipline and educational approaches in general are needed so that these can be more explicitly communicated in teacher training.

Special provision for the needs of children with emotional and behavioural difficulties was comparatively late in being made. The first two voluntary child guidance clinics were established in the late 1920s and about the same time a few independent schools began to cater specially for nervous and difficult children. The first day school for such children was opened in Leicester in 1932 following the appointment of Cattell as educational psychologist in 1931. The first LEA child guidance clinic was set up by Birmingham in 1932. By 1939 there were twenty-two clinics wholly or partly maintained by LEAs as well as several voluntary or hospital clinics.

The Second World War gave an impetus to these beginnings of work with maladjusted children. Evacuation revealed many children with behaviour problems and hostels were set up for unbilletable children; child guidance workers were spread through the country to help in evacuation areas. As a result, the need for child guidance and residential treatment for maladjusted children became more widely recognized and by 1945 the number of clinics had risen to seventy-nine.

The Handicapped Pupils and School Health Service regulations of 1945 introduced a category of maladjusted children who were defined as 'pupils who show evidence of emotional instability or psychological disturbance and require special educational treatment in order to effect their personal, social and educational readjustment'. This, as well as war-time experience, gave an impetus to the provision of child guidance clinics and special schools. In 1955 the Underwood Committee reported on the treatment of maladjusted children within the educational system, and made comprehensive recommendations for the development of work with maladjusted children including the need for every local education authority to have a child guidance team (one psychiatrist, two educational psychologists, three psychiatric social workers) for every 45,000 schoolchildren. More use of day treatment was recommended by means of day special schools and part-time special classes in line with the view that residential treatment should be given only if there was no hope of treating a child successfully while at home.

In 1968, there were 367 child guidance clinics which treated 61,358 children (one in every 124 children); 8,602 children were receiving special education (4,315 in special schools, 2,592 in independent schools, 1,695 in 159 special classes). The important role of boarding education is shown by the fact that fifty-nine of the schools were boarding and twenty-eight day schools.

Special schools for maladjusted children are usually small (thirty to fifty pupils) with the small class groups that would be expected when children have been brought together who for a variety of reasons cannot manage in ordinary schools. The main aim is to provide a therapeutic environment in which children can learn to relate to adults and other children, can be helped to understand themselves and to overcome their difficulties. The security of familiar school routines is combined with greater flexibility and tolerance of individual children's anxieties, aggressions, attention-seeking and immaturity. The most important special feature is the teachers' insight into troubled behaviour and their ability to handle situations and problems so that children can learn from them – acquiring trust in others and trust in themselves. Creative, practical, physical and academic activities are used as a means of knowing pupils and helping them forward. An important element is remedying poor attainments, since many pupils are very retarded.

There is usually close contact with the Child Guidance Clinic. The contribution of psychologists and psychiatrists is often one of supporting staff by discussion of individual pupils as well as seeing pupils when required. The psychiatric social worker continues to work with the home; some schools have their own psychiatric social worker. A few schools have a psychotherapist on the staff (Barron, 1969; Shields, 1962).

But the problem of helping emotionally disturbed children is not confined to these special schools. It is a problem for ordinary schools and for other kinds of special school, since maladjustment is a frequent additional handicap.

Processes in emotional and personality development

Before considering what steps can be taken by schools and teachers to help emotionally disturbed children, we need to consider the nature of personality development and the dynamic processes which underly emotional disturbance. This is a vast subject to which justice cannot of course be done in a short summary; references to further reading are given at the end of the chapter.

It is useful to have a framework of ideas about the developmental tasks which are to confront the child (and those who care for him) at different ages. One framework is provided by the theories of Erikson (1965) who sees the main tasks as acquiring (1) a basic sense of trust in babyhood up to about eighteen months of age; (2) a sense of autonomy in the toddler up to about four years; (3) a sense of initiative (from about four to seven years); (4) a sense of industry (about seven to twelve years) and (5) a sense of identity in adolescence. Each phase has problems of adaptation to inner urges and environmental pressures, which must be solved if there is to be satisfactory development at that stage and readiness for the next stage of personal growth.

We start from the fact that every human being has powerful drives serving the biological purpose of survival and maintaining the organisms' functioning. Parents recognize these needs – for food, love, security, activity, etc. – and meet them according to the methods of child-rearing customary in their own society and sub-culture and also according to their personal capacity for providing materially and emotionally. The regularity and consistency with which bodily needs are met and the continuous dependable mother-child relationship develop a basic sense of trust which enables the baby to overcome the sense of mistrust involved in new experiences, in the frustrations inherent in learning in what ways needs may be satisfied and what gratifications must be given up or denied.

In the next phase, the child develops 'awareness' of himself as an independent being. The maturation of locomotor abilities and speech as well as other physical and mental skills contribute to this Selfhood (the Ego). He reaches out, experiments and expands his world growing as a person in his own right – parents often find their amenable baby has a will of his own and is not so easy to manage. But at the same time, the child feels the pull of dependency and the risk of failure or loss of self-control as he tries himself out and explores his environment. As Erikson puts it, he has to develop a sense of autonomy as well as combating a sense of doubt and shame. He needs the security of parental guidance and firmness as well as the freedom to experiment.

During the next phase, from about four years, the marked development of physical, perceptual and thinking skills enables the child to understand better the world around him and makes him more established as a person. His language skills, his questions, his increased social experience with others and his ability to function in more varied ways in a wider environment increase his 'sense of initiative'. At the same time, he is more aware of parental and social expectations; he internalizes some of the values and prohibitions of his parents, developing a conscience (or super-ego) which acts as an inner self controlling his own behaviour.

Many children by the age of school entry have gone a long way in this direction and others do so during the infant school, so that by about seven years they are moving into the next phase which Erikson describes as acquiring a sense of industry and fending off a sense of inferiority. If previous development has gone well, it is a period of mastery—in the sense of learning basic physical, mental and educational skills, a basic understanding of the environment and social skills of getting on with other children. This period is important for developing self-esteem and attitudes towards work and effort as a basis for the even more demanding tasks of the next stage.

The adolescent's main task is to acquire a sense of identity while overcoming a sense of identity diffusion, e.g. he needs to experiment with a wide range of roles, yet emerge eventually as a person knowing what he wants to be and do; he needs to explore a variety of opinions, ways of behaving and ideals, but arrive eventually at a 'philosophy of life'. Bodily changes, mental development and environmental influences make for a re-patterning of personality. How well the main tasks of adolescence are accomplished obviously depends upon the completion of tasks at earlier stages and how they are also affected by personal and environmental handicaps.

Even with this brief outline, we can begin to discern some of the possible origins of unsatisfactory personality development. Some of the basic needs for acquiring a sense of trust may have been imperfectly met through disruption of the mother-child relationship. The child's developing sense of Self may have been impeded by insecurity or disturbed relationships with parents. Inconsistent methods of child care or lack of training may have resulted in the child not internalizing standards with the result that he is at the mercy of impulses or, on the other hand, parental discipline, and expectations may have been so severe that the child develops an overpowerful conscience with excessive feelings of guilt and conflict – or he reacts with rebellion.

Much maladjusted behaviour can be seen as the expression of conflict and anxiety. Growing up inevitably involves conflict between basic impulses, for example, between the desire for dependence and the emerging one for independence; between love for mother as a supplier of needs and hate for mother as a prohibitor and denier of gratification; between love and jealousy for a sibling. Conflict occurs between basic impulses and the awareness that certain forms of behaviour are not acceptable and may be punished by adults. There is also conflict when impulses are not allowable by the child's own inner standards and conscience and, strangely, these can be more punishing than any externally given – this is the explanation of the excessive distress of some children when they have had an 'accident' or broken something. They sometimes even blame themselves for things which they have had nothing to do with. Children brought up in a loving consistent, nurturing environment learn to accommodate these conflicting desires but many of the children with whom we are concerned have not been able to resolve conflicts and may continue anxiously to live them out with teachers and other children in the classroom.

Growing up also involves anxiety in situations which may lead to punishment, loss of love or loss of self-esteem. Failure to control basic impulses, to learn skills expected of the child, to tolerate the brief separations inevitable in becoming independent, and inability to control aggression arouse anxieties which are comfortably handled by the child in a stable, tolerant family environment but may become disruptive in the child on whom discipline and demands are severe, or markedly inconsistent.

In essence the child's task (and that of those who care for him) is to harmonize the satisfaction of basic needs and drives with the development of a personality which enables the child to live 'with himself' and to function in a social environment. By the kind of discipline he experiences and also by his identification with parent figures, he develops an inner Self which gradually takes over the regulating function of parents.

These are all dynamic processes and it is not surprising that even in normal development it is usual to find conflict and anxiety showing in symptoms of unsettled behaviour. When there is conflict or anxiety the individual tries unconsciously to cope with impulses by repression, regression, compulsions and other defence mechanisms. These are commonly observed in the behaviour of schoolchildren and are demonstrated in extreme form in maladjusted children. Some insight into their function contributes to wise handling of the child.

Regression or reverting to a childish or more immature form of behaviour is one way of resolving conflict, especially when new demands are being made (e.g. starting school). The tendency to regress may be activated by a parental tendency to over-protect or by earlier deprivations, e.g. deprived children may seek attention, cuddles or food like children very much younger. With some children, it is sufficient to 'bolster the ego' so that they can face up to new demands. With others, however, it is valuable to recognize the healing functions of regression and provide opportunity for it in a therapeutic environment with a view to helping the child forward from there. Thus in young children dramatic play often provides the opportunity; some children's need for regression may be at a more primitive level of play with water, sand, clay and paint. With adolescents, free drama can be used to offer opportunities.

While regression as a habitual response to frustration and difficulty is not healthy, it is, within limits, an adaptive response in normal development. Children and adults find relief through mild regression in play and recreational pursuits. We can say with justification that it is an essential feature of education for mental health and particularly in the education of disturbed or handicapped children. How much must some of the latter need to regress after the efforts they make to overcome their disabilities!

Another means of adjusting is *compensation*. The place of this in education is well recognized as a means of enabling the handicapped child, the backward child or the intelligent non-reader to obtain satisfaction and success in ways other than those prevented by his handicap. Failure to do this can be damaging to the child's stability and self-esteem. However, over-compensation may occur. Sheila, a withdrawn, socially-isolated ESN (educationally sub-normal) child, put everything into reading in which as a result she achieved a level exceptional for an ESN child but made no progress in other ways. Some backward readers compensate practically or socially so well that they are undisturbed by their failure. Compensatory reactions become more of a problem to the teacher when they result in boasting or exhibitionistic behaviour; when inner feelings of inadequacy are compensated for by unruliness, rebellion and dare-devil behaviour. It is obvious that tackling the symptom by punishment is not enough, that the underlying sense of inadequacy needs to be remedied or alleviated. This applies also to compensatory stealing and eating. In all these cases, while much can be done within the classroom, the remedy requires co-operation with the home.

A common way of coping with anxiety and feelings of guilt is by *projection* – attributing to others the unpleasant feelings or impulses one finds unacceptable in oneself. Thus the disturbed child claims that it was not he who started the row but the other child. Or it is the teacher who is being unjust. In more extreme forms the child has a grudge or 'chip on his shoulder' which makes it difficult to break through to the child in order to make a relationship. This mechanism points to the need for means of expression through which projection can occur without side-effects – in play, in free drama, art and creative writing. Externalizing unpleasant feelings and tendencies in this way not only affords relief without feelings of guilt but may help the child to distinguish fact from fiction, to test his fantasies against reality.

In the process of *displacement* feelings and attitudes are shifted from their origin to a substitute. A common manifestation of this is the displacement of aggressive or rebellious feelings towards parents on to the teacher (the reverse process sometimes happens at home!) or towards discipline, authority and society more generally. As a feature in normal socialization Susan Isaacs describes how the hostility of two children towards a third is due to the displacement of aggressive feelings on to the outsider so that the two are left with positive feelings of love towards each other. It is a common situation in the friendships and rivalries of the infant and junior playground and one which is bound to occur in groups of older disturbed children as they struggle through stages of social development normally experienced by much younger children.

An obvious way of coping is to *deny* the reality of urges, wishes or unpleasant facts. Thus a handicapped child or his parents may refuse to face up to the handicap, perhaps even nourishing unrealistic ambitions. A deprived child in a boarding school may create in fantasy a good mother in place of the absent or inadequate one. A child may be difficult to help because he refuses to face up to his failure in reading, or denies his delinquency even though caught in the act. Perhaps in these cases it is wise to realize that in one sense the desire to see one's self in good terms has a positive side to it (a tendency we all share). The teacher can help by communicating acceptance, by promoting achievements which ensure real achievements which maintain the Self and by gradually leading the child to face reality.

Helping the maladjusted child in school

Much has been written about the causes and nature of emotional disturbance in childhood. There are also some stimulating accounts of methods used by notable headteachers of schools for maladjusted children but little has been written about the way emotionally disturbed children are helped within ordinary schools and classes, although much is in fact done by teachers to prevent and relieve emotional problems. It is, however, a task for which most teachers have had little specific preparation in their training.

What factors are important in helping maladjusted children in the school setting? Some general issues will be considered first and more specific problems and practices will be considered later.

THE NEED TO OBSERVE CHILDREN

Emotional and behavioural characteristics should be observed as carefully as progress in school attainments so that the early signs of unsettlement can be detected and alleviated. Observing the child's interaction with other children, his relationship to the teacher, his response to a variety of learning situations, tendencies to frustration, persistence, his reactions to new or difficult situations, all provide clues which can lead to wiser handling. It is often suggested that aggressive, awkward children are noticed, and quiet, withdrawn ones get overlooked – though some recent surveys indicate that teachers are alert to the possibility of this bias. Good observations are of the utmost value both to the teacher himself and to child guidance workers should the child be referred.

There is ample opportunity for observing; the difficulty is understanding the significance of what is being observed. Set discussions or case conferences about individual children can help to increase this understanding especially if an educational psychologist or social worker can participate occasionally. Many schools have found that using the Bristol Social Adjustment Guides have been helpful here. The mere fact of having to underline phrases describing the child's behaviour on a form which has a comprehensive coverage of behaviour in everyday school situations draws attention to facets which had been overlooked. More importantly those descriptions which are known to be symptoms of unsettled behaviour are picked out and recorded on a diagnostic form and sorted into different types of behaviour – withdrawal, attention-seeking, hostility to adults and/or children, restlessness etc. From inspection of this scoring it is possible to get some indication of the seriousness of the behaviour and also of the kind of behaviour pattern the child is showing. One common pattern, for example, is that of the child who seeks attention and approval from adults but at the same time shows hostility towards adults. It is natural that in the classroom it is the hostile behaviour which the teacher is most aware of and he may feel that giving the child attention is being unfairly rewarded by hostility. The Adjustment Guide analysis, however, does indicate there is a hopeful side – the child seeks attention and approval which is something positive to build on. There are other cases where the pattern revealed by the Guide indicates that the child has begun to 'write adults off', is showing unconcern for their attention and approval. Unless a good relationship and sympathetic understanding can be achieved it may become increasingly more difficult to get through to the child.

These Guides are no more than a way of systematizing the teacher's impressions. They are fairly crude compared with the observations and 'hunches' which enable a teacher to know when an attempt to get a withdrawn child to make a step forward in group participation is likely to be successful; whether a certain task is just that bit too difficult for a child and liable to cause frustration; when a child is in a 'mood' and must be tactfully handled. The ability to be observant and some insight into the dynamics of behaviour are basic requirements.

THE IMPORTANCE OF FULL INFORMATION

It is important to know as much as possible about an unsettled child since this often provides clues to the sources of difficulty. Naughtiness or apparent disobedience can be due to something as simple as a hearing loss; a specific difficulty in speech, perception, co-ordination or basic subjects may underlie behaviour difficulties. Lack of acceptance by other children may be due to some characteristic in the child which the teacher can do something to remedy – the child may lack simple games skills like skipping or catching; over-demanding or bossy behaviour may be modifiable by the teacher's intervention.

THE IMPORTANCE OF HOME/SCHOOL CO-OPERATION

Carrying the enquiry further, contact with the parents may reveal any of a great range of facts in the child's previous history or his present situation at home which help in understanding and tackling the problem.

There have always been some teachers who have visited homes to gain a fuller picture of children's situations and to enlist the parents' co-operation. Lesley Webb (1967) provides an excellent account of this kind of work in an infant school. Most special schools have close contact with parents but would welcome more social work assistance.

Secondary schools are increasingly seeking ways of promoting liaison between home and school (Schools Council, 1970). Appointments are being made of teacher/social workers and counsellors with training and experience in this field. Without this knowledge of the home and without parent co-operation, the school is working in the dark.

EMOTIONAL CLIMATE OF THE SCHOOL

The organization, class grouping, aims and discipline of the school exert a profound influence on the pupil's emotional and social development. It is a common observation that a child can be an unhappy misfit in one school; in another his problem is minimized. A school organization which emphasizes the difference between good achievers and poor achievers, relegating the latter to inferior status and communicating their unworthiness, is likely to have continued trouble from less successful pupils as they live up to the low expectations and as they react to an unsatisfying school experience. High standards and achievements are not incompatible with an atmosphere which in many subtle ways communicates that all pupils are of equal worth as persons even if they are not equal as scholars or equal in potentials. Co-operation is more productive of achievement and personal growth than competition. Those who emphasize competition overlook the fact that its benefits apply to a limited band of better achievers who stand some chance of success; and success itself often tends to be narrowly interpreted. Believers in co-operation are able to draw upon the natural competitiveness of children at all levels – to do better than their friends or another group or to do better than they themselves did before.

Many schools are finding that more flexible methods of organization benefit not only educational attainments but also personality development. Mixed ability grouping in secondary schools reduces the negative attitudes and low morale of less academic children. Family grouping in primary schools creates a situation in which it is easy to provide for different levels of emotional maturity and to 'contain' restless and awkward children.

TEACHER/PUPIL RELATIONSHIPS

The crucial factor is the making of a teacher/pupil relationship. As the quotation from the Underwood Report suggested about maladjusted children: 'Receiving is as difficult for them as giving and they appear unable to respond to simple measures of love, comfort and trust.' Not all maladjusted children in a class are as disturbed as that. Some respond quickly; with others it is a long process to break through their insecurities and hostilities. Attempting it and partially succeeding can be the most valuable help a teacher can give.

But what is meant by a good teacher/pupil relationship? It does not mean that the teacher must love or even like the unhappy child. Obviously the teacher's task is easier if he has a sympathetic, affectionate concern for him but it is often the case that the aggressive, over-active, selfish or unpredictable child is difficult to like. What is required is an unsentimental compassion for the child and an acceptance that it is part of the teacher's professional responsibility and skill to do something about it. The key word is *acceptance* which avoids on the one hand emotional over-involvement and on the other hand the rejection implied by ignoring the problem or trying to keep the lid on it purely by disciplinary means. Acceptance communicates to the child that his situation is not hopeless and that someone has the matter in hand (if not always under control). This realization itself often brings about an initial improvement.

Acceptance should include, of course, a feeling of warmth and communicate to the child a feeling that he is valued as an individual though this should stop short of over-anxiety and over-concern. What is needed is empathy not sympathy – empathy is the perception or understanding of what it is like to be in someone else's situation rather than a gush of sympathy. Sympathy can more easily distort judgment in those situations which so often arise when you need the wisdom of Solomon.

Acceptance gets across to children partly by what one says. Studies of the verbal interactions in classrooms show that the way commands and requests are phrased and the amount of praise bestowed has a marked effect on the co-operativeness and tone of the class. But acceptance is also communicated *non-verbally* – by gestures, facial expressions, the giving of time, the provision of suitable activities and materials. Giving, providing and satisfying needs are basic elements in forming relationships.

The discipline and emotional climate of the class

It is often stated that maladjusted children need a 'permissive' discipline. This is a vague word, increasingly gathering overtones of meaning, and is best avoided. It suggests that maladjusted children should be allowed to do what they like with few demands being made. There are some severe degrees of maladjustment where something of this kind is a desirable part of the therapeutic process as a preparation for more active intervention of the therapist or teacher and it is probably fortunate that there are a few boarding schools which are able to go to these lengths as part of a particular policy in the healing process with very disturbed children. In ordinary schools and special classes this is not possible; nor is it desirable.

We can state what is required more positively by saying that the class atmosphere should allow and provide for the expression of feelings and accept the manifestations of unsettled behaviour. It is only through such expression that the teacher gauges the child's needs and, more important, that the child learns to know himself, learns to cope with his emotions and learns through trial and error to make relationships with others. It is for these purposes that expressive activities in dramatic play, free drama, dance, art and creative English are so important.

While rules, routines and expectations may not be conspicuous, there are limits; indeed both the child and the teacher need to know what these are for their own security and confidence. What the limits should be depends on the nature of the group. With younger children and with more disturbed children the limits will be set wider, particularly at first; as children progress it is possible to set the limits more narrowly. There must be some flexibility to allow for tolerance of behaviour from one child which would not be expected from others and for the inevitable failures which arise from temporary distress and upset. How the limits are set will also depend upon the teacher. Some can work well in a loosely organized régime and others need a more organized situation to be happy and effective.

In this context, it is useful to quote an investigation (Cohen, Lavietes, Reens and Rindsberg, 1964) at the Children's Day Centre, New York. They observed over a period two teachers working in the Centre with seriously maladjusted children. Both were successful teachers yet each was a strikingly different person working in a style unique to herself. Each had distinct viewpoints. *Teacher A* was quiet in personality and manner. She did not talk a lot but controlled the class by giving freely of her personal attention and by providing ample activity and ample materials. She was quietly alert to avert or divert problem situations; the discipline was relaxed with broad limits. Standards and achievements were not stressed; order and tidiness were not considered of first importance. *Teacher B* ran a more traditional classroom. There were well-defined rules and academic achievement provided clear goals. There was ample praise and encouragement. The classroom was well organized and orderly. The teacher's hold was gentle, persuasive and firm. While Teacher A was unobtrusive, allowing children to grow in a nurturing environment, Teacher B was a forceful and colourful person both in dress and manner, who tended to carry pupils along with her enthusiasm.

At the end of the periods of observation, the researchers reported certain common features in such otherwise contrasting styles. These help us to identify what is required:

(1) Both enjoyed children. They were both kind and positive towards them and communicated a sincere interest and basic concern as well as a wish and an ability to help them.
(2) Both were conscientious and well organized. This communicated strength and stability to the children.
(3) Both were generous and able to *give* at different levels – one in response to basic emotional needs; the other in response to the child's need for success. Each communicated to the child her personal enjoyment of *giving* rather than withholding or restricting.
(4) Both avoided power struggles.
(5) Both took the child's abnormal behaviour in their stride. Neither was panicked by it. One showed this by a kind of neutrality, a non-registration of moral indignation; the other by not emphasizing failure and bad behaviour, and by helping the child to forget it.

The authors of this study go on to point out that the question is not which style of teaching is better for the maladjusted child *but which is better for which kinds of maladjusted children.* The relatively unstructured approach which emphasized the meeting of emotional needs and gave freedom for making and experimenting with relationships is clearly applicable to younger children and children who are in the early stages of treatment. In particular, it suits children who are withdrawn as a result of over-bearing parents or detached, emotionally cold parents. It suits children who have been emotionally deprived and those who need to learn that acceptance does not depend on being able to achieve. It seems the right environment for children who have experienced power struggles with adults and have learnt all the techniques of winning and non-conforming. The authors suggest that the more structured approach benefits the child who is reaching the stage where he wants to be like others and is ready to try to adapt and to conform; children whose backgrounds have not provided them with models of behaviour or achievement or who have been allowed to remain at an immature level of adaptation; certain children who have not developed an organized sense of self who need the feelings of success and mastery or the external controls to acquire behaviour patterns.

Individual levels of motivation

Rather than contrasting so-called permissive approaches and so-called structured ones, a way is required of defining children's needs in classroom or educational terms, which recognizes that some disturbed children at one extreme are not able to accept the tasks of learning, of adjusting to the group and relating to the teacher, and that at the other extreme less disturbed children or children who are recovering may be able to benefit from more normal routines and expectations. Hewett (1964) has outlined a series of levels of educational tasks based on experience of working with emotionally disturbed children in a clinic in California. He calls it a hierarchy of educational tasks in which seven levels are distinguished. At the *primary task level* the child is unable to respond to social controls or is totally resistant to learning and the teacher can motivate the child only through basic rewards such as food, sweets or affection. The teacher has to establish contact on the child's own terms as a basis for achieving more control and direction later. We can observe this level in some mentally handi-capped children, autistic children and occasionally in disturbed child-ren of infant age. This is the level at which operant conditioning is undertaken (see p. 87).

The *acceptance task level* is one in which the teacher attempts to establish the beginnings of a relationship and the child shows the be-ginnings of a response, though contact is still on the child's terms. For example, a withdrawn non-communicating child may show some interest in a piece of apparatus the teacher offers, may look at pictures with the teacher or make some tentative show of playing with sand, clay or other material. It is a beginning but no more.

At the *order task level* the teacher aims to get the child settling for a short time to specific tasks which are carefully chosen to suit the child's capacity and to ensure completion and success. The child has begun to accept some of the conditions for learning.

The *exploratory task level* emphasizes exploration of the environ-ment through multi-sensory experience. It is the level at which we can engage the child through interests and activity. With young children a full participation in play within a well organized environ-ment such as is provided in nursery and infant schools epitomizes this level. With older children, the use of a wide range of activities in practical, creative work and environmental studies provide this. In remedial teaching, it is often necessary to start at this 'interest' stage.

The *relationship task level* is one in which the child accepts, con-trols and applies himself to tasks because he is beginning to be con-cerned with gaining approval and recognition from the teacher and the group. At this level the relationship between teacher and pupil becomes an important force for motivating learning and developing social attitudes. Moreover children can begin to work together in pairs or in group projects.

The levels so far described are 'readiness' levels which have been achieved in a measure by most normal children during the infant stage. The next one – *the mastery level* – is one where the child is ready to apply himself to tasks for the sake of achieving; he is no longer dependent on motivation through interest or teacher's approval. He wants to learn; he wants to conform. At this level the teacher's task is to assess the child's needs and plan learning and experience which ensure progress. In remedial teaching, for example, the child can often have the immediate programme outlined to him and his progress can be expressed in tangible form through graphs and check lists, e.g. lists of books read. At the last level – *the achievement task level* – the child is fairly consistently self-motivated, is achieving successfully, eager for new experience and learning and is well integrated into the classroom.

Teachers of maladjusted and backward children will recognize this series of levels as a codification of ideas inherent in their own practice. A remedial group or a class of maladjusted or backward children commonly contain children spread through the levels from acceptance to mastery. One cannot assume, as one can (though not always correctly) with a normal class, that the children are able to function at the mastery level. A survey by Sampson (1968b) into the work of remedial teachers shows that they recognize very clearly the need to start many pupils at least at the exploratory or relationship task levels. Moreover an individual child may be at different levels in different tasks. Michael, for example, was a very withdrawn, over-protected child. In reading he was at the mastery or achievement level. In number he was at the order level in the sense that he would comply with a very simple task, but with anything more complex he would escape. Socially he was at the low acceptance level – he avoided contact with other children and adults and any participation in group activities. He had a limited acceptance of his teacher which was far from being a relationship. It is difficult (though not impossible) for a teacher in an ordinary class to recognize and provide for these different levels in one or two children while the others are operating at the mastery level. We have to have the confidence to set demands and devise activities at the levels children can function at in the hope of working up through them.

Finding and providing the appropriate levels for children means that the classroom should have available a wide range of materials and learning experiences. Hewett in a later article describes a classroom 'engineered' for emotionally disturbed children, i.e. the room is organized to provide for three major levels in the hierarchy of educational tasks. There is a mastery-achievement centre where academic assignments can be undertaken in a desk area or in two study booths designed to eliminate visual distraction. There is an exploratory centre with art and science materials and there is an order level centre where there are available puzzles, exercises and materials emphasizing concentration and routine. This idea is much more fully worked out and practised in English nursery and primary schools and in many kinds of special class where the environment is carefully organized to provide spaces where different kinds and levels of activity can go on and which are appropriately supplied with materials. It is accepted that some children will be working individually or in a group at academic work while others may be engaged in readiness work or in some experimental or practical work having completed an assignment. In schools using vertical grouping, where a class unit contains children of several different ages, it is essential to work in this way and clearly it facilitates the provision of materials and space for the different levels of maturity of children.

While it might appear to the casual observer that this kind of organization is a soft option for the teacher, the reverse is, of course, true. It requires not only careful organization of materials but careful record keeping so that the teacher knows what individual children are capable of doing, what they actually do, what they can be guided into doing and what they actually achieve. Though this kind of classroom is often referred to as an unstructured classroom, it is in fact a good deal more structured than a conventional one – the structuring being both in the organization of the room and its materials and, more importantly, in the framework of ideas within which the teacher works. The teacher has to be clear about his aims and how the materials and activities are utilized to achieve them.

The possibility that this kind of classroom is too distracting and over-stimulating for some disturbed children has been suggested by a number of writers. In fact teachers of maladjusted children point out that the highly stimulating approach needed to arouse the interest and motivation of educationally subnormal children is often not appropriate to groups of maladjusted children. In the USA Strauss and Lehtinen (1947) outlined an educational method for brain injured children which was designed to minimize the effects of distractibility, perceptual disabilities, impulsiveness and hyperactivity which, it was claimed, are characteristic of these children. Emphasis was given to reducing extraneous visual and auditory stimuli, reducing excessive physical activity and movement during study periods, providing well ordered and well graded learning tasks and insistence on accuracy and completion of work. Cruikshank (1961) who continued this kind of work has applied it to emotionally disturbed children organizing classrooms with carpeting and sound proofing, and all potentially distracting visual stimuli are removed. The approach emphasizes the development of academic skills in an orderly, timetabled, well planned programme of educational tasks. Haring and Phillips (1962) have also advocated this kind of approach. For example, children had to complete assigned work before play or recreational opportunities were allowed. Most of the academic work was done in the morning – physical education, art, music and free play periods came in the afternoon provided a child's work was 'up to par'. During the morning 'water in the classroom sink was kept off; art materials were kept under cover to minimize distraction'. Limits were set upon the amount of movement about the class.

There are certainly children who for one reason or another are highly distractible and benefit from the opportunity to work in a quiet corner or from individual teaching in a remedial room. There are also children who benefit from clear routines and guide lines, who are required to complete a task before moving on to a preferred one. For example, children whose experience at home is of a lax and indulgent discipline often need the support of a definite framework if they are to progress in learning. They are not so much maladjusted as untrained. But to generalize that all maladjusted children require a highly structured programme is naïve and smacks of reacting to a bogey of extreme permissiveness which is rarely observed in a school setting.

It would be a great advantage if there were more studies like that quoted earlier of teachers' methods of class control for many teachers feel the need for an account of classroom practice. Redl (1957), an American psychiatrist who worked closely with very disturbed adolescents, provides an interesting list of seventeen kinds of intervention which the teacher can employ depending on the child and the situation. The following summary cannot do justice to his account; his full discussion of each tactic is well worth reading. All of the tactics are well known to teachers but the list, together with their deliberately amusing labels, focuses attention on them.

(1) *Planned ignoring*: the skilled teacher knows that sometimes attention-seeking or provocative behaviour is best ignored.

(2) *Signal intereference*: sometimes unacceptable behaviour can be inhibited by a gesture, facial expression or verbal prohibition. As everyone knows, whether this will succeed depends on the child, the situation and the relationship between teacher and child.

(3) *Proximity and touch control*: misbehaviour, restlessness, anxiety or excitement may be reduced by the physical proximity of the teacher or, if insufficient, by touch control -- holding the child's hand or a touch on the shoulder.

(4) *Involvement in interest relationship*: a child losing interest in an activity or about to be distracted into misbehaviour is refocused on the activity when teacher displays interest in it.

(5) *Hypodermic affection*: an 'injection' of affection or praise

may enable the child to cope with anxiety or frustration.

(6) *Tension decontamination through humour* speaks for itself.

(7) *Hurdle help*: when the child is coming up against frustration in play, work or social activity, the teacher gives help before a crisis arrives so that the child is able to cope with the difficulty.

(8) *Interpretation as interference*: the teacher interprets to the child a situation which he has misinterpreted or not perceived so that he understands why he was feeling jealous, awkward or hostile.

(9) *Regrouping*: placing a child in another group or class to avoid negative reactions.

(10) *Restructuring*: when excitement, noise and disruptive activity are building up, the activity can be changed for a different or quieter one.

(11) *Direct appeal*: depending on the child it may be effective to appeal to a child's sense of co-operation, fair play or kindness.

(12) *Limitation of space and tools*: limits have to be set. At times there is no alternative but to withdraw privileges or materials, e.g. when there is an element of danger and loss of control.

(13) *Antiseptic bouncing*: there are times when a child has to be withdrawn from a group for his own or other children's sake. The word 'antiseptic' stresses that it should not have psychological side effects, e.g. intensifying the child's feeling of rejection or being pleasurable and rewarding.

(14) *Physical restraint*: the necessity for this may arise in an infant or an adolescent. Redl's discussion of the problem is essential.

(15) *Permission and prohibition*: there are occasions when positively to permit an activity is sometimes sufficient to remove its attractiveness. It is also necessary, of course, to make quite clear that some things are positively prohibited.

(16) *Promises and rewards* and

(17) *Punishments and threats*: are such complex issues that it is essential to read Redl's ample discussion of them.

Redl calls these 'techniques for the antiseptic manipulation of surface behaviour', i.e. they do not get at the root of the trouble but may be a means of minimizing symptoms and avoiding crises. Their use is hedged around with qualifications and safeguards depending on the child, the teacher-child relationship and the total situation. They are in fact all techniques which experienced teachers use without thinking about it but being aware of them and their possible applications can be a help.

Another approach to the treatment of maladjusted behaviour is offered by *behaviour modification* techniques which are aimed at changing specific patterns of inappropriate behaviour, e.g. over-activity, attention-seeking, nervous habits, uncommunicativeness and over-talkativeness. The essence of the approach is first to decide what inappropriate behaviour should be decreased and which should be increased. Secondly, to examine what rewards or reinforcement of the unwanted behaviour should be avoided and what reinforcements should increase the occurrence of the desired behaviour. Thirdly, the avoidance and application of reinforcements are applied consistently and, ideally, a record is kept of changes in behaviour.

It is a common situation in class that nuisance behaviour gets rewarded by teacher's attention (and often by the approval or annoyance of the children). Behaviour modification suggests ignoring the attention-seeking behaviour and ensuring that desirable behaviour, such as sitting quietly and getting on with work, is rewarded by attention, praise or some other reward. This sounds commonsense. Teachers often do try to ignore the attention-seeker but they are perhaps less likely to reward consistently when he does settle to the task in hand. A common reaction is likely to be: 'Thank goodness X is quiet; I can attend to Y.'

While the underlying principle is understood by teachers the full possibilities of selective and systematic reinforcement of behaviour have probably not been fully utilized. Rather than just hoping to stimulate a withdrawn child to come out 'of his shell' or a non-communicator to talk, a more careful assessment of what rewarding consequences favour participation or communication and a more systematic application of rewards will accelerate progress. A considerable number of research reports claim good results. (A short account is in an article by Thomas (1965).)

It is worth noting that unusual or odd behaviour is sometimes unwittingly reinforced. The child who tells a 'tall story' may be rewarded and encouraged to repeat the performance if it is given too much attention and pursued in an attempt to get the child to see its unreality. It is often hard to avoid reinforcing an obsessive interest in a certain topic, plaything or activity, but a programme could be devised for strongly rewarding any widening of the range of interest. Only too often, the obsession or isolated display of knowledge and skill is reinforced by being something to point out and discuss with others.

The behaviour modification approach is sometimes criticized as not getting down to the root of the trouble. The sensible thing is to use whatever methods are effective and, if behaviour modification principles can help the teacher to alleviate particular difficulties, it would no doubt help the larger aims of effecting teacher-pupil relationships and creating a therapeutic environment.

Further reading

BLACKHAM, G. J. (1967), *The Deviant Child in the Classroom*, N.J.: Prentice-Hall.

BURNS, M. (1956), *Mr Lyward's Answer*, London: Hamish Hamilton.

CHAZAN, M. (1963), 'Maladjusted pupils: trends in post-war theory and practice,' *Educational Research*, 6, 1, 29-41.

DEPARTMENT OF EDUCATION AND SCIENCE (1967), *The Education of Maladjusted Children*, Education Pamphlet No. 47, London: H.M.S.O

ERIKSON, E. H. (1965), *Childhood and Society*, Harmondsworth; Pelican.

EVANS, M. (1967), Chapter in *What is Special Education?*, 1966 International Conference, Association for Special Education.

EVANS, M. AND MARTIN, F. (1968), 'Two Children at Chalcot', *Special Education*, 57, 1, 22-5.

HARING, N. G. AND PHILLIPS, E. L. (1962), *Educating Emotionally Disturbed Children*, New York: McGraw-Hill.

HEWETT, F. (1964), 'A hierarchy of educational tasks for children with learning disorders', *Exceptional Children*, 34, 4, 207-14.

KAHN, J. AND NURSTEN, J. P. (1964), *Unwillingly to School*, Oxford: Pergamon.

LANSDOWN, R. (ed.) (1970), *Day Schools for Maladjusted Children*, Association of Workers with Maladjusted Children.

LENNHOFF, F. G. (1960), *Exceptional Children*, London: Allen & Unwin.

MACLEAN, I. C. (1966), *Child Guidance and the School*, London: Methuen.

MINISTRY OF EDUCATION (1955), *Report of the Committee on Maladjusted Children* (The Underwood Report), London: H.M.S.O.

REDL, F. (1957), *The Aggressive Child*, Chicago: The Free Press.

SHIELDS, R. (1962), *A Cure for Delinquents*, London: Heinemann Educational.

STOTT, D. H. (1966), *Studies of Troublesome Children*, London: Tavistock Publications.

—— (1966), 3rd edition, *The Social Adjustment of Children* (Manual to the Bristol Social Adjustment Guides), University of London Press.

WILLS, D. (1960), *Throw Away Thy Rod*, London: Gollancz.

four

Intellectual handicaps

Retarded mental development in its various degrees of severity is the commonest disability for which special educational help is needed. Few teachers have not met pupils whose capacity to learn is well below that of average children; most people know of some family in which there is a mentally handicapped child. Among children with physical and sensory handicaps, low intelligence is a common additional disability and many multi-handicapped children tend to be rather severely mentally retarded. The need to understand, therefore, the nature of mental retardation and to evolve effective methods of education is an important one but, it would be fair to suggest, progress has lagged behind work in other fields of handicap.

One reason for this is historical. Education for deaf and blind children was started early in the development of special education and there was always an optimistic belief that special methods could do much to overcome visual and hearing impairments. For the mentally handicapped, however, the view was rather the reverse at times. They were thought to have limited potentialities for improvement by education and training and for the first half of the century the conception of care for the mentally handicapped tended to be a custodial one and even special schooling was rather limited in aim and scope by the feeling that too much could not be expected of 'defective' children. It is mainly during the last twenty years that greater efforts have been made to develop the subnormal's potentialities through training and work in hospitals and in the community and to develop centres for children in the community. These trends have culminated in the severely subnormal children being brought under the responsibility of education services rather than health, the implications of which have still to be thoroughly worked out.

One result of these earlier conceptions was that, apart from a few devoted pioneers, there was a shortage of people interested in research and in experimental methods of treatment. Since the Second World War, however, there has been a marked change. There has been a considerable amount of medical research into the causes of mental handicap so that some of the causes are better understood; some can be prevented, some treated and the search for other causes and treatments continues. Research by psychologists has led to more optimistic views about the learning and work-capacity of subnormal individuals, and research into their limitations of thinking, language and learning has begun to provide tentative findings which have implications for methods of education. The educational and social aims of teaching for the moderately retarded have become clearer, and with the replacement in 1945 of the category of mentally defective by the category educationally subnormal a big expansion of special educational provision has been paralleled by a very much broader and varied scope of special educational approaches. For the severely subnormal the amount and quality of provision has improved and an important task in the immediate future is to develop a distinctive and progressive educational approach for them.

These stirrings of progress have not come a moment too soon. The disability of low mental ability is as much as anything a social handicap; rapid development and change in society increase its significance and consequences. The educational requirements and social competence skills required for a minimal adjustment to living and working in modern communities are considerably greater than those of urban, and even more of rural, life half a century ago. There are fewer unskilled jobs – for example, farm labouring which used to be thought something of a haven for the least intelligent is now a job requiring skills and adaptability; domestic service has diminished and the kind of help needed has changed. For those who get married and raise a family, living itself raises greater complexities especially when a large family and low income leave no margin for error and incompetence. The organization and methods of educating the least able pupils in our schools is not therefore a matter for a casual or *laissez-faire* approach nor for doctrinaire remedies. It requires a clear-minded assessment of their present educational potentialities and their future social needs.

As well as technical and organizational changes in society, there are changes in attitude and belief which affect work with the mentally retarded. A more educated and liberal society is less willing to tolerate custodial care as a long-term solution for those who cannot manage. Sheltered employment, hostel accommodation and social work services for families are increasingly needed. At the same time, more flexible concepts about human differences, more optimistic views about the extent to which abilities can be improved and greater awareness of social and group influences on learning have led to a profitable questioning of many customary methods of organizing education. From many points of view, therefore, the policies and methods of education and care for the mentally limited are ready to seek and take new directions.

Degrees of intellectual handicap

In order to discuss the different kinds of education and care needed by children with intellectual limitations, it is necessary to distinguish different kinds of problem, though it must be stressed that such distinctions have to be flexible since the problems overlap. The most frequently used grouping is according to the *severity of the disability*.

Thus ten to fifteen per cent of the normal school population are sufficiently below average in intelligence to warrant special consideration as *slow learners*. They are later than average children in learning basic educational skills such as reading and writing; their learning needs to be carefully graded and organized, particularly to ensure the acquisition of concepts since their limitations are relatively more marked in abstraction and generalization and in the use and acquisition of language. With appropriate and well-planned teaching, they can make reasonable progress and make a successful transition to life after leaving school.

A smaller group of children can be distinguished in whom these limitations are more marked and often complicated by adverse environmental circumstances, poor health, physical and sensory defects. While they can learn to read and write and to use arithmetic for normal everyday purposes in living, their academic achievements are limited. Their emotional and social development is also slower and a particular emphasis in their education is ensuring that they achieve sufficient personal maturity and social awareness to facilitate their adjustment to post-school life. Most of them fit satisfactorily into the community after leaving school, but a proportion are less successful and ways need to be found of avoiding such failures or partial failures. Special schools for somewhat less than one per cent of the school population are provided for these educationally subnormal children, but at least an equal number in ordinary schools require special consideration of the methods and organization of their education.

The most limited of these children merge into those who until recently were considered 'unsuitable for education' and were provided for in junior training centres or in hospitals for the subnormal. These severely subnormal children are in general not able to benefit from the usual academic aspects of education. Considerable emphasis has to be given to developing their personal and social competence so that they can become more self-reliant and less dependent on their families for supervision and care. But there is considerable scope for education, not narrowly conceived in academic terms, to promote their physical, emotional and intellectual development and to provide special training to improve key functions such as perceptual and motor ability, language and thinking. Developments in this work will be of value to mentally retarded children in other groups of handicap.

A further group of children in hospitals or special-care units are so mentally and developmentally retarded, often multi-handicapped, that it is less a question of providing them with an educational programme as providing basic sensory-motor experiences so that they have the opportunity of making such progress in mental and physical functioning as they may be capable of. The end result may be to make them less bed-bound or chair-bound, less completely dependent on others, but there is always the possibility that in some cases the masking effects of multi-handicaps may be withdrawn, leading to much greater progress than expected. The ways of doing this and the preparation of nurses and other helpers for doing so have scarcely been explored as yet (Mittler, 1969).

The grouping briefly outlined above indicates the different educational aims for children with increasingly severe intellectual limitations and the degree to which modifications of normal educational methods and organizations are required. These will be considered in more detail later. Meanwhile it is necessary to consider whether different causes or combinations of causes of mental retardation have implications for educational aims and methods.

POOR INHERITED POTENTIALITY

Some mental backwardness is related to poor genetic endowment. Just as some children are innately bright, there are others who are innately limited in intellectual potentiality. At one time, the assumption of low inborn capacity tended to be accepted as sufficient explanation of poor educational achievements, but this view is now modified by the view that intelligence as it is observed in a child's behaviour is the product of learning through activity and experience. Many children in the lower ranges of intelligence have experienced as infants, and continue to experience during childhood, environmental experiences which are less productive of intellectual development. Though the environment may provide sufficient perceptual and motor experience it is often the case that the stimulation to thinking and the use of language is meagre. This does not always apply, of course. In school one meets dull children from intelligent and well educated families whose home background has promoted their optimum intellectual and educational development, and the teacher's task is rather to guard against the negative effects of feelings of failure arising from comparisons with other brighter children in the family.

Modern views of the nature of developing intelligence, together with a fuller realization of the many emotional, social and personal factors which affect educational progress and achievement, all imply an important role for the educator. Though native ability may be poor there is much scope for engineering the best conditions for learning and adjustment.

SOCIAL AND CULTURAL FACTORS

In the first uses of intelligence tests early this century psychologists were impressed with the finding that low intelligence was often associated with a variety of social failures – depravity, incompetence, prostitution and delinquency. They concluded that mental retardation caused these evils, a conclusion which for a time led to restrictive attitudes and held back the development of more positive and remedial treatment – and still has lingering effects on public attitudes. We now tend to see the relationship operating the opposite way. Unstable families, defective family care, inadequate mothering, economic and cultural poverty and other very adverse environmental circumstances do not provide the emotional and cultural basis required for developing attention, perception, thinking and language, nor for developing good attitudes towards education. In some cases, children surprisingly rise above such circumstances. In others, either because of the severity or unrelieved duration of the adversities, because of additional physical or sensory disabilities or because of inherent limitations of intelligence, the resulting intellectual limitation is sufficient to require special educational help. How far such effects are reversible by education is uncertain. Clarke (1954), testing adolescents in a hospital for the subnormal, found that in the period following admission there were gains in IQ. Looking more closely at the results he found that these gains were largest in a group of patients coming from the most adverse home environments, judged on criteria such as poverty, child neglect, families with no fixed home. A number of investigations into the effect on mentally retarded children of special educational experience find that improvement is most readily obtained with the children from sub-cultural environments. Kirk (1959) for example, found that a pre-school experience for mentally retarded children aged four to seven had greater effect on children from poor homes than those whose retardation had an organic or physical basis.

Recognition of a group of retarded children in whom social-cultural factors are influential has important implications for practice. It raises such questions as what can be done to *prevent* retardation by providing pre-school education, by social and advisory help to parents, by intensive teaching programmes aimed at remedying weaknesses significant for education (e.g. in perception and language). In many of these children we may hope for quicker progress than in those who are inherently limited or suffering additional sensory or neurological disabilities. The generalizations about the needs of socially disadvantaged children made in Chapter 7 apply to this group.

EMOTIONAL CAUSES OF INTELLECTUAL HANDICAP

It is a common observation that emotional disturbance affects a child's learning in school and may also depress a child's mental functioning. Often in a congenial school atmosphere such a child improves and makes better use of his ability. It is not perhaps so easily accepted that low intelligence may be the result of very adverse emotional conditions earlier in the child's life. Russell Davis (1967) has hypothesized that low intelligence is sometimes due to the inhibiting effect of severe emotional upset occurring at critical periods of the child's life – a family crisis, serious illness of the mother or the child at the age when speech or exploration of the environment was just beginning. How far such effects can be reversed is uncertain but one must act on the educator's belief that they can be.

ORGANIC FACTORS IN INTELLECTUAL HANDICAP

A great variety of pathological conditions affect the organism's growth and functioning. In Down's disease (Mongolism) the characteristics of facial and bodily structure are easily recognizable. The skull is small, flattened and shorter than it is wide, eyes often appearing slanting; short stature; short, broad hands and feet; large tongue; loose, easily-roughened skin. There are many other less obvious differences and associated disorders including heart disorders. Many used to die in infancy as a result of respiratory infections but more now survive. After many years of investigation which implicated a large number of factors (for example, the older age of a proportion of the mothers), the cause was eventually tracked down to extra chromosomal material in the cells of mongol children.

About 20 per cent of all severely retarded children suffer from

Down's disease, and in junior training schools about 40 to 50 per cent of the children are mongols. The range of ability varies from severe to mild retardation; quite a number of them are able to benefit from special school work at least during the primary years and some become very competent at taking responsibilities and participating in social activities at home. Much depends on their education and care.

Metabolic disorders as causes of mental retardation have been known for a long time. Probably the best known is phenylketonuria discovered by Folling in 1934 who found phenylpyruvic acid in the urine of two young defective brothers. It was found that a protein substance in food, phenylalanine, is not metabolized owing to an inborn defect in the metabolic process. As a result phenylpyruvic acid and other incomplete metabolites are released into the system bringing about retardation and other physical abnormalities. In the 1950s ways were found of providing a diet which had only the essential amount of phenylalanine so that with careful dietary control, starting very early in babyhood, there is a good chance of the child developing within the normal range. In order to ensure early detection, simple tests have been devised whereby babies can be screened in the first few weeks of life in order to discover the 1 in 10,000 children who have the disease and to have dietary treatment instituted. The success of treatment depends, of course, not only on biochemical control but also on the ability and willingness of mothers to supervise the diet, to co-operate with regular medical checks and generally to provide as normal conditions for the child's development as possible. Though phenylketonuria is the best known metabolic disorder, many others have been studied and the search for others continues (O'Gorman, 1969).

Various kinds of damage to the brain are responsible for a variety of problems ranging from severe subnormality to mild learning difficulties in an otherwise normal child. Knowledge of brain functions is of relatively recent origin. In the period after the First World War, useful knowledge was obtained from studying the consequences of head wounds sustained by soldiers – the reduced ability to think abstractly, the tendency to react to stimuli which people normally ignore, difficulties with comprehension and expression in language. In the 1920s these findings influenced the study of similar cognitive and language disorders in handicapped children, particularly the speech defective and the mentally retarded.

About the same time distinctions were being made between different kinds of retarded child. One kind of distinction was between a *pathological* type and a *sub-cultural* type. The former included all cases due to infection, organic damage, hydrocephalus, epilepsy and various other clinical conditions. The latter included retardation which is the low extreme of normal variation in intelligence and retardation due to environmental handicaps. A similar classification distinguished primary mental defect (due to inheritance or to clinical conditions such as mongolism) from secondary defect (due to disease or other injurious factors). During the 1930s, Werner and Strauss, two refugees from Germany, were working in the USA studying the perception and thinking of the mentally retarded. Their work led to the publication of *The Psychopathology of the Brain Injured Child* (Strauss and Lehtinen, 1947) in which Strauss made a distinction between ordinary mental defectives (whom he called the endogenous) and those who had experienced brain damage before, during or after birth (which he called the exogenous). He claimed that the latter showed characteristic patterns of disability in learning and behaviour. Later in the book, Lehtinen, a teacher, described special methods of teaching she developed for these children.

The main characteristics which Strauss described were: *disturbances in perception* – e.g. difficulty in distinguishing figure from ground; *distractibility* – a tendency to be distracted by perceptual stimuli which are normally ignored; *perseveration* – a tendency to continue some action or mental activity beyond the point needed; difficulties in *concept formation* – e.g. a tendency to sort things in unusual ways or to group things which are only tenuously connected; *disturbance in behaviour* – erratic, unco-ordinated, uninhibited, impulsive behaviour. It soon became apparent that this cluster of symptoms occurred in children in whom there was no history of brain damage or no evidence of neurological abnormality and the term 'Strauss syndrome' rather than 'brain damaged' was proposed.

This account certainly matches the behaviour of some children in special schools and it is not surprising that Strauss's account aroused a considerable and continuing interest, provoked much research comparing groups of endogenous and exogenous children and led to further developments in educational methods. Two people who worked with Strauss early in their careers continued to follow up this work. Kephart (1960) described methods for developing basic motor patterns and perceptual-motor integration. Cruickshank (1961) and his associates investigated the perceptual and conceptual difficulties of cerebral palsied children, proposed detailed methods for teaching brain injured children and advocated special classrooms designed to remove distracting auditory and visual stimuli. In several books he has described a structured programme of teaching methods and home care for 'brain injured children'.

The concept of 'the brain injured child' as an *educational* label is however an unsatisfactory one. Birch (1964) has discussed some of the difficulties. Some children show Strauss syndrome characteristics with no evidence of neurological abnormality; in others, neurological abnormalities are present but with no or few signs of disordered behaviour! Moreover, brain damage can mean very different things according to its cause (e.g. accident or infection), the type, place and extent of the lesion in the brain. Its effects on behaviour will vary according to the stage of the organism's development at which it occurred, according to the individual's genetic potentialities and capacities and according to the many environmental experiences which modify the individual's development (the parents' management of the child, the quality of schooling, the child's capacity for compensation and adaptation). As Birch remarks, 'The behavioural disturbance of children who come to our notice are developmental products and not merely manifestations of a damaged portion of the brain.' All these considerations suggest that we should avoid the stereotype of the brain injured child (and the term) and should keep in mind that, for educational purposes, it is behaviour which is important and, moreover, that behaviour is influenced by developmental and environmental factors.

In other words, teachers and psychologists should observe and assess disorders and severe developmental lags in perception, perceptual-motor, thinking and language skills so that teaching can be prescribed to remedy the weaknesses. Awareness that there may be an organic basis for these difficulties is important for avoiding the assumption that emotional factors or inadequate teaching methods are primary causes. Ordinary experience at school and home will probably be insufficient to remedy matters; indeed children often avoid what they cannot do.

Slow learning children

Until 1945, there was a fairly sharp distinction between the 'dull and backward' in ordinary schools and the 'mentally defective' in special schools. Recognizing that such a distinction is inappropriate, it has been the practice since 1945 to think of a large group of backward children, a few of whom require education in a special school, and a larger number able to be educated in ordinary schools. The term 'educationally subnormal' strictly applies to the whole group but in practice it is often used to refer to children who go to a special school for educationally subnormal children.

The term educationally subnormal was introduced in the list of categories of handicapped children given in the Handicapped Pupils and School Health Service regulations 1945. The 'definition' was: 'pupils who by reason of limited ability or other conditions resulting in educational retardation, require some specialization form of education wholly or partly in substitution for the education normally given in ordinary schools.' This defined an educational need and thus marked a change from the pre-war requirement of ascertaining children with 'a mental defect' which required special schooling. Moreover, it recognized that marked educational backwardness could be due to limited ability or other conditions – minor physical and sensory disabilities, maladjustment, environmental handicaps. It was suggested that 10 per cent of the school population might be considered educationally subnormal in this broad sense and Pamphlet No. 5 (Ministry of Education, 1946) clearly hoped that delineating this broad group of backward children would lead not only to more special school provision for the very backward but also a variety of ways of providing special educational help in ordinary schools.

PROVISION IN SPECIAL SCHOOLS

In 1968 there were about 50,000 educationally subnormal children in special schools. About 9,000 of these were in residential schools which are required in thinly-populated areas (where day schools would be unsuitable), and also required in large urban areas for very backward children with emotional and social difficulties or very adverse home conditions.

In large urban areas, this special school provision is available for about 1 per cent of the school population. In some very rural areas, the amount is very much smaller owing to the difficulty of gathering together sufficient numbers of children over large distances for a day school.

Day schools frequently do not admit until seven years of age but, as suggested earlier, it is desirable that children needing special help should be transferred as soon as possible after that age. An increasing number of schools do, however, have classes for children of infant age. Such classes often perform an assessment function making it possible to assess whether the child is likely to benefit from the kind of education given later in the school or would be better placed in a school for severely subnormal children. Most schools are all-age schools continuing the child's education through to sixteen years, the statutory leaving age for special schools.

In the pre-war period the small number of places in schools for 'mentally defective' children and the required process of certification meant that these special schools catered largely for children with IQs below 70. Since the war, the broader definition of the category and the generally progressive quality of the education given has led to more children with higher IQs being referred for special education. In South Wales, Williams (1967) found that 161 children in ESN schools included twelve with IQs below 60, forty-three between 61 and 69, thirty-five between 70 and 79 and ten above 80. In other words, there were nearly as many above IQ 70 as below; the trend is probably not untypical of the country. Williams also showed that the excess of the boys over girls is greater in the higher IQ ranges, which may be due to the greater incidence of reading backwardness among boys or the tendency of boys to show more behaviour difficulties. Further light is shed by Williams's study of fifty-seven children who had been returned from special to ordinary schools. The mean IQ of this group when they were examined for special schooling was 73 with a range from 54 to 83. (When their social competence was assessed on the Vineland Maturity Scale after leaving special schools the mean Social Quotient was 103). Discussing other factors in their records, Williams notes that in contrast with mentally retarded children, they passed the milestones of development normally and showed very few speech problems. As a group, however, they had experienced adverse environmental factors – there was some financial anxiety in families often related to father's poor occupational record, and families were often large. An outstanding feature running through the group was a strong element of lack of mothering. We might see them as children in whom lowish ability combined with environmental factors resulted in poor initial progress in school. In spite of the fact that they were not ascertained for special school until the average age of nine years two months (range six to twelve years) they made good progress in a special school and were able to return to ordinary schools. One is tempted to wonder whether this improvement could not have been brought about in ordinary schools.

The other end of the educationally subnormal range is illuminated by Williams's examination of forty-seven children who had been excluded from special schools as 'unsuitable for education'. At the time of ascertainment, their mean IQ was 55 with a range from 72 to unassessable. A defect of speech was noted in half the group, more than a quarter had some degree of motor inco-ordination, three had a hearing loss and four a defect of visual acuity. In comparison with the previous group, these children came from adequate and good homes and the distribution of social class was closer to that of the general population. Why were these children unsuccessful even in a special school? We ought perhaps to ask whether a more thorough assessment of the assets and deficits of children like these should be made and more carefully programmed methods of teaching and training attempted to remedy the weaknesses.

By studying the extreme ends of the range of children being educated in ESN schools, Williams has brought out clearly two kinds of educational need being met in the special school, the environmentally and the organically handicapped, and in the middle of the range are children who have fairly marked mental retardation, sometimes combined with adverse environmental factors, sometimes with organic ones, sometimes with both. It may be appropriate for the ESN school to cater for this range but with the assimilation of the severely subnormal to education, the possibility might be considered of some restriction of the range to permit a more thorough attack on the very special educational needs of the intellectually handicapped and the children with organic deficits. With the current emphasis for providing for the handicapped child wherever possible in the ordinary school, it is desirable to consider whether the remedial function which was so successful with Williams's high IQ group could not be organized in ordinary schools. Putting the issue explicitly, the question is whether the trend since 1945 to broaden the criteria for admission to special ESN schools does not need to be somewhat reversed.

PROVISION IN ORDINARY SCHOOLS

The crucial issue, of course, is what can be done in ordinary schools. Special educational help in ordinary schools is less easy to evaluate since there are no published statistics nor any large scale surveys of the amount and kind of provision. Some of the more obvious signs of progress are the increased number of remedial teachers and remedial services. Many secondary schools have a remedial department and a teacher with special responsibility for backward children. An unknown number of primary schools are able to organize a special class for backward pupils or give remedial teaching in some way. A few authorities have developed a more organized provision of special classes to supplement special schooling, and have arranged for in-service training of special class teachers.

The question is one of prevention as well as of organization. We can look forward hopefully to increased nursery school and nursery class education to give more of the children with low abilities and limited cultural background an opportunity for acquiring the perceptual, motor and language skills as well as the emotional maturity known to be important in readiness for learning in the infant school. Without this, infant schools have to make up for these deficiencies as well as begin to make a start on more formal educational skills. Prevention also means more contact and interaction with parents in schools in areas which so frequently supply the waiting lists for special schools. More social work, remedial work and case study at these early stages might enable some children to make better progress in learning and adjustment and promote earlier identification of those children whose truly low ability or combination of minor disabilities warrants special treatment. Many infant teachers, of course, already do just this (Webb, 1967). But we need to stress the importance of the infant stage in prevention and identification and combat the rather complacent view that the very backward child is happily catered for in the infant school; that the junior school is early enough for remedial teaching and decisions about special education.

The need to look early and closely into the reasons for delayed development and difficulties in learning arises from our changed conception of the origin of such difficulties. At one time, we should have viewed them as the result of inherently slow maturation and, of course, this is true in a proportion of cases. We are now much more aware of the possibility that adverse environmental, emotional and physical factors are influential – as they were in Williams's environmentally damaged group. The sooner we can start to tackle them the better the prospect for the child.

What kind of special help is needed in ordinary schools for slow-learning children, i.e. for children in the intelligence range IQ 70 to 80 or 85, and particularly for those whose ability to learn is further limited by environmental factors and additional minor disabilities? One can agree with the suggestion in the Plowden Report that 'slow learning children are best served by the approach which characterizes the most progressive primary schools of today'. The activity and experience, the group work and the greater degree of individualization (for example, as required in non-streaming), make it easier to help the slow learner than was the case formerly when class teaching and lock-step methods were the rule. But as the Plowden Report goes on to note: 'Somewhat different provision may be required by those children who will always develop slowly and those who, with help, should be able to make relatively rapid strides.'

The Department of Education and Science Pamphlet No. 46, *Slow Learners at School*, points out the advantages of a special class for the most backward pupils in the first two years of the primary school, but also points out that its success depends on the attitude of the rest of the school – it can become at worst a group of rejects from other classes taken by an unwilling and inexperienced teacher – and also points out that in a large school a second class is really desirable to match the amount of need and to avoid too wide an age range and to provide progression. The Plowden Report wisely cautions against the danger of a remedial or opportunity class becoming a dead-end through lowering of aims and expectations in both teachers and children.

Although it is not always easy in practice, a distinction should be attempted between a remedial and a special class. A special class should cater for slow learners whose slower development and more limited capacities in learning and thinking require a modified approach in the curriculum as a whole, not only in basic subjects. More intelligent children who are very retarded need remedial teaching individually or in groups by a remedial teacher on the school staff, or a peripatetic teacher. Confusion of the two needs should at least be avoided to the extent that the slow learners' class is not permanently used for the backward child of average abilities who is likely to suffer from the slow pace and the lack of stimulation of normal companions. If an all-purpose remedial or opportunity class is the only solution, every effort should be made to get the more able child functioning sufficiently well to take his place in normal classes.

At the age of transfer to secondary schools, many slow learners have attainments at an eight- or nine-year level – some below this. Moreover their mental development – their ability to comprehend ideas, events and processes – have more in common with the junior age child than the average-to-bright twelve-year-old who is ready to respond to the more academic approach of secondary schools. Many slow learners are somewhat immature in their general personal development, the more so if their educational and personal needs have been inadequately met in the primary school. It is most desirable that they should come under the care of teachers who have real concern for these pupils and who understand their needs. Such teachers often smooth the transition by visiting backward children in their primary schools prior to transfer.

Whatever method of organization is adopted, these children need a person who can try to ensure a sense of security. A method of organization which has usually been favoured is a series of special classes or a remedial stream with smaller numbers in the classes. In the first or second years, it is good that they should meet their teacher for much of the timetable with the amount of specialization being limited. As Pamphlet No. 46 says; 'specialization confronts them with a dismembered field of learning in which their limited intellectual powers find it almost impossible to impose any pattern'. It depends, of course, how specialist teachers are used. When specialists can work as a team within an agreed framework of topics suited to the slow learners' capacities and needs, there is great advantage in the specialist contributing his particular skills and knowledge to a stimulating and meaningful scheme of work.

Various alternatives to this streamed organization have been tried in recent years so that backward pupils are included in groups of mixed ability but 'set' for basic subjects or withdrawn at suitable times for remedial work. Some of the alternative methods of organization are usefully discussed by K. Williams (1969), and by Gordon and Wilson (1969). The two great advantages of this are first, that it avoids segregation and the poor attitudes which often result – both in the pupils themselves and from the school as a whole – and second, it exposes backward pupils to the mental stimulation of brighter pupils, improves their motivation and indeed may enable them to demonstrate good abilities in some activities in spite of low achievements in others. The success of this and any other method or organization depends a great deal upon the headteacher and the staff, upon the importance and value they give to this work. If backward children and their teachers are obviously regarded low in the priorities, success is less likely.

Educational needs of slow learning children

The term 'slow learner' is an umbrella term which includes several different types of backwardness, but as the Plowden Report suggested there is a need to distinguish those who will always develop slowly. One must be cautious about making such a prediction about individual children but the fact remains that some children are certainly slower in their general development and in their learning, even when care is taken to present learning in the most suitable ways. More care is needed to develop concepts, to point out relationships, to fit explanations to their level of understanding and language comprehension, to grade steps in learning more carefully, to ensure generalization and transfer of learning. While they need an active approach emphasizing learning by doing and concrete experience (partly to ensure interest and good motivation), they probably benefit less from incidental learning. What is important and relevant in their learning needs to be more clearly brought out; they need help to grasp the purpose of their learning. Retarded language affects their progress in many ways and needs special emphasis. The fact that they are retarded in their development and their ability to learn means that their needs are comparable to those of children a stage younger as the following outline indicates.

Slow learners of infant age

Infant schools are accustomed to providing for children with very different levels of personal and mental maturity and all save the most severely retarded can be satisfactorily catered for although, as suggested elsewhere, it would be beneficial if there were more resources for early remedial work with children who have special needs of various kinds.

A few slow learners are so retarded or additionally handicapped that they start their schooling in a special school or are transferred at an early date. Their mental development is likely to be comparable to that of children aged two to four years, though this is apt to be a misleading comparison since their growth is often discrepant –

they may be quite well developed in physical skills but more retarded in language, in fine motor skills and in ability to attend, to persist and be interested in activities. Many in fact show over-active, distractible behaviour and other behaviour associated with neurological impairments. Additional disabilities are common.

In keeping with their retarded development, the approach of the infant class is comparable to that of a nursery school in which a wide range of materials and opportunities are available for activities promoting different aspects of development. The function of the teacher is to guide and stimulate activity in the group as a whole as well as to emphasize activities which her knowledge of individuals shows to be necessary. Compared with nursery school teaching, considerably more guidance is needed because spontaneous activities tend to be more short-lived, and there is less experimental, constructive and imaginative play. More specific teaching is required in language, in perceptual development, and in acquiring fine motor skills, e.g. in dressing, feeding and other self-help skills. While some may be relatively advanced in larger movements, there will be others who are clumsy and awkward, needing help in large physical and rhythmic movements.

Since 1961 assessment or diagnostic units have been set up, mainly taking children up to eight years and mainly subnormal children, with a view to assessing their educability and the educational placement needed. A survey of these by Brennan and Herbert (1969) suggests that school observation units might be a better name though a more diagnostic function could no doubt be developed if there were closer relationship with local services for comprehensive assessment.

Slow learners of junior age in special schools and classes

Children in the age range seven to eleven years have usually had several years of unsuccessful school experience and the first requirement is to establish a happy adjustment to the new environment and to provide activities similar in essentials to the ones just described. There is a need for the assessment and observation of development and abilities; ideally these children should have a thorough psychological assessment on entry – of a kind which provides a basis for individualizing teaching.

Certain generalizations can be made about backward children of this age. Their requirements for learning and the way the class is organized have much in common with an infant class. The aims may be listed as: (1) Learning to be members of a group: relating to the teacher and other children; (2) acquiring positive attitudes towards self through feelings of success and achievement; (3) learning how to play and how to learn; (4) developing thinking and language skills;

(5) finding means of expression through language, art, drama and physical movement; (6) increasing awareness and knowledge of the environment; (7) promoting readiness for basic educational skills; (8) ensuring a successful beginning for those who are ready.

The atmosphere and organization of the class should be such as to provide many opportunities for children to play and work together, to experience success in creative and practical activities and to practice thinking and language skills. While many of these activities help to promote readiness for learning, special care needs to be given to specific requirements for reading – language, visual and auditory discriminations.

A great deal of research and teaching experience, drawing upon Piaget's studies of the development of number concepts, has demonstrated the importance of adequate readiness experiences in mathematics to develop concepts of conservation, seriation, classification and measurement and the necessary vocabulary. A useful account is provided by Nicholls (1963) and further ideas are suggested in Chapter 3 of *Primary Mathematics* (Schools Council, 1966). Readiness for writing skills is important and as slow learners begin to write in connection with their reading, it is important to ensure that they are forming letters in the right way. Adequate preparation and teaching of these basic skills at this stage saves a lot of trouble later when it is difficult to remedy wrong habits and poor attitudes.

It is important to ensure the continued development of social competence skills (self-help, independence) and sociability (the ability to get on with other children and relate to the teacher and other adults). It is common to find a number of children who are unsettled or maladjusted – some showing inhibited behaviour, others awkward hostile behaviour, attention-seeking and restlessness. Chazan (1964) found that about one-third of ESN children showed more than twenty symptoms of maladjusted behaviour when assessed on the Bristol Social Adjustment Guides compared with 14 per cent of a normal control group. This underlines the importance of a therapeutic element in the education of ESN children. The relationship with the teacher, the atmosphere of the class, expressive activities, feelings of achievement both in academic and non-academic activities are rightly stressed by teachers. But Chazan's results suggest that a major factor in maladjustment is a social one. The nature of maladjustment indicates 'that they need positive and secure relationships with adults and protection from strain producing situations, especially from a feeling of rejection'; 45·6 per cent of his sample came from homes where the father was an unskilled labourer or unemployed or where there was no father because of separation, desertion or death. Half were in families with five or more children; 10 per cent from families with nine or more. It seems reasonable to suggest that the work of the teacher in the classroom needs to be supported by increased efforts to influence and help parents, a task which schools themselves can do something towards (Herbert and Clack, 1970) but also requires preventive and rehabilitative work by social workers. Ideally ESN schools need the services of a teacher-social worker or a social worker on account of social problems just as much as they need the help of a school medical officer on account of physical and health problems.

Junior slow learners are liable to be much less aware of the environment than are normal children, surprisingly lacking in knowledge and experience and in the vocabulary which helps to make everyday experiences meaningful. They need the teacher's prompting to be curious and interested as much as they need special help in reading and number. Experience is a basis for language work as well as a preparation for the topics and social studies which will follow at the secondary stage. The following outline suggests some of the basic topics:

Home and family. Members of the family. Relations. Mother's and father's work. Home as shelter; kinds of home; rooms in the house; furniture; heating and lighting.

Neighbourhood. Where other children live. How they come to school; different kinds of transport. What they see on the way to school. What they see going to town. Different kinds of shops and what they sell. Places the family goes to – schools, places of work, cinemas, parks, post office, hospitals, etc.

People in the neighbourhood. Relations, neighbours, friends. People who help – policeman, postman, fireman, tradesman, etc.

The natural environment. Town/country/sea. Where food and milk come from. Features of the country. Simple classification of animals, plants, non-living things. What living things need for life and growth; growing seeds and caring for pets. The seasons and weather.

Health. Care of self – food, rest, clothing, appearance and cleanliness. Doctor, dentist, clinic, hospital. Safety.

Many details could be listed under these headings according to the opportunities and the needs of the children. They are starting points for many kinds of activity and experience in school and can be taken as far as seems needed by the age and ability of pupils. Though children have some knowledge of these things, understanding can by no means be taken for granted.

Slow learners of secondary age in special schools and classes

The transfer from a junior school or department to a secondary one takes place about eleven or twelve years of age, though in the case of the special school this is flexible to take account of children with marked immaturities. The mental development of ESN children aged eleven to thirteen may be indicated by saying that their mental ages would range from about six to ten years. Put another way, they will be beginning to develop the reasoning processes of Piaget's concrete operational stage – the ability to see similarities and differences, to order and classify and generally to think more logically about processes and events. It is the kind of thinking which enables the normal junior child to understand his environment and interpret his experiences by more or less stable systems of thought. Researches indicate that many ESN children are slow to develop this kind of thinking, some not even by the age when they are about to leave school. They are of course further handicapped by lack of experience and by less of a tendency to be curious and enquiring and to verbalize about their experience.

At the comparable stage of mental development in the normal junior child, there is a gradual but pronounced turn of interest and attention to a wider environment, promoted partly of course by the child's ability to read and also his ability to comprehend it as his mental powers grow. This is often matched in junior teaching by topics, projects and centres of interest and reading information books. Many juniors show the desire to 'master' the environment by knowing it just as they also enjoy mastery in basic 3R skills and physical accomplishments. With ESN children, this period at the end of the junior special school and the first few years of the secondary school is a place for a similar kind of emphasis. Bell (1970) stresses the ESN child's lack of experience and understanding of quite ordinary places and things and considers it essential that the school should try to remedy the lack by well chosen Units of Experience planned over a period of time. This work can build on the topics suggested for the junior stage, and can also be preparation for the social knowledge required at the next stage preparatory to school leaving. Topics provide a background of experience and language for reading and can be a basis for purposeful talk and discussion. An outline of possible topics for social education at the secondary stage is given in the Appendix.

An important task at this stage is consolidating reading and writing skills and ensuring systematic but well motivated teaching for those who are still in the earliest stages. The latter in special schools are not infrequently joined by others who are transferred late from ordinary schools. The next two or three years are crucial for establishing reading skill. Important elements in this are firstly ensuring that children have a sufficient knowledge of phonic and other recognition skills and secondly developing the language and the use of context to support recognition skills. A third problem is creating sufficient motivation for practising and using reading skills without which fluency and comprehension will remain inadequate. Many ESN children are limited in so many of the abilities which underlie reading – thinking, generalizing, language, experience and desire to read for enjoyment and information – that it is not surprising that several researches have found an average reading age of about eight years. Some do very much better, of course, and the average is depressed by those children who have a marked inability to read – sometimes in spite of a keen wish to.

The need to promote social competence is an important element all through the ESN school, but at this stage teachers realize the need to stress learning which will help children to meet the social and vocational requirements of life after leaving school. The basis for this is the atmosphere and life of the school through which children are helped to develop confidence, make relationships with adults, take responsibility and develop good attitudes. On this foundation, social education becomes a unifying purpose in the curriculum. Social arithmetic focuses on money, time and measurement in relation to budgeting, wages, insurance, hire-purchase, timetables, time required to get to places, etc. Communication skills include conversing, letter-writing and asking for help and information. Home management stresses functional skills in relation to home and family – planning a day's work in the home, planning meals and shopping, looking after children, making and mending. Health and sex education, education for leisure and handling simple machines are other important themes. Most schools concentrate in the last two terms at school on an even more thorough Leaver's Programme in an attempt to ensure that pupils are well prepared with knowledge of working life and have thought about some of the problems that may arise (Tansley and Brennan, 1965).

Special schools, especially those for ESN pupils, are strongly attracted to the idea of providing Work Experience programmes through which pupils could, while still at school, have experience of working one or two days a week or for short continuous periods. The experience would be supervised; difficulties and problems could be fed into the discussions of the leaver's group. The pupil would have some familiarization with working conditions and likely difficulties in work adjustment could be recognized and helped. Unfortunately, work experience for pupils still at school contravenes various laws. For the most part, therefore, schools have to make the best use of opportunities within the school – for example, in practical work – for promoting habits of work and the experience of doing a job well. Some have attempted to simulate working conditions introducing time clocks and other features. But the school cannot reproduce the conditions of working life.

While many ESN school leavers have relatively little difficulty in coping with working life, a few are still personally immature at leaving age. One school tackled this problem by setting up a workshop separate from the school in which work was done for outside firms in conditions which were very close to those in industry (Jerrold, 1968). The boys not only acquired confidence in using machinery but improved in habits of work and ability to stick at a task. This was regarded as an 'end-on' course comparable to other courses in secondary schools. Another experiment with older pupils (Burden, 1969) arranged for selected pupils to attend a local further education college, the courses taken by individuals ranging from art, building, car maintenance and carpentry to cookery, needlework, decorating and welding. This experiment was stimulated by the finding that in a group of forty ESN children aged thirteen to sixteen performance on a non-verbal test of mechanical ability spread well into the average range. That some pupils have near-average potentialities in some directions is well known in the school but, as Burden points out, teachers are sometimes reluctant to return pupils to ordinary schools unless arrangements for backward children are really satisfactory. This observation together with Williams's findings about an environmentally handicapped group emphasizes the importance of special teaching in secondary school and also the need for further education opportunities.

Further reading

BELL, P. (1970), *Basic Teaching for Slow Learners*, London: Muller.
DEPARTMENT OF EDUCATION AND SCIENCE (1964), *Slow Learners at School*, Education Pamphlet No. 46, London: H.M.S.O.
GULLIFORD, R. (1969), *Backwardness and Educational Failure*, National Foundation for Educational Research.
GORDON, M. AND WILSON, M. (1969), 'Helping the inadequate – a flexible approach', *Remedial Education*, 4, 2, pp. 76-8.
KIRK, S. A. AND JOHNSON, O. (1951), *Educating the Retarded Child*, London: Harrap.
SAMPSON, O. C. (1969), 'Remedial education services', *Remedial Education*, 4, pp. 3-8, 61-5.
SMITH, R. M. (1968), *Clinical Teaching Methods of Instruction for the Retarded*, New York: McGraw-Hill.
TANSLEY, A. E. (1967), *Reading and Remedial Reading*, London: Routledge & Kegan Paul.
TANSLEY, A. E. AND GULLIFORD, R. (1960), *The Education of Slow Learning Children*, London: Routledge & Kegan Paul.
WILLIAMS, A. A. (1970), *Basic Subjects for the Slow Learner*, London: Methuen Educational.
WILLIAMS, K. (1969), 'The role of a remedial department in a comprehensive school', *Remedial Education*, 4, 2, pp. 66-72.
WILLIAMS, P. AND GRUBER, E. (1967), *Response to Special Schooling*, London: Longmans.

Severely subnormal children

One of the pressing questions for the immediate future is what education should mean for the severely subnormal – for the children who have until now been the responsibility of Health Departments and provided for in junior training centres and those who are in subnormality hospitals.

These children have until recently been considered 'unsuitable for education', that is, for education in the sense of acquiring basic educational skills of reading, writing and simple calculation. Some in fact do acquire some simple skills of this kind and more may do so in the future, but for them education means developing motor, perceptual, conceptual and language skills which we usually think of as being preparatory to school learning. The skills of the educator are just as appropriately applied to improving the thinking or language of a twelve-year-old subnormal as they are to a four- or five-year-old. Apart from the immediate benefits to the child, such teaching also has diagnostic function showing how much a retarded child is capable of further development. Only too often in the past, it has been assumed that little progress can be expected. It is also important that the subnormal child has emotional and social experiences at home and school which help him to develop as a person. Again, it has often been assumed that certain personality characteristics were due entirely to the subnormality, whereas more enlightened methods of care and education have shown that at least some of the characteristics were by-products of our low expectations and methods of treatment.

An important aim of education with severely subnormal children is that of improving their social competence – their ability to look after themselves in feeding, dressing, toileting; to perform simple tasks and responsibilities such as routine household ones; to be able to communicate with other people, to make social relationships and appropriate social responses; to engage in simple occupations leading eventually to sheltered, or even open, employment. These social competence skills are valuable first of all because they benefit the child – they put him increasingly in situations where he has to think for himself; they enable him to widen his experience and increase his motivations for learning communication, manipulation and other skills. They are basic to the process of developing as a person. They also, of course, make it easier for the child's family; they will still, however, need to give him some supervision and help even into adulthood.

The present attainments of severely subnormal children

Marshall (1967) made one of the few surveys of the abilities and attainments of severely subnormal children attending junior training centres. The survey covered 165 children in nineteen centres in three areas. Children were seen in their last two years at centres, i.e. aged fourteen to fifteen, in order to assess their attainments and how far they were achieving up to their potential; 45 per cent of the children were mongols; in 10 per cent there was evidence of brain damage, 10 per cent were classified as familial, 10 per cent mixed causes, and in 25 per cent the causes were not known. The high incidence of additional disabilities was illustrated by the fact that 48 per cent suffered from some other minor disability, 9 per cent had mild cerebral palsy and 15 per cent had epilepsy. One quarter had been in schools through their primary years.

A variety of educational and social assessments were made. Gunzburg's Progress Adjustment Charts were used to assess social competence. These consist of 100 items representing achievements and skills divided into four categories; self-help (concerning dressing, washing, eating etc.); communication (speech production and comprehension, concepts of colour, time, number etc.); socialization (concerning responsibility, co-operative play, etc.) and occupation (the ability to play and work on one's own; to master routine tasks and motor control). The items are graded according to the order of achievement by normal children and are credited pass or fail by a teacher who knows the child well.

Marshall found that the children in her sample did best in the self-help skills in which there was 80 per cent success. The main failures were not being able to move unsupervised about the neighbourhood and being unable to tie a bow (e.g. a shoelace). In dressing, feeding and looking after self at toilet this sample had achieved independence.

The hardest category was communication in which percentage success was between forty and fifty per cent. While most of them were comprehending simple instructions and conversing in short sentences, only about half were able to relate coherently a simple experience, to use sentences with plurals, past tense, simple prepositions or to define simple words. The expected weakness was on items relating to simple educational skills – reading a few words at sight, writing a name, dealing with simple number concepts, money and time. On both vocabulary tests given, the mean vocabulary age of these fourteen- to fifteen-year-olds was just under six years.

Scores for socialization and occupation were rather higher than for communication. The weakest items in the socialization section were, 'Is trusted with money', 'Goes to shops and fetches specified items', 'Answers the telephone'. In the occupation section, 'Builds elaborate structures with suitable materials', 'Cuts cloth with scissors', 'Cuts very carefully round outlines' were the weakest.

The pattern of these results conforms to expectations – that communication involving concepts and language would be the weakest; certain other skills reflect lack of opportunity as well as inability. The greater success with self-help skills was no doubt due to the emphasis given them in centres, since self-help skills are basic to independence and self-reliance and ease the task of parents and others caring for the child. The lower communication scores are partly due to insufficient attention to language, to uncertainty about methods of promoting language as well as the inherent difficulties of the children. One of the challenging educational tasks with subnormal children is to explore methods of improving language. It is also necessary to explore ways in which constructive, manipulative and creative activities (comparable to nursery-infant methods) can be used to promote other psychological and educational developments.

An educational approach based on the methods of nursery education was shown to be very effective in an experiment reported by Tizard (1964). A group of children aged five to ten years with IQs in the range 25-30 were moved from a large subnormality hospital and cared for in a small hostel, Brooklands, which was run on family-group lines as in a modern children's home. During the day a nursery school teacher and assistants provided an environment and stimulated activity on nursery lines. The experimental group learnt to engage in activity very much like pre-school children: experimenting with physical skills of climbing, tricycling, manipulation and movement; constructive and dramatic play with a wide range of materials; proceeding through the usual sequences of social and co-operative play; responding to visits in the environment and to the closer adult contact which the régime provided. At the end of the three-year experiment, comparison with a control group which had remained in hospital showed considerable gains in emotional development and verbal development. This experiment encouraged many centres to work on similar lines and there is no doubt that the education of subnormal children of primary age should be based on the kind of approach which has been so well developed for nursery-infant schools.

The difficulties of doing this well should not be underestimated. In the first place, the organization of a nursery-school environment as well as the guidance and stimulation of children's activities is not as easy as it appears. It depends on the training and expertise of the teacher; what may appear a deceptively simple provision of suitable materials and opportunities does not necessarily create the situation in which the optimum learning and development takes place. The teacher needs to be clear about her aims, to be observant of children's development and needs to know how to foster new activities and interests.

In the second place, the methods used with normal children cannot be applied without modification to the severely subnormal. The ordinary nursery school is able to draw upon children's normal curiosity and drive, their spontaneous urge to be active and exploratory. Their activity is guided and elaborated by processes of thought and language which are developing quickly between three and five years of age. The severely subnormal are retarded in speech and language, have fewer experiences and ideas to incorporate in play. They need and benefit from more guidance, direction and participation from teachers and helpers. A careful account of points of difference are summarized by Kirk (1951) based on his work in the early education of mentally retarded children.

Clarke (1970) has raised some criticisms of the Brooklands approach. He points out that the children improved verbally but not in nonverbal abilities and he advocates specific training of certain perceptual and conceptual skills. He supports his case by the results of learning experiments with severely subnormal children. In one experiment, they were given the task of sorting photographs of common objects – animals, clothing, furniture, tableware and human beings. They were then divided into groups and each group was given different kinds of practice training in sorting geometrical shapes which were varied in difficulty and complexity for different groups. After training, they were retested on the original photograph-sorting task and were shown to do significantly better, i.e. there had been a transfer of effects from the training on to the original task. Furthermore, the transfer effect was most marked in the group which had been given the most difficult training tasks. Clarke argues from this that more can be expected of subnormal children and particularly that we should try to locate *key activities* which will help to promote and accelerate the development of thinking skills.

Most people would be in sympathy with this point of view so long as key activities are located and promoted within a general developmental and educational context. Without the latter, there is a danger of a fragmented programme of specific training activities. A whole curriculum for all-round personal development is needed within which it is appropriate, indeed it is essential, to remedy particular areas of weakness and delayed development and to emphasize key activities. There are many sources of information about specific methods for promoting mental and physical developments which are usually accomplished by normal children early in the primary school stage. Some of the remedial methods for children with learning difficulties are relevant: Kephart's approach through perceptual-motor skills;

remediation activities proposed for deficits revealed by Kirk's Illinois Test of Psycholinguistic Abilities; perceptual training programmes such as Frostig's. Morganstern's (1966) practical training for the severely handicapped and Frankel's (1966) account of McGloe's functional teaching of the mentally retarded suggest activities and materials derived from practical experience.

Piaget's studies of intellectual development have already contributed to the theory and practice of work with retarded children, more especially the ESN. Woodward (1963) has found Piagetian tasks useful for assessing the mental development of subnormal children, especially in the six stages of sensory-motor development. Most severely subnormal children in school will be in a pre-operational stage of development and few will be showing more than the beginnings of concrete operational thinking by the time they leave at sixteen.

Unfortunately, little of Piaget's work has been directed to that period of pre-operational development between eighteen months and four and a half years. In this period the normal child is no longer dependent on sensory-motor patterns of behaviour (which enable him to *act* in and on his environment). There is the development of the symbolic function, shown for example in 'pretend' play, the comprehension of pictures and the beginning of language. This, especially for mentally retarded children, is an important step forward from action-dominated behaviour – from manipulative and locomotor behaviour. A book is no longer treated as an object to be manipulated; a brick can represent a boat or train (or, for an ESN child quoted by Sampson, a lamp outside a toy house). The child is extending his ability to act in his environment with the beginnings of an ability to think about it and represent it to himself. Encouraging symbolic, imaginative, constructive and experimental play would be an important aim at this period of mental development.

Most of Piaget's studies of pre-school thinking are concerned with the transition from intuitive to concrete operational thinking between ages four and seven (e.g. in concepts of number, measurement, space, time and classification), though in few cases (e.g. spatial concepts and classification) he does include children of two and three years. Thus Piaget shows that the ability to classify bricks of different shapes and colours has a discernible beginning in the way three-year-olds play with them, just as there is a well known sequence from scribble in babyhood to drawing a man in the primary age groups. Greater understanding of such sequences would indicate what help could be given to promote the thinking and activity of subnormal children at this stage. Woodward (1967) has made observations of the way subnormal children tackle a task such as replacing a nest of beakers decreasing in size.

As subnormal children move into the intuitive stage (becoming aware of amount, size, time, relationships and simple concepts) there is more experience to draw upon; for example, the number readiness activities which, influenced by Piaget, have been developed in ESN schools. Piaget's studies of spatial concepts, ideas about measurement and about the real world provide a valuable means of interpreting observations of children's activity and matching learning experiences to children's stage of development.

An important aim is the improvement of language – as a means of social communication and personal expression and as an aid to thinking and learning. The reluctance of the subnormal to verbalize is often commented upon. Luria (1961) would explain this as a failure to develop the regulatory function of speech which normally by seven years becomes internalized speech and an essential component of thought and action. A practical implication of this is the need to encourage subnormal children to talk to themselves as they play, to verbalize actions and processes in learning motor skills. Another explanation is that they are emotionally reluctant to express themselves; certainly an encouraging atmosphere, good relationships, feelings of success and enjoyment are required. Reluctance is also an indication of lack of language skills – poor vocabulary and sentence structures.

Mental limitations and additional handicaps only partly explain the subnormal's retarded language. They are less exposed to situations which provoke the use of language. Even in good homes, parents may be uncertain how to provide the level of language experience needed for a child with retarded development; the normal child's numerous opportunities for acquiring and practising communication skills in play and social experience are much reduced in the subnormal. So a first requirement is that the school should maximize opportunities for talking about experience, for comprehending instructions, for acquiring and enriching vocabulary.

This informal experience can be given some 'structure' as suggested in Chapter 6 by the teacher who is fully aware of the language possibilities of the environment *and*, from observation of the language children use, of the level of attainment reached. In this way, the teacher's 'feedback' of language can be used to match their capacity. Sampson's (1964) description of the spontaneous expression of a group of subnormals shows how useful this observation can be for sharpening awareness of those children who are beginning to show occasional signs of mature sentence structures, expressing simple relationships, reasoning, and imagination. Observation of the wide range in a group enables the teacher to vary and extend their talk as she joins in a play activity, in daily living activities and in conversation with individuals or groups. Renfrew (1959) has described her approach with young subnormal children, participating in house-play, tea-parties, telephoning and similar activities. She carefully edited her own vocabulary and sentence length and encouraged children to expand their one-word utterances. Games were played such as hiding an object, the child having to explain where he found it before he could have his turn to hide it. The games revealed limitations of vocabulary (e.g. prepositions such as under, behind, beside). The content of language programmes referred to in Chapter 6 suggest ways in which the verbal interaction between teacher and pupils can be used to promote conceptual thinking and the use of language structures.

Some children who are virtually non-communicators may not respond to a motivating language-experience approach. Step by step methods may be required, starting if need be with imitation of words and phrases, reinforced by tangible rewards such as sweets. (Sampson (1968) found pieces of potato crisp useful.) Sloane and MacAuley (1968) provide accounts of operant conditioning procedures for a variety of speech and language problems – including attempts to modify echolalic speech (parrot-like repetitions).

Physical education is another important aspect for the subnormal. Many subnormal children have less opportunity for the physical activity – climbing, skipping, ball play – through which normal children spontaneously practise and acquire physical skills. They lead a more restricted life and are less likely to be involved in the play group of children from neighbouring homes. Apart from the contribution of physical education to general health and well-being, we know that it promotes mental health, particularly through feelings of achievement and improved general motivation. While with older children it contributes to the development of good self-concepts, with younger ones it helps to develop more a basic awareness of the self – an awareness of the body, its position in space, rhythm, laterality – as well as being a means of personal expression compensating for limitations in verbal and other means of expression. The use of movement in dance and its valuable effects on personal adjustment and response have been well described by Sherbourne (1969).

The learning of subnormal children

It used to be rather taken for granted that subnormal children and adults had very little capacity for learning, but in recent years there has been an attitude of cautious optimism. Research by psychologists in the 1950s into the learning of adult subnormals led first to a reappraisal of their potential for simple industrial tasks (Clarke, 1965). Briefly, this research showed that when subnormals were well motivated and when tasks were broken down into simple and well taught (ensuring correct learning from the beginning; verbal cues for move-ments; spaced practice and over-learning), they could learn things better than would have been predicted from their IQs or their initial level of performance. These findings were partly responsible for the increased provision of simple industrial tasks in senior training centres and hospitals.

One thing which seems fairly clearly established from comparisons of normal and retarded children of the same mental age is that it is in *the initial stages of learning* a new task that the mentally retarded have most difficulty. They are less able to focus attention on what is most relevant and useful for making discriminations, e.g. between objects, pictures, shapes, letters, etc. O'Connor and Hermelin (1963) have shown that they are helped if the stimulus is made to stand out more prominently or by reducing the complexity of the task. Another factor is poor short-term memory. When a child hears a verbal in-struction, or part of a nursery rhyme, or is asked to copy a movement, short-term memory determines the amount he can 'take in' and the time he can retain it for associating with other impressions. Once something is really learnt, however, subnormal children retain it rela-tively well. In practice of course this depends on the child's oppor-tunities for using the knowledge and skills he has learnt.

These findings suggest that we can put less reliance on 'incidental learning' and that care should be taken to present material in an amount and in a way that helps them to focus on what is relevant. A readiness to observe and to see relationships can be built up and, as Clarke has shown, has some transfer to similar learning tasks. The subnormal child is also less likely to use language to direct his atten-tion, to guide and reinforce his learning of actions and to categorize his experiences, e.g. by using words such as round, big, long. The play, problem-solving and learning of normal children at the pre-school stage is continually assisted by verbalizing and this needs to be en-couraged with the subnormal.

All this does not, however, mean that the subnormal child should be restricted to set tasks and formal learning situations. As in any learning situation, there are times when the teacher perceives that certain children are ready for a particular piece of learning to be brought clearly into focus using well prepared and well graded material. There is also need for the teacher to seize opportunities in informal activities for directing attention to features of the experi-ence – by pointing out a comparison, by supplying a key word, by describing an action or event in words, by rewarding with praise or attention. But all this can occur within a situation in which children are encouraged to be active, interested, constructive and experimental and through which some of their motivations for learning can be found.

Further reading

CLARKE, A. M. AND A. D. B. (eds.) (1958), *Mental Deficiency – the Changing Outlook*, London: Methuen.

FRANKEL, M. G., HAPP, F. W. AND SMITH, M. P. (1966), *Functional Teaching of the Mentally Retarded*, Springfield, Illinois: C. C. Thomas.

GUNZBURG, H. C. (1960), *Social Rehabilitation of the Subnormal*, London: Baillière, Tindall & Cox.

MARSHALL, A. (1967), *The Abilities and Achievements of Children Leaving Junior Training Centres*, National Association for Mental Health.

MORGANSTERN, M. (1966), *Practical Training for the Severely Handicapped Child*, London: Heinemann Medical.

NEALE, M. D. AND CAMPBELL, W. J. (1963), *Education for the Intellectually Limited Child and Adolescent*, Sydney: Novak.

ROBINSON, H. B. AND N. M. (1965), *The Mentally Retarded Child*, New York: McGraw-Hill.

ROTHSTEIN, J. H. (ed.) (1965), *Mental Retardation*, New York: Holt, Rinehart & Winston.

SAMPSON, O. (1968), 'The language of the subnormal', *Special Education*, 57, 1, pp. 15-20.

STEVENS, M. (1968), *Observing Children Who are Severely Subnormal*, London: Edward Arnold.

TIZARD, J. (1964), *Community Services for the Mentally Handicapped*, Oxford University Press.

five

Specific learning difficulties

Teachers are aware of children who have marked difficulty in learning certain things although their achievements may be fairly normal in other ways. Outstanding examples are severe difficulties in reading, writing, spelling and mathematics, but disabilities often show up in other ways – distinguishing left from right, perceptual and language weaknesses or some clumsiness in hand and eye tasks. Indeed, although the term *specific* learning difficulties is sometimes used, there is usually a cluster of signs of abnormal or delayed mental functions – in motor development, attention, perception, thinking, language. In general, it is assumed that there is some impairment – perhaps slight – of brain functioning, though evidence for this cannot always be found. The term 'minimal cerebral dysfunction' has been used, but in an educational context it is preferable to refer to *learning disability* since, as was pointed out on p. 68, the important thing for the teacher is the pattern of difficulty in learning and behaviour. It is, however, important to realize that some difficulties in learning are not just due to failures in teaching or adverse environmental and emotional factors – that there are real difficulties which need to be carefully assessed so that teaching can be planned to remedy and take account of them.

Progress in understanding these difficulties has been held back by the difficulty of distinguishing them from failure due to low intelligence, emotional disturbance, environmental handicaps or sensory defects. A discussion of reading disability will illustrate the problems and indicate the uncertain, even controversial concept of special learning disabilities. Most backwardness in reading is due to a combination of adverse factors. Social and cultural inadequacies, coupled with lowish ability, result in pupils being ill prepared perceptually, linguistically and motivationally for reading in school. Even when they have made a start, environmental factors provide insufficient support for progress in higher reading skills. Various school factors (lack of continuity, insufficient teaching and remedial teaching of reading in the junior school) are also involved. Another group of backward readers are emotionally unsettled children in whom poor concentration, poor motivation and inconsistent work habits contribute to reading failure.

There are other backward readers whose failure cannot entirely be explained in these ways. Indeed, the problem is shown most clearly in intelligent children from good home backgrounds who have experienced good teaching and yet have failed to learn. Sometimes they have learnt to read but with a poorer level of skill than might be expected from their ability and with only partly resolved difficulties in spelling and handwriting. (The same difficulties, can, however, be observed in children from poorer environments and in ESN children, but are perhaps more likely to be explained on other grounds.)

There has been considerable controversy about whether a specific disability in reading can be distinguished from other kinds of reading backwardness. Neurologists and paediatricians refer to these severe reading difficulties as dyslexia (Critchley). Teachers and psychologists tend to be averse to the term, partly because conflicting descriptions have been offered and partly because they are not convinced that what is being referred to is really a separate problem. The important thing is that some children *do* have special difficulties and that early recognition of these should lead to remedial teaching which includes an attack on the weak functions rather than a generalized approach to remedial teaching.

Several kinds of difficulty have been indicated. Ingram (1964) suggests that some children have *visuo-spatial difficulties* in recognizing and distinguishing written symbols; in reproducing letters or groups of letters correctly; confusing or reversing letters and the order of letters in reading and writing. These children often have higher verbal than performance quotients on intelligence tests. Other children have *speech-sound difficulties* – in synthesizing words from their component sounds; in relating words to meanings. Most of these show a history of late or slow speech development, often with continuing minor articulatory defects and hesitancy in verbal expression. They tend to have verbal quotients lower than performance quotients. A third group have *association* difficulties – e.g. in associating speech sounds with their symbols in reading and writing – and this also tends to be the case in the other two groups. Weaknesses in a number of functions seem to be critical ones: weakness in integrating information from several sensory channels; weakness in symbolization; in sequencing and ordering material, e.g. the order of letters in reading or spelling; in orientation and direction. Delay in acquiring speech and language with persistence of some speech difficulties seems strongly indicated in at least some of the cases and suggests a milder form of the receptive and expressive language disorders referred to in Chapter 6. A genetic or familial basis has been argued but the evidence is unclear. Uncertain laterality and mixed cerebral dominance are other controversial points. The main thing is that weaknesses in function should be looked for with a view to modifying teaching methods.

Bowley (1969) made a survey of children aged seven to ten-plus in Kensington junior schools, looking for those who showed characteristics of 'minimal cerebral dysfunction' – poor manual dexterity, general clumsiness, distractibility and restlessness, slow language development and marked reading, writing or spelling disabilities. Out of 2,280 children she found thirty-four who showed a cluster of these characteristics, i.e. about 1·5 per cent. On closer study these children showed weakness in language development in almost all cases, notably slow onset of speech, poor auditory or visual memory and sequencing and reading retardation of two to four years in most cases.

The possibility of an earlier identification of children who are likely later to have severe difficulties in reading is suggested by the results of a study by de Hirsch (1966). She attempted to find out what deficiencies in development at five years were associated with later failures. She identified a group of children, mainly boys, of average intelligence who appeared over-active, disorganized, impulsive and immature. They were poor in motor abilities and in visuo-motor tasks (e.g. copying patterns); their drawings of a man were crude and lacking detail; they were poor in expressive language skills and had difficulty in word finding. From the large number of tests used, she selected a small number which could be used as a predictive index of future progress – five were of visual perception, three oral language, and one was conceived with visual-motor performance. She argues that these children need remedial training in the infant school suited to their individual weaknesses and before failure has aggravated the original difficulties by emotional problems.

A disability in spelling is frequently noted. Bizarre spelling is a symptom which often occurs in severe reading retardation and some cases of specific weakness in spelling seem to be a continuation of difficulty in pupils who have overcome their reading disability. Weakness in visual memory and sequencing are particularly apparent and some continue to show crude phonic attempts at spelling. Being shown a technique of learning words suited to the child's strengths and weaknesses is a minimum requirement; older pupils get some help from spelling rules.

Handwriting difficulties merit attention. In many backward children poor handwriting is related to their late progress in reading, to poor motivation for writing and lack of clear guidance on how to form and join letters. This leaves others, sometimes quite intelligent, who have difficulty in managing the spatial relationships involved in forming and spacing letters and words and in hand-eye co-ordination. Additional practice in visuo-motor skills and careful teaching of writing movements is needed.

Severe retardation in mathematics has not attracted as much attention as reading failure, but there is no doubt that in addition to those who have difficulty because of lack of experience, inadequacies in teaching and dislike of the subject, there are some children who have a marked lack of 'number sense'. Often they (and their families) are upset and bewildered by their failure. Some failures are associated with the kind of difficulty referred to in the last paragraph – difficulty in distinguishing differences in shapes, sizes and lengths and visuo-motor difficulties. Not infrequently verbal abilities (including reading) are good but there are several signs of difficulty in the integration of non-verbal experience. Various kinds of visual perceptual difficulty are obviously liable to interfere with practical work in mathematics, with interpreting diagrams and charts; auditory perception and sequencing are factors in other kinds of mathematics. The question merits more attention since there are certainly children with marked mathematical difficulties.

In addition to disabilities affecting particular subjects there are disorders which have more general effects.

The term 'clumsy children' has been used for those who are awkward in gait and posture and late in acquiring skills such as doing up buttons and tying shoelaces (Gordon, 1969). Some have minor articulatory defects. Some are weak in tasks involving co-ordination of hand and eye. In a survey in Cambridgeshire, Brenner and others (1967) found 3·8 per cent of 810 children had marked visuo-motor disabilities – in writing, craftwork, using scissors, copying patterns – although all of them had IQs above 90. Fourteen of the more severely handicapped children were observed for three years and only two made satisfactory progress in school. The main weaknesses were in spelling and arithmetic but several were good readers. Only one of them had been referred for any kind of specialist help and that was on account of emotional disturbance. There is a danger that such problems are overlooked or attributed to laziness, carelessness or low ability.

Sometimes one meets children with difficulty in spatial orientation – they bump into things, cannot estimate distances or even get 'lost' in a building. Teachers of cerebral palsied children are familiar with this kind of disability and also with children who have disturbance of 'body image' – who are very much delayed in awareness of parts of the body and their movements. Some children are very poor at understanding social situations – for example in playing with other children, or appreciating the 'rules' or routines of a game and even other people's expressions and gestures.

Some children have abnormalities of attention showing in distractibility, in perseveration, in disinhibition (switching from one idea to another, often inappropriately, like the talkative hydrocepahalic children referred to on p. 183). In general these children benefit from a more ordered routine and more carefully programmed work than is usual in a special or remedial classroom, though the aim of reducing extraneous stimulation and distraction should not lead to a meagre educational experience. Helpful suggestions for each of these characteristics are suggested in Johnson and Myklebust (1967).

The assessment and treatment of learning difficulties

In order to observe and assess these difficulties a framework of ideas is needed about the several mental processes involved, particularly since the current interest in perceptual difficulties has tended to overshadow other equally important processes.

Perceptual difficulties are of course a first source of possible weakness. It is a common observation in school that some children are poor in visual or auditory perception; it is not so obvious that the difficulty may be one of integrating information from several sensory channels, e.g. the visual and auditory aspects of reading. Wedell (1968) has given a clear account of the factors involved in perceptual-motor difficulties, as when a child fails to copy a shape or letter.

A neglected possible source of difficulty is imagery by which sensations are recalled. Burt devoted many pages of *The Backward Child* to a discussion of the marked differences in people's capacity to visualize, to image sounds and movements. This may well be a factor in reading, spelling and other difficulties.

The next source of weakness may be in attaching meaning to symbols such as spoken words, or printed symbols (letters and mathematics symbols), or non-verbal symbols such as gestures and expressions, the clock face, diagrams and other representations. Apart from weakness in these 'inner languages', some children seem to have weaknesses in receptive and expressive aspects of language. Some degree of speech and language difficulty is a recurring theme in the study of learning difficulties.

Much research has explored the tendency of neurologically impaired individuals to be inferior in conceptualization – being over-influenced by the perceptual attributes of objects, tending to relate things in less obvious ways, tending to be concrete and particular in thinking rather than abstracting and generalizing. Such difficulties might, of course, be related to underlying perceptual or language difficulties.

In addition, there can be variations in attention, memory and in ordering and sequencing information.

Psychologists do not claim to have adequate methods of exploring these problems, though a number of recent tests have been found useful. The Wechsler Intelligence Scales, apart from providing a general assessment of intelligence, can be examined to compare performance on sub-tests involving conceptualization (comprehension, similarities and vocabulary), or visuo-motor abilities (picture completion, block design and object assembly), or sequencing (repeating digits, sequencing pictures and coding). Knowing the content of tests in these groups would suggest to the teacher what to observe in class. The Illinois test of Psycholinguistic Abilities was developed as a means of assessment of particular functions so that remedial teaching could be planned according to the profile of abilities revealed. For example, a child could be weak in decoding (receptive) processes or in encoding (expressive) processes, or there might be weaknesses in the visual rather than the auditory channel. The ITPA also distinguishes between two levels – a higher level involving interpretation and association, and a lower though not less essential level at which, for example, there are tests of the ability to recall and reproduce digits or pictures in sequence. Frostig (1968) found that in a group of seventy-eight children with learning difficulties, performance was particularly poor in these two tests of memory and sequencing functions.

There are a number of tests of visual perception (e.g. the Frostig tests, the Bender Visual-Motor Gestalt test) and auditory perception (e.g. the Wepman test). A number of procedures for assessing perceptual processes are described by Tansley (1967).

For remedial work there are no simple rule-of-thumb remedies nor could they be expected. The essential thing is to assess by tests and observations the child's strengths and weaknesses, and to plan to provide additional work directed at the area of weakness. For visual perceptual weakness, Frostig's worksheets and Teachers' Guide suggest many activities for improving eye-motor co-ordination, perception of form and spatial relationships. Familiarity with these would suggest to the imaginative teacher many uses of ordinary classroom activities in nature study, art and creative work. Frostig herself suggests that drawing to scale, making maps, diagrams, maps of the stars and planets, etc., are excellent alternative exercises in spatial relationships. Work of this kind is often of interest to an intelligent, failing child and is productive of other learning as well as helping with basic difficulties. Likewise, the child with a visuo-motor difficulty manifested in writing difficulties needs remedial instruction in the correct writing movements, but if the remedy is to be effective he needs topic work or some other interesting writing activities which motivate him to use his improving skills. There are now many suggestions for remedial activities suited to weaknesses in the processes assessed by the Illinois Test of Psycholinguistic Abilities (McCarthy and Kirk, 1966). These are best viewed as illustrations of possible activities from which the teacher will proceed to devise activities suited to the particular children and their interests. The suggestions and programmes for improving language referred to in Chapter 6 would have relevance to children whose difficulties are in speech and language.

An important theme in the writing about learning difficulties is concerned with the importance of body awareness and movement for developing a system of reference for spatial awareness and perceptual-motor abilities. Kephart's *The Slow Learner in the Classroom* is a source book for this. Oliver and Keogh (1967) have shown how a motor inco-ordination can be analysed and retrained.

The remedial teacher specializing in these problems now has a wide range of material to consult, though in the present stage of theory and practice he has to seek a coherent view of the field for himself. Books by Strauss (1947), Cruickshank (1961) and especially Johnson and Myklebust propose a variety of approaches. Tyson (1963) and Francis-Williams (1970) propound a British view of the problem.

Concern with the learning problem should not lead to neglect of broader issues of care. It goes without saying that the effect of the learning disability on the child's view of himself, his emotional reactions, his social development and the reactions of the family to the problem must be attended to. An important point is that the school should recognize that the child is not just lazy, careless, wilfully inattentive or dull and should attempt to stress and value what he can do relatively well. It would be an advantage too if schools would more readily accept that a child who has difficulty in learning through reading and writing could perhaps be learning through other means (orally, practically, with audio-visual aids) and that progress in general subjects could be assessed by means other than a written examination. One not infrequently meets young men who have developed ways of adjusting to their disability in responsible jobs in adult life, e.g. always using a dictaphone rather than making written notes of job requirements. One wonders whether this process of adaptation could not have been started at school.

Further reading

BATEMAN, B. (1964), 'Learning disabilities', *Exceptional Children*, 31, 4.

BRENNER, N. W. (1967), 'Visuo-motor difficulty in school children', *British Medical Journal*, 4, pp. 259-62.

CRUICKSHANK, W. M., BENTZEN, F. A. RATZBURG, F. H. AND TANNHAUSER, M. T. (1961), *A Teaching Method for Brain-injured and Hyperactive Children*, Syracuse, N.Y.: Syracuse University Press.

FRANCIS-WILLIAMS, J. (1970), *Children With Specific Learning Difficulties*, Oxford: Pergamon.

FROSTIG, M. (1967), *The Frostig Program for the Development of Visual Perception*, Chicago: Follett.

GORDON, N. (1969), 'Helping the clumsy child in school', *Special Education*, 58, 2, pp. 19-20.

JOHNSON, D. J. AND MYKLEBUST, H. R. (1967), *Learning Disabilities: Educational Principles and Practice*, New York and London: Grune & Stratton.

KEPHART, N. C. (1960), *The Slow Learner in the Classroom*, Columbus, Ohio: Merrill Pocks.

MITCHELL, R. G. (1966), 'Minimal disorders of cerebral function', *British Journal of Disorders of Communication*, 1, No. 2, pp. 109-13.

STRAUSS, A. A. AND LEHTINEN, L. E. (1947), *Psychopathology and Education of the Brain Injured Child*, New York and London: Grune & Stratton.

TYSON, M. C. (1963), 'Pilot study of remedial visuo-motor training', *Special Education*, 52, 4, pp. 22-5.

——(1970), 'The design of remedial programmes', in Mittler, P. J. (ed.) *The Psychological Assessment of Mental and Physical Handicaps*, London: Methuen.

WEDELL, K. (1968), 'Perceptual-motor difficulties', *Special Education*, 57, pp. 25-30.

six

Communication difficulties

Speech and language disorders

The growth of speech and language is one of the most fascinating aspects of children's development. The baby's first words at about twelve months of age and his first two-word phrases at about the age of two years are noted with parental pride in which surely there is an element of wonder at the spontaneous emergence of this new skill. By four years of age, nearly half of children have acquired complete skill in the pronunciation of English sounds and by five years most children have learnt the principles of how words are strung together to form the basic sentence structures of English. There is, unfortunately, a small number of children who have persisting difficulties in articulation, and apart from the many who have poor knowledge and use of their mother tongue, there are a few who have special difficulties in acquiring, comprehending and using language.

The most common defect is faulty pronunciation of certain sounds including (1) substitution of sounds for one another, e.g. using the t sound for k as well in *I tan't tate my toat off*; (2) omission of one or more consonants in a cluster like *pay* for *play* or *cool* for *school*; (3) distortions where a non-English sound in some respects similar to the English sound is used; (4) sequencing where the sounds or syllables of a word are spoken in the wrong order, e.g. *bikissill* for *bicycle*.

Morley (1965) studied the development of speech in a sample of normal children at Newcastle upon Tyne in the 1950s, assessing them at ages $3\frac{3}{4}$, $4\frac{3}{4}$ and $6\frac{1}{2}$:

Table 1   *Development of articulation in children* (Morley, Table IX)

Age	3¾	4¾	6½
	Percentages		
Normal speech	42	64	95
Weak on *th* and *r*	27	22	4
Some defects of articulation	20	9·5	4
Unintelligible	11	4·5	1

The results (Table 1) show that just prior to beginning school 10 per cent have some articulatory defects and 4 per cent are still unintelligible, but that by 6½ years much of this has cleared up. Increased maturation of the neuro-muscular systems involved in speech is no doubt largely responsible for the improvement, but increased opportunities for practising and hearing language and speech in the infant school also plays an important part.

There are still, however, at 6½ years about 4 per cent of children who have some articulatory difficulties. While some of these are minor ones and some will continue to improve spontaneously, the most serious ones will benefit from assessment by a speech therapist who will decide whether regular treatment sessions are needed and will advise on what can be done in school. Some of these children will not be unduly troubled by their articulatory defect but, depending on the degree of unintelligibility and also on the child's personality, it may impede social contact with other children and participation in school activities. It can also be a factor in reading backwardness. Rutter and his co-workers (1966) in the Isle of Wight survey found that 14 per cent of retarded readers aged nine to twelve years still showed defects of articulation – a figure which did not include ESN children among whom defects of articulation are commonly found in as many as one-third.

Clearly children with poor articulation at seven years of age are somewhat 'at risk' educationally and, apart from seeking the advice of a speech therapist, it is worth taking extra care in the teaching of reading and spelling. For example, training in auditory discrimination as a preparation for phonic work in reading may be even more important for these children. At the same time, learning how speech sounds are symbolized by letters and combinations of letters is likely to contribute to improved speech and this is part of the answer to the question which teachers often ask, 'What can we do to help?' It is important, of course, that the child should not be made self-conscious about his difficulties. Help best takes the form of general encouragement to expression in speech and language with incidental and unobtrusive assistance towards clear speech for all children.

Table 1 illustrates the considerable improvement in speech between three and six years – from 31 per cent showing some defects or unintelligibility to 5 per cent. This could be taken as evidence in support of the advice sometimes given to mothers of late or poor talkers: 'Don't worry; he will grow out of it'. While this is certainly true of a large proportion of children it is significantly not true of a few children. Late talkers and those with unintelligible speech should always be seen by a paediatrician or speech therapist in the pre-school years if only to exclude the possibility of other conditions to which the speech defect is secondary. These other conditions to which defective speech may be due are: *a perceptive hearing impairment* in which there is loss of certain frequencies, especially the high ones resulting in characteristic consonant defects. A hearing aid may make a considerable difference to speech progress; the advice of a teacher of the deaf will be needed. Poor speech may be related to *mental retardation*, and if this is the basic problem there is likely to be retarded language development – a small vocabulary and expression limited in form and content. For the pre-school retarded child, nursery school or play group experience is ideal and much can be done at home if it is realized that the kind of language experiences required are those appropriate to normal children a year or two younger, communicating about everyday experiences in and around home, giving simple instructions about helping tasks, reading and telling stories and giving time for listening to the child's attempts at communication – even though it is often quicker to say it for him. Much the same remarks apply to the retarded child in the infant school. As Renfrew (1959) has pointed out, the backward communicator is often on the fringe; more vocal children inevitably compel teacher's attention. A basic form of help therefore is ensuring that the slower child is brought into the group, is encouraged to communicate and feels himself to be in an atmosphere which values his contribution.

There are a variety of other factors in poor articulation. Some children are unable to appreciate the difference between the sound they make and what others say. There are those who can hear the difference but don't know how to imitate it. In other children, articulatory defects are the persistence of faulty habits from the early stage of rapid speech development, or there is imitation of faulty speech patterns (owing to exposure to different dialects or parents' foreign accents or otherwise defective speech in a close member of the family). Emotional immaturities due to over-dependence and lack of social interaction with other children occur and in some cases serious emotional disturbance holds back both language and speech development.

A group of disorders which particularly need assessment by a speech therapist with a view to treatment are those which result from abnormalities in the structures involved in speech (teeth, lips, tongue, palate, pharynx) or from inco-ordination of the muscles involved in making the fine adjustments required. From her knowledge of how speech sounds are produced the therapist can assess how far the breathing or the directing of air through the speech organs, or the placing and co-ordination of the tongue against the palate and teeth or the positioning of lips are at fault.

Language disorders

Among children with disorders of speech can be distinguished a group who not only have difficulty in producing speech sounds but in producing phrases and sentences. The language forms they produce are those of much younger children They tend to omit words such as prepositions, articles, auxiliary verbs and conjunctions (often described as telegraphic speech) and often have difficulty in finding words when they want to use them. They have difficulty in mastering the 'rules' by which words are put in sequence in different kinds of utterance (statements, questions). There is a disorder in the thinking and language processes affecting language expression, the term expressive aphasia or, in milder cases, dysphasia being used. The ability to comprehend speech is also often affected (receptive aphasia and dysphasia) and in the more severe cases it is difficult to distinguish between receptive and expressive dysphasia. There may be some hearing loss but the language difficulty is out of proportion to the impairment. While some are retarded in general development, others are not, although perceptual difficulties and difficulties in thinking limit their general knowledge and awareness, and their learning of educational skills. That they have much in common with other children who have specific learning disorders is well brought out in an account by the headmistress of the John Horniman School (Palmer, 1962) which was opened in 1958 for children with severe language disorders. Moor House School now for senior children, was opened in 1947. Lea (1968) has described some of the problems and methods at this school. Of the receptive aphasic children, some have no speech, some have a few words or phrases, others have jargon interspersed with words. Some of them cannot distinguish sounds, e.g. a whistle from a bell, nor music – even the rhythm. Some cannot interpret gestures and facial expressions. Lea has devised a method where different parts of speech are associated with different colours so that in answering a question in writing, the kind and order of words required are cued by colour to help the child form sentences. Since many of these children are better at visual perception, use has been made of written language and finger spelling as a means of communication and as an aid to speech.

An American approach is the McGinnis (1963) association method in which the child learns to make sounds, to combine them into words and to associate them with their written symbols. When articulation is clear, the word is associated with its meaning, with writing, lip-reading and also listening to it. Repeating, matching and writing the word assist attention and memorization and after a small vocabulary is built up, teaching proceeds by small steps to simple language structures. Another account of a method is by Barry (1961).

Although few teachers will meet children as severely handicapped as this, the account of methods of teaching using different channels of communication is a good example of experimental approaches which are also needed for other children with severe learning problems.

About 250 children are at present provided for in either three special schools or in about twelve special classes. Surveys have shown, however, that there are other children needing special teaching on account of language disorders. These include a variety of conditions which need thorough assessment and diagnosis by hearing and speech specialists, as well as special teaching in which the skills of the teacher and the speech therapist are intermingled. In some cases it is difficult to distinguish the disorder from associated mental retardation and emotional and personality problems. In other cases, referred to as central deafness or auditory imperception, it is difficult to distinguish language disorder from hearing impairment – there may be no response or inconsistent response to sound. Sometimes these have indeed been placed in a deaf school. Clearly there is a possibility that children with this disability may retreat into a world of their own and show features of the autistic syndrome which is increasingly viewed as a condition in which perceptual and language problems are primary and withdrawal secondary.

Ingram (1964) and others consider these language disorders to be part of a large group of specific developmental speech disorders. In cases of moderate difficulty, there may be some articulatory defects and reading and writing difficulties. As mentioned earlier, Rutter (1966) has noted the frequency of speech and language difficulty in backward readers. Very often there is a family history of slow speech development, of difficulty in learning to read and write, of left-handedness and ambidexterity. The relationships between various language and learning difficulties are not completely elucidated.

Stammering

Pauses, repetitions and hesitations of various kinds are so common as to be a normal feature of speech. Stammering, however, is a disturbance of the normal rhythm of speech which occurs to such a degree or with such frequency that it interferes with communication or causes distress to the speaker or his audience. In comparison with normal non-fluency there is visible tension in the breathing and speech organs while attempting to articulate. Surveys show that it occurs in 1 per cent of the school population and is four times more common in boys. It is reported to occur in as many as 9 per cent of mentally retarded children. Many start to stammer as they begin to talk; others are said to start when they begin school and a few start during the school years but rarely after ten.

Stammering in the pre-school child has a good prognosis – threequarters or more growing out of the tendency by five or six years – but this occurs less frequently in school-age children. However, in a survey in Newcastle, Andrews and Harris (1964) found that more than 50 per cent remained only mild stammerers with little or no communication problem. The developing pattern of stammering shows comparatively little emotional reaction and avoidance of speech during the early primary age groups, but later, awareness, and perhaps avoidance of certain speech situations and a tendency to substitute easier words, often begins to occur. In adolescence and early adulthood, the disability becomes more of a personal problem, the stammer being anticipated, special difficulty occurring in particular words and situations. Word substitution, avoidance of speaking situations and emotional reactions may complicate the difficulty. In adulthood, many stammerers learn to manage the disability quite well and may be relatively unhampered by it.

Many explanations for stammering have been advanced in terms of psychic conflict and stress, neurological dysfunctions and maladaptive learning. Almost certainly there are a number of primary causes and even more certainly the effect of secondary factors – emotional and environmental – are important. In common with many abnormalities in learning and behaviour, it is necessary to think of *predisposing factors* (genetic ones; familial attitudes to non-fluency; a history of delayed speech – the poorer and slower development of speech increasing the chances of wrong learning and emotional interference) and *precipitating factors* (anxiety, emotional stress such as hospitalization, sibling jealousy, difficulties in social adjustment, adverse parental attitudes and expectations, beginning school or other school factors). Once stammering has started, it can be viewed in terms of learning, the unwanted speech habits being continually reinforced and associated with particular situations and generally aggravated by emotional factors. It should be pointed out, however, that there is little evidence to support the common view that stammering is a symptom of emotional disturbance – emotional factors may well be involved in it and in maintaining it and the way it is treated by the family, teachers and other children. Teasing can be a factor and teachers can help to prevent this by encouraging a co-operative atmosphere in which personal idiosyncracies are accepted without fuss.

EDUCATION AND TREATMENT

With the pre-school and young primary age child, the emphasis is preventive. Parents and teachers should avoid anything which makes the child self-conscious about his lack of fluency – attempting to correct him, telling him to speak slower or to repeat words, discussing the stammer in front of the child or scolding. Positively, the aim should be to develop confidence in spoken expression through play, activities and interests in a relaxed atmosphere. It is important to promote the child's general personal adjustment through a sense of achievement and confidence and to discover, remove or alleviate any home or school circumstances causing stress. The child who is socially rather isolated and retarded can be provided with opportunities for mixing with others and for communicating in free situations where speech occurs spontaneously and unselfconsciously.

Clearly it is most important that measures of this kind adopted by the teacher and speech therapist are fully supported by others, particularly the parents whose possible worry needs to be talked through. The teacher obviously has an important role here, especially as the shortage of speech therapists means that there are not enough to perform the supportive and advisory functions for all the children who need it. However, if the stammer is quite marked, it is better to refer early to a speech therapist rather than wait until the problem is exacerbated by the child's increasing preoccupation with it and by other secondary factors.

In class, the stammerer should be accepted and treated like any other child (except in so far as any special help is needed to ensure that he participates normally and grows in confidence and personal maturity). An unhurried waiting for him to say what he wants to and a general policy of de-emphasizing the hesitation is required. Whether or how much he reads aloud in reading or takes a speaking part in dramatic work depends on the child. The general aim is gradually to increase the amount of his participation. Some do so freely; others will do so with encouragement and in a favourable atmosphere. As has been often noted, joining in puppet work, choral speaking and singing can be helpful.

The speech therapist's approach will be very similar especially with younger children, aiming at relaxation, confidence and easy expression. In some cases, a more frankly psycho-therapeutic approach may be indicated and in a few cases the help of other members of the child guidance team may be called upon. A more direct approach to speech will be used only when the child is aware of his stammer and beginning to show the characteristics of the stage of secondary stammering – making efforts to avoid, disguise and stop stammering.

A variety of methods have been advocated. Some have the effect of distracting attention from the difficult sounds on to some other technique such as the timing and rhythm of speaking or breathing, or learning to stammer in a manner which is tolerable to the stammerer and to others. Another form of therapy aims to lead to an appreciation (depending on the child's age and ability) of what he is doing when he stammers; how his effort increases the difficulty of making certain sounds. When he is shown that making the sound is not inherently difficult and his anxiety about it is reduced, the change in attitude often brings about progress.

It is important for teachers to realize that a child going to speech therapy is not necessarily going for 'a cure'. Some children do improve very considerably but the therapist's work is equally concerned with easing the child's difficulty so that he is not hampered by it and so that the problem does not become more complicated.

A problem which sometimes causes puzzlement in school are children referred to as *elective* mutes. They are averagely intelligent, have the ability to speak but remain completely mute in certain situations or with certain people. Commonly they have never been heard to speak at school or only in a whisper or only with a playmate out of class. In the family they may talk normally. It is a defensive neurotic reaction to anxiety, the reasons for which are often difficult to identify. It is resistant to treatment even in a relaxed school atmosphere or by child guidance treatment. An article by Haskell in Renfrew and Murphy (1964) discusses the condition and one by Sluckin and John (1969) describes the slow progress of treatment. The problem should not be confused with the much more common uncommunicative and very shy child.

Further reading

ANDREWS, G. AND HARRIS, M. M. (1964), *The Syndrome of Stuttering*, London: Heinemann Medical.

BARRY, H. (1961), *The Young Aphasic Child: Evaluation and training*, Washington: Alexander Graham Bell Association for the Deaf.

LEA, J. (1966), 'The education of children suffering from receptive aphasia', *Slow Learning Children*, 13, 2, pp. 72-87.

LEA, J. (1968), 'Language and receptive aphasia', *Special Education*, 57, 21-5.

MCGINNIS, M. (1967), *Aphasic Children*, Washington: Alexander Graham Bell Association for the Deaf.

MORLEY, M. E. (1965), *The Development and Disorders of Speech in Childhood*, Edinburgh: Livingstone.

PALMER, M. (1962), 'Educational problems of the aphasic child', *Special Education*, 51, pp. 13-19.

RENFREW, C. AND MURPHY, K. (1964), *The Child Who Does Not Talk*, London: Spastics Society and Heinemann.

SLUCKIN, A. AND JOHN, D. (1969), 'A behavioural approach in the treatment of elective mutism', *British Journal of Psychiatric Social Work*, 10, 2, pp. 70-3.

WYATT, G. L. (1969), *Language Learning and Communication Disorders in Children*, London: Collier-Macmillan.

Retarded language development

How teachers can improve language skills is an important issue in many branches of special teaching. Apart from the special problems of children with hearing impairments and language disorders and those learning English as a second language, there is the larger problem of slow learners and of many others whose experience of language at home is an inadequate preparation for the language used in school.

What are the deficiencies in language which we hope to remedy? It is easy to think that the main task is to promote the growth of vocabulary – more words and better understanding of their meanings. This is of course important, but language is more than words. It is a system by means of which words are ordered and inflected in different ways to convey different meanings. Average children of five have acquired a good grasp of the 'rules' of syntax regulating the order of words in English sentences as well as the factors of intonation, stress and rhythm. They also have a good grasp of the inflections – e.g. plural *s*, adding *ed* and *ing*; indeed, some of their 'mistakes' such as 'catched' or 'teached' show how they are applying the rules they have generalized.

To illustrate this, we can compare two five-year-olds describing a colourful picture. John said: 'That's a blue telephone and a man 'phoning – there's a house on fire and it's got the chimney smoking and he's telephoning the fire brigade to put it out. If not he won't have a house.' James said, 'It's a fire – house on fire. Now he's get out – that man on fire – out his house. It's on fire – man said "It's on fire."'

An obvious difference is John's more coherent understanding of the event and it is difficult to know how far James's understanding was handicapped by his limited language. John seems to have the right words for what he wants to say and he can put words together in phrases and sentences which combine several details in the picture and even go beyond it to interpret purpose (he's telephoning the fire brigade to *put it out*) and condition (*if not*, he won't have a house). James not only seems to have difficulty in finding words (he repeats *fire* five times) but each utterance is simple in structure and he seems to omit certain words (that man('s *house is*) on fire; out (*of*) his house) – rather as a toddler hearing mother say *Put the dolly on the chair* will say *Dolly chair*.

If this sample of his language is typical, we can assume that James will get less help from the pictures in his reading books, will be less 'at home' with the sentences he meets in learning to read and will not find it easy to use language to talk about experiences in the class-room and to use language in even the early stages of mathematics. He needs not only a better vocabulary but greater facility in con-structing sentences.

Why was James so poor at this task? In the first place, he pos-sibly lacks experience of things like telephones and fire brigades. Per-haps he lacks experience of looking at pictures, talking about them and hearing other people talk about them. He is perhaps slower in mental development – in understanding what is happening in the picture as well as in holding in mind the words and forming the structures of his sentences. Note the ease with which John produces 'If not he won't have a house'. Clearly James could do with much more attention from the teacher – enriching his experience, widening his vocabulary, prompting him to notice, helping his understanding and developing ways of varying the structure of sentences to convey different meanings.

We should not forget, however, that as well as *expression* we need to assess *listening* and *comprehending* in following instructions, listen-ing to stories, comprehending explanations. For one thing, this helps the teacher to match communication to the child's capacity for understanding it, but even more we want to know how well children can use language to assist their thinking and learning. We are often conscious that words and ideas occurring in stories and lessons are unfamiliar, but the length, complexity and style of communications are also important. It is sometimes difficult to assess this since the context, gestures and tones of voice provide additional clues.

In addition to the meaning and the form of communication, child-ren may be limited in the range of purposes for which they use language. In teaching, we are especially interested in the use of language for thinking and learning – asking questions, acquiring con-cepts, reasoning, comprehending and explaining processes and events. Closely related to this is verbalizing as a commentary upon and guide to action. Young children can be observed talking to themselves in their play and this link between language and action continues as an inner verbalization in learning in school. Some slow learners need to be encouraged to use language in this way – for example, as they manipulate mathematics material, learn physical skills and tackle many kinds of practical and problem solving situations.

Language is of course important for *social* communication between children and with the teacher. This is one of the justifications of the typical nursery-infant approach and of co-operative and group work with older children in which they learn the language of sharing, taking turns, making friends and being part of a group. Language also functions as a means of becoming aware of one's own identity through individual expression. With some handicapped children, this self-awareness needs establishing at the level of bodily awareness. With all children this *personal* language serves to heighten awareness of one's own thoughts, feelings and personal qualities, a need which reaches a peak in adolescence. A related purpose is the *imaginative* one – using language for make-believe, dramatic play, making up and listening to stories continuing into free-drama, creative and imaginative writing. It is a way of assimilating personal experience, of sorting out fact and fiction, of trying out personal and social roles. While school tends to emphasize the language of instruction, it is important that these other functions of language should not be overlooked since language development is influenced by the whole of personal growth (Halliday, 1969).

Improving language in school

It is only too obvious that many children in our schools have in-adequate command of vocabulary and of the sentence structures of their mother tongue, lack facility in expression and are poor in listen-ing and comprehending. Many are restricted in their use of language as a tool for exploring their environment, for examining their ex-perience, for developing personal awareness and social communication. An early start on remedying these deficiencies is needed in nursery and infant schools. Any generalizations about methods which can be made for young children will have relevance for slow learners in the junior school and for sub-normal children.

Normal nursery-infant methods have always emphasized that the wide range of activity and the social interaction between children and with teachers provides excellent opportunities for promoting language growth. While language is not taught formally, opportu-nities are taken for talking about play activities and new experiences, conversing at mealtimes, listening to stories and in many other situations. In recent years the heightened interest in children's language and especially the belief that improved language will increase children's abilities and school progress has stimulated interest in special methods of teaching language. It is useful to examine what has been suggested if only to consider whether there are methods which could be incorporated in traditional approaches.

In the USA, compensatory pre-school programmes for giving socially disadvantaged children a better preparation for schooling has resulted in a variety of approaches ranging from some which are comparable to British nursery-infant methods to others which are highly structured programmes of step-by-step instruction in thinking and using language.

Susan Gray (1966) describes activities in The Early Training Project, a pre-school programme for socially deprived children in Nashville. Many of the methods used were comparable to those adopted by nursery-infant teachers, though activities were more closely guided and directed. The use of language was encouraged in the course of activities (asking for a particular toy; conversation at meal times), reinforcing verbal responses (providing something only if the request was framed in a sentence), listening to children talking about their own experiences and activities, story-telling, dramatization, puppets and tape-recording. There were also units of experience on such topics as the weather, people in the community and the neighbourhood. More specific language work was done through the use of a filed collection of pictures, picture sequences and picture puzzles. Patterns were copied on pegboards and used to develop concepts such as left/right, top/bottom, middle, long/short, between, beginning, ending, around, inside, outside, next to and colours. Brick building was used in a similar way and especially for positional concepts and words – up, down, top, bottom, underneath, between, in front of, behind.

Another American language programme is the Peabody Language Development Kits – a series of expensively produced kits covering the age ranges from 3 to 9½ years (Dunn 1967). Each kit has a teacher's manual with about 180 lessons outlined and provided with materials (puppet, pictures, records, objects, a manikin, geometric shapes, etc.). It is so designed that groups of up to twenty children can be taught in lessons of about twenty minutes each. The aim is to stimulate oral language development and thinking. For example, twenty-one plastic fruits are used for a variety of purposes – learning their names, teaching concepts of size and length, noting similarities and differences, dramatic play, tactile and visual sense training and a variety of classificatory tasks, e.g. which grow on a tree, on a bush, on the ground? which have juice in? what meals would you have them at? Geometric shapes are likewise variously used for teaching concepts of colour, number, shape, size, length, for classifying and other mental tasks. Other material helps to develop auditory discrimination, listening, remembering, describing, following directions and other thinking processes.

Blank and Solomon (1968) consider that a broad enrichment programme for disadvantaged children is likely to be ineffective if it does not tackle their basic deficiency which they identify as a failure to develop 'the abstract attitude', i.e. the ability to go beyond perceptual experience of objects and to think of the *properties of things* and *relationships*. They argue that these children need not only a rich and stimulating environment but also a symbolic system (i.e. concepts and language) with which to organize their experience. Moreover they need the 'feedback' which is provided in the middle class but not the poor home. So they provided individual sessions daily. The nursery school teacher who did this used normal nursery school materials and activities but was trained to emphasize certain features of the teaching. Some of these were: (1) selective attention – comparing objects and noticing their features; (2) ability to categorize – sorting and classifying; (3) cause and effect reasoning, e.g. in relation to weather and other natural events; (4) categories of exclusion – emphasizing the boundary between one concept and another. Thus: 'This is an animal. Tell me something which is not an animal.' 'Something big and not big'; (5) imagining future events; (6) training inner verbalization – getting the child to verbalize what he is doing. Even if individual sessions like these could not be arranged, it would be useful to have these aims in mind.

A programme by Bereiter and Englemann (1966) has aroused considerable controversy because it proposes a rigorous tutoring method very different from our normal language experience approaches. They worked with 4½-year-old socially disadvantaged children in the USA who were retarded by a year or more in language and reasoning, though not in other abilities such as short-term memory and rote learning capacity. They argue that these children must learn faster in order to catch up and that it is not enough to provide an enriched language experience. In their beginning programme, all the tasks revolve round two simple statement forms: *This is* – (a dog, etc.) and *This – is* – (e.g. this dog is black). These are used to make statements about a variety of toys and objects. The child learns to transform the statements into question and negative forms and later to handle a variety of concepts and words referring to attributes and relationships; and later still to categories ('This building is a house').

According to the authors, in the beginning programme the child learns 'the fundamental conceptual framework of logical thought' – he has learnt to examine his experience, to express what he has perceived and to ask questions. In a further stage, the concepts *and, only, or all, some, if, then are* dealt with. Although the programme can be criticized, if only on the grounds of dullness, it provokes awareness of aspects which probably do need more attention with language-retarded children. Much of it could be made more interesting and attractive by a teacher.

Is there a place for such methods in the education of children with retarded language? Most teachers are reluctant to make use of such techniques because of the artificiality of the situation. The genuine need and desire to communicate which occurs in informal situations is lacking, and there is not the same sense of communicating to a genuine listener which we know to be important. Rather, teachers prefer to make use of the rich possibilities for acquiring and using language in everyday situations – with younger children through play and with older ones through activity and discussion. Here language can arise from concrete experiences and real needs for communication. Moreover, language experience can be more broadly based, providing for the language functions previously noted – the personal, social, imaginative – which seem to be lost sight of in the stress on language as a tool for thinking and forming concepts.

The informal, incidental approach could, however, run the risk of being so casual that opportunities are unused or not exploited fully, or that the children who talk most gain attention while the silent ones who need it most will get insufficient attention. Another possible weakness may be that the teacher is very vague about what she is hoping to achieve in language. Improving language is not like teaching reading or number where the sequences of teaching have been made clear by staff discussion and by the books and materials to be used.

Both these weaknesses can, at least to some extent, be avoided by an attempt to make more explicit what language learning is being aimed at (just as the teacher in the Blank and Solomon research was asked to emphasize certain features in her teaching). One way of doing this is to examine and observe the language possibilities of the classroom environment – the language likely to arise as children use different kinds of material or engage in different kinds of play (e.g. constructive, experimental, imaginative play; Wendy House, sand and water, painting and clay). This leads to an awareness of the vocabulary and language forms which can be brought in and the kind of explanation, discussion and description which can be provoked. With older children, it is useful to consider the vocabulary and the special, sometimes unfamiliar, uses of words in different subjects and the kind of language structures required for comprehension and expression.

This procedure needs to be complemented by observation of the language children use. Making a few records of spontaneous expression is an illuminating experience. Comparison of good and poor talkers (like John and James earlier in this section) make one aware of differences and indicate those children who can do with more help as well as those remarks which could be expanded by the teacher. The awareness on the one hand of the language children use and on the other hand of the language possibilities of the environment should help to avoid overlooking the needs of individuals and failure to exploit the possibilities of the environment.

In some of the American approaches which have been referred to the teacher has a very active teaching role. In an informal approach what does the teacher do? The teacher, of course, provides materials or experiences and initiates activities which, it is hoped, will arouse interest, comment, questioning and communication. The teacher draws attention to things children have not noticed or do not know about; supplies information; asks questions (there is much skill in posing questions which lead to description and explanation rather than one-word replies). Opportunities are seized for bringing in words for activities which children, especially slow learners, would be content to undertake without any verbalization. Particularly important is ensuring the emotional atmosphere favourable to communication – with the poor communicators a good teacher-pupil relationship is a first step. Mistrust and failure in relationships is often a major factor in retarded language development.

Perhaps the most important thing is providing 'feedback'. In the development of language in young children, the mother's expansion of the child's expression provides him unobtrusively with the correction he can learn from. *Child*: Pussy milk. *Mother*: Yes! The pussy cat is drinking the milk. *Child*: Pussy drink milk. This feedback takes various forms – supplying words, meanings, information, expanding sentence structures, giving approval and rewards. In this continual process of feedback the child modifies his own language and gradually approximates to adult linguistic forms. An important feature of this is that most mothers are able to match their responses to the child's stage of development, reducing the 'linguistic load' though not to the point of over-simplification and failing to 'stretch' the child.

It is this close verbal interaction with a parent that many language-retarded children have lacked and the conclusion seems inescapable that they should have the maximum verbal interaction with an adult for a short period as often as possible. Nursery-infant teachers often achieve this to some extent through small groups for stories, talk and news-time, but there is no doubt that it would be a great advantage to be able to organize 'remedial language' sessions for individuals and small groups of language-retarded children for ten to twenty minutes a day. This would be additional to the general language work of the class. For most schools, this is an unrealistic ideal but there are some situations where something of this kind could be organized.

It is interesting to note that many American programmes have tried to influence the mothers by having them observe the pre-school programme occasionally, and in some cases by having a worker visit the homes. In Susan Gray's programme this had a diffusion effect – brothers and sisters benefited and other mothers also began to be influenced by what went on in the training project. The need for this is underlined by several investigations in which the verbal inter-actions between mothers and children have been observed. The educa-ted mother gives explanations and answers questions. The lower-class mother is likely to disregard questions and in her verbal comments in relation to an experience is likely to name things rather than to give explanations or initiate a verbal interchange with the child. As Bernstein and others have suggested, the teacher's task is not just to 'give more words' but to develop a different attitude towards the use of language in relation to experience.

Further Reading

BEREITER, C. AND ENGLEMANN, S. (1966), *Teaching Disadvantaged Children in the Pre-School*, N.J.: Prentice-Hall.

BLANK, M. AND SOLOMON, F. (1968), 'A tutorial programme to develop abstract thinking in socially disadvantaged children', *Child Development*, 39, 379-89.

GRAY, S. W., KLAUS, R. A., MILLER, J. D. AND FORRESTER, B. T. (1966), *Before First Grade*, New York: Teachers College Press.

GULLIFORD, R. (1960), 'Teaching the mother tongue to backward and sub-normal pupils', *Educational Research*, II, 2, pp. 82-100.

RENFREW, C. (1959), 'Speech problems of backward children', *Speech Pathology and Therapy*, April.

Early infantile autism

A puzzling and unusual group of children has attracted much interest and concern in the post-war period. The term autism derives from the Greek word *autos* meaning self, and autistic children indeed appear to be living in a world of their own. Their characteristics were usefully delineated in nine points drawn up by a committee in 1961 (Creak) – though, as we shall see, recent work suggests a different emphasis in the description. The nine points were :

(1) *Severely impaired relationships.* They are usually aloof, making little contact and relationships with adults and children. This has a different quality from the behaviour of the withdrawn child. They wander about a room uninterested in what others are doing, unresponsive to what is offered them. They appear not to perceive others as persons and some will use others or parts of them impersonally, e.g. lifting teacher's arm to get something.

(2) *Lack of a sense of personal identity.* Some tend to explore their bodies visually or by posture as though it were an unfamiliar object.

(3) *Pathological preoccupation with particular objects.* E.g. a piece of shoe lace or a small stone may be constantly manipulated.

(4) *Resistance to change in the environment* and a striving to maintain or restore sameness; for example, excessive reaction of anxiety or rage to a new person, a new thing or rearrangement of routine or environment.

(5) *Abnormal perceptual experience* – ignoring sounds, refusing to look at things or people, insensitivity to pain or temperature. At the same time, some children continually explore objects by putting them in the mouth; some bring objects to the nose or near to the eyes. Some fixate on lights or moving objects.

(6) *Acute, excessive and seemingly illogical anxiety.* Quite ordinary things (e.g. changed routine) may cause this while, on the other hand, fears of real dangers (traffic, heights) may be lacking.

(7) *Speech and language retardation.* Some children never learn to talk and the majority are late in talking. Many unusual features of speech and language occur : the tendency to echo what has just been said (echolalia); 'telegraphic' speech omitting small words; confusing pronouns, similar words or the order of words; difficulty in comprehension of anything more than simple verbal instructions; being literal and concrete in their use and understanding of speech.

(8) *Unusual movements* – excessive movement and wandering about or extreme passivity; bizarre mannerisms such as rocking, spinning themselves or objects, hand flapping.

(9) Generally a low level of mental functioning in which islets of normal or near normal performance may appear, e.g. in doing jigsaws; in memory for certain kinds of fact; music.

It is important to recognize that some of these characteristics *taken by themselves* are observable in normal children during the course of their development. Some features are frequently observed in other kinds of handicap – the mannerisms of some blind children and sub-normal children and children with multiple handicaps. This is really a warning not to use the word autistic indiscriminately. It is often difficult to make the differential diagnosis between autism and sub-normality, sensory defect or other severe communication problems. Some cases of blind or deaf children showing autistic behaviour make very good progress towards normality.

There has been considerable speculation about the nature and causes of autism since Kanner first distinguished it from other conditions in 1943. He himself thought that there was some inborn defect aggravated by emotional coldness on the part of parents; others emphasized even more psychological factors in the child's rearing and the view was at one time held that the mothers of autistic children were cold and withdrawn. This view was perhaps fed by the relative frequency of intellectual and professional parents and also by the fact that a mother baffled by the lack of response from her child is very likely to appear not to relate to him. (This confusion of cause and effect must have added to the unhappiness of many mothers and is an object lesson for us in child guidance and education. It is often easy to perceive failings in the child as being due to parental faults and mismanagement, but in some cases parents' behaviour is a response to difficulties in the child. In all cases, it is better to see each parent-child relationship as a unique interaction which it is necessary to evaluate in an undoctrinaire and sympathetic way.)

An obvious hypothesis to consider is whether autism is the result of brain damage. This is supported by the fact that encephalitis can lead to an autistic condition and there is evidence of brain damage in one in four autistic children. Moreover, some of the defects in perception, thinking and language are reminiscent of those occurring in brain damaged children. However, evidence of brain damage is lacking in at least half the cases of autism.

The current view is that the basic disability may be an inability to use and interpret sensory experiences, especially hearing and vision, probably due to a defect in the brain's processing of sensory information. It is further suggested that the difficulty particularly applies in interpreting symbols which could account for the language difficulties as well as for several other characteristics. For example, the impaired relationships may be partly due to not comprehending the meaning of non-verbal symbols such as facial expressions, actions and gestures. Their play is manipulative and lacks the make-believe element of normal children, which suggests a failure to develop the *symbolic function* which Piaget has shown as emerging out of sensory-motor behaviour in the second year of life.

Viewed in this way, the nine characteristics of behaviour can be reorganized to provide a more integrated and meaningful system of symptoms. As major elements there are: avoidance of, or over-reaction to, visual and auditory stimuli; the special interest in certain perceptual experiences; the disorders and oddities of speech and language. The unusual motor behaviour, resistance to change and extremes of emotion and mood can be seen as reactions to their incomprehensible world. A reorganized statement of symptoms in autism has been prepared by Wing (Mittler, 1968).

The education of autistic children

It is estimated that between two and four out of every 10,000 children suffer from this condition, which means that there may be 3,000 in the whole country. There is no clear policy about their education. According to Elgar and Wing (1969) slightly under half the children are in subnormality hospitals, the remainder in special schools for the subnormal, various kinds of special schools and in ordinary and private schools. There are, however, a number of units attached to hospitals or set up by local education authorities and the National Society for Autistic Children runs two schools and hopes to set up more.

Lack of complete understanding of the condition and even more of the educational methods needed have tended to hold back the making of special provision and it is also sometimes suggested that it is beneficial for autistic children to be in a mixed group with other children. On the other hand, the symptoms previously described suggest that a concentrated and informed search for ways of overcoming the disabilities is needed rather than placing them with children of a similar level of functioning and hoping for the best.

Education aims to assist the autistic child to make sense of his environment, since as we have seen he appears unable to interpret and organize his impressions and sometimes finds perceptual experience so disturbing that he avoids them or shuts them out. He needs therefore a settled environment with established routines rather than a free one, though within these limits he needs freedom to act and behave in his own way; attempts to direct and control often provoke a strong reaction. One stable element will be the teacher from whom is needed a considerable amount of individual attention in order to develop self-awareness and a relationship. Several teachers (Clark, 1965; Furneaux, 1969) have stressed the importance of minute observation of the child to find what he can do, what are his preferred sensory channels, what comprehension there is of speech even though there is no spoken language. Both stress the value of taking some preferred activity and trying to expand and develop it by bringing in new materials. Thus, a child playing obsessively with a shoe-lace might be provoked into threading beads onto the lace; a child who spends much time obsessively pushing bricks along the floor might have pictures or letters added to the bricks.

The fact that auditory and visual stimuli are sometimes unacceptable to the children suggests experimenting with tactile or olfactory experiences. Often materials which provide simple manipulative experiences rather than perceptual discrimination may be favoured. Elgar and Wing (1969) report the use of Montessori material, but the teacher experienced in nursery-infant work will know of a great variety of materials and activities which can be drawn upon once a foothold has been gained in the child's participation. Elgar and Wing describe a varied programme of activities – P.E., swimming, cooking, simple needlework, music and dance – which become possible as children improve. Of particular importance is language. Many autistic children never learn to talk; some do so at quite late ages. As with all children, a first aim is comprehension of spoken language and autistic children often comprehend language and situations much better than is supposed. An assessment of verbal comprehension can provide therefore another starting point – for stories, following instructions and many other activities.

What progress do autistic children make? Rutter (1967) followed up sixty-four children who had been seen at the Maudsley Hospital between 1950 and 1958 and found that only a few make a good social adjustment by the time of adolescence (two in employment and five doing some kind of remunerative work) and about a half remained severely handicapped and incapable of independent existence (a third were in long-stay hospitals). However, only twenty-nine of these had received even as much as two years' schooling, most of them less than ten years, and nine for less than five years. It will obviously be important to follow up progress of children who have been receiving education and to evaluate its different forms and methods. Rutter's results indicate that while many factors have a bearing on future progress – IQ, response to sounds, acquisition of useful speech before five years, additional disabilities – the amount and type of schooling has a discernible effect.

Further reading

CLARK, G. D. (1965), (in Weston, P.T.B., ed.) *Some Approaches to Teaching Autistic Children*, Oxford: Pergamon.
CREAK, M. et al. (1961), 'Schizophrenic syndrome in children', *British Medical Journal*, 2, pp. 889-90.

ELGAR, S. AND WING, L. (1969), *Teaching Autistic Children*, College of Special Education.

FURNEAUX, B. (1969), *The Special Child* (Ch. 9), Harmondsworth: Penguin.

MITTLER, P. J. (1968), *Aspects of Autism*, British Psychological Society.

RIMLAND, B. (1965), *Infantile Autism*, London: Methuen.

RUTTER, M. (1967), 'Schooling and the autistic child', *Special Education*, 56, 2, pp. 19-25.

——(1970), 'Autism: concepts and consequences', *Special Education*, 59, 2, pp. 20-4; 59, 3, pp. 6-10.

WING, J. K. (ed.) (1966), *Early Childhood Autism*, Oxford: Pergamon.

seven

Social and cultural differences

Disadvantaged children

There is a long tradition of concern in this country for children living in very adverse social conditions. Early in this century, Margaret Macmillan campaigned in Bradford for school meals and medical inspection; later in Deptford she set up open-air nursery schools for children living in slum conditions. Nursery schools, unfortunately too few in number, have continued to see compensation for environmental disadvantages an important element in their work. Special schools, particularly those for backward children, have always accepted welfare functions as a part of their work. Likewise teachers in backward classes and 'remedial' departments have always known that they were dealing not just with backward children but invariably with a proportion of socially disadvantaged children who gravitated to the lower streams. There have always been good teachers who sought to make their schools into oases of happiness and learning in the drab inner areas of towns.

What is new at the present time is the growing determination to do something about it. Certain schools have been designated as schools in educational priority areas with some increases in resources, staffing and other forms of help. Several programmes of research and action research have been instituted. Some training courses in compensatory education and teacher-social work have been instituted both for experienced teachers and for teachers in training. For the first time for many years some new nursery schools and classes are being started in urban areas. There is considerable discussion about how the content and methods of education need to be modified to compensate for the effects of disadvantage; how schools may influence parents and the neighbourhood community and can undertake 'pastoral' and social work functions.

Paradoxically, this determination has come at a time when improved economic circumstances of families and the effect of welfare legislation have brought about a general improvement in the physical condition and care of children. Nevertheless, the Child Poverty Action group and the researches of social workers have compelled attention to the problems of a not insignificant minority whose circumstances are detrimental to educational development and social adjustment. And while the Education Act of 1944 opened up the possibility of educational opportunity for all, it has become apparent that some children were seriously hindered in taking advantage of educational opportunities.

In fact, the mitigation of the worst material inequalities has only served to highlight the psychological influences on educational achievement. In the 1950s, the first incursions of sociologists into education showed that working-class children were under-represented in grammar school selections. The Ministry of Education's report on Early Leaving showed that children of unskilled and semi-skilled workers did not do as well in grammar schools as children from higher social groups with similar abilities and attainments at eleven plus. Subsequent education reports amplified the same theme. Although educational opportunities were equal in theory, in practice many children were held back educationally, their response to education being limited by cultural and social factors.

Researches began to show what factors were important. Fraser (1959) studied the relationship between various environmental factors and school achievement in 400 children in Aberdeen. The three most important were income, parents' attitude to education and to the child's future occupation, and abnormality of home background. The importance of parental attitudes was further confirmed by the longitudinal studies of Douglas which found that the degree of parental interest and encouragement was even more related to achievement in working-class than middle-class children. It was this kind of evidence which led the Plowden committee to stress parent-school relations so that parents who would not otherwise do so might be encouraged to take a positive interest in their children's progress.

The factor of abnormal home background scarcely needs stressing. Both schools and children's departments have considerable experience of dealing with families that are broken or functioning badly as a result of desertion, death, poverty, bad management, unemployment or mental and physical illness in the parents. Wilson (1962) has provided a vivid account of the various combinations of adversities which produce family situations lacking not only the basic requirements of physical care but also the psychological conditions necessary for personal growth and readiness for school learning.

An additional fillip has undoubtedly been given to the idea of special help for disadvantaged children by the great flurry of activity in the USA. In the early 1960s Federal legislation and private foundations began to provide resources for tackling the effects of poverty and educational disadvantage. In 1965 the Headstart programmes began, designed to provide a pre-school experience for disadvantaged children. Many school systems and universities initiated programmes of compensatory action and research and a vast literature is available. While American experience has much to offer, some caution is necessary before assuming that research findings and, especially, practical remedies have direct relevance in a British context. Differences in ethnic, political and economic factors have significance for the nature of the problem. Differences in the educational system (its administration, financing, training and deployment of teachers) and, not least, differences in educational philosophies and practices must be taken into account in drawing upon American experience.

The nature of the problem

Several different terms are used interchangeably to refer to the children under discussion – culturally deprived, socially disadvantaged or environmentally handicapped. A common element in all descriptions is that these are children who are at a disadvantage for making progress in school and for successful adjustment to life and work after leaving school. Disadvantage may show in various combinations of the following characteristics: failure to develop fully abilities in attention, perception and thinking; retarded language development; limited experiences of the kind assumed in school learning; poor motivation for learning and limited educational and vocational aspirations; difficulties in behavioural and emotional adjustment. The causes of these limitations are many: inadequate child care associated with poverty, bad housing, large families and inefficient family management; methods of child rearing which do not develop the mental capacities and attitudes favourable to school progress; emotional deprivation or disturbance resulting from breakdown of normal family pattern, over-burdened or otherwise preoccupied parents; lack of parental interest in education or lack of understanding of the aim and methods of education. In addition to home and neighbourhood factors, school factors must also be considered: the failure of schools to adapt the timing and approach of teaching to the deficiencies of these children; failure to provide effective remedial and special teaching and to modify curriculum and methods to meet their needs;

failure of the community to organize the extra teaching and material help needed by schools in poor areas.

The last point was recognized by the Plowden Report which recommended 'positive discrimination' should favour schools in neighbourhoods where children are most severely handicapped by home conditions and that local education authorities should apply various criteria to identify schools needing special help – occupation levels of parents, size of families, supplementary State benefits, over-crowding and sharing of houses, poor attendance and truancy, pro-portion of retarded, disturbed or handicapped pupils, incomplete fami-lies, children unable to speak English. The fact that certain schools tend to have many children with environmental handicaps should not lead to the error of assuming that all children in educational priority area schools are disadvantaged, that all children from poor homes are deprived, that all parents in poor areas are not interested in their children's education. Many indeed are concerned for their children's welfare though they do not always know how to help.

Disadvantage can occur in rural areas (poor or isolated homes; gypsy children with sporadic school attendance) and it is also impor-tant to recognize the effects of disadvantage and stress in more favoured areas.

The educational needs of disadvantaged children

There is now a considerable amount of evidence which shows that a very deprived cultural background may retard mental development, limit verbal development and fail to develop other capacities required in learning. This is an important idea since it emphasizes that teach-ing, especially with young children, is not simply concerned with improving school attainments but with promoting mental growth. It is generally accepted that the early years of childhood are most critical in this respect, which results in the emphasis on nursery education and in the USA has also led to efforts to influence the kind of experience children have at home by providing play materials and by involving mothers in the pre-school programmes. Emphasis on the early years does not however mean that improved mental functioning is not sought in the middle and later years of childhood particularly through the improvement of language and thinking skills.

The effect of poor environment is most often discussed in relation to children with low IQs, but it may equally be true that some child-ren with average IQs have genetic potentialities, the full realization of which has been prevented by a very poor environment. Nor should low IQ in disadvantaged children be taken necessarily to imply low capacity for learning. Jensen (1967) reports that in experimental learning tasks lower-class children with low IQ are superior in learning ability to middle-class children with low IQ, i.e. there are children in the low social class group who have abilities for learning which are not fully utilized. This provides further support for the point of view expressed in Chapter 4 that the backward child with inherent intellectual limitations should be distinguished from the environmentally handicapped child. While both need good teaching, the former needs an education adapted to his poorer capacity for learning, while the latter needs an education designed to motivate him and help him use his better ability more fully. In short, we should be careful not to assume that the special content and methods required for slow learners are sufficient for all disadvantaged children.

Research evidence shows that environmental differences have an even greater effect on attainment than on intelligence. The important factors are not so much material ones as parents' attitude towards education and to the child's progress, their degree of interest and encouragement. This implies that an important element in compensatory education is trying to involve and interest parents. Attitudes to school are sometimes hostile, more often apathetic, but, often, more susceptible to influence than is assumed. Some families are so disorganized or burdened with problems that it is not surprising that schooling has a low priority. Even in these cases it is sometimes surprising what schools can achieve by providing such children with security and acceptance, practical help and ensuring compensatory achievements and interests.

The need for good motivation goes deeper than providing interesting activities, though this is important. Disadvantaged children are unlikely to appreciate the short-term and long-term goals of learning. They have less experience of working towards a delayed gratification. If they fail to progress, a sense of failure and inferiority is liable to set into a generalized dislike and rejection of school, and it is not surprising that a high rate of truancy is a common result – which, of course, further aggravates the educational problem.

A critical factor is the child's readiness for school learning. The ordinary child comes to school having learnt how to play constructively with materials and to attend to what an adult has to say or show. The disadvantaged child needs to be taken through such pre-school experiences before he learns not to flit from one thing to another, before he learns that manipulating and experimenting with materials leads to new possibilities which can be explored, before he learns that what the teacher is saying or providing has meanings which are worth attending to and looking for. Primary schools can go a long way to rectifying these deficiencies. Where, however, children are prematurely confronted with demands to sit still and conform to formal learning requirements, their basic problem of learning how to learn, of being curious and spontaneously interested will be untouched

In a class with a high proportion of disadvantaged children one of the main problems is likely to be unsettled behaviour. Children who have not learnt to find satisfaction through activity nor experienced the rewards of persistence are likely to have a short attention span, aggravated in some by emotional insecurities and difficulties in relationships with others. Many are not tuned in to listening to an adult nor sustained by the desire to achieve or the feeling that they can achieve. The routines of a classroom in which there is some pattern in the sequence of events is an alien environment in comparison with the homes of many children. Invariably some children, not only in the younger groups, are continually seeking affection and attention. Many of the points discussed in Chapter 3 about the need for a framework of routines, for flexibility in interpretation of rules and for adapting expectations to children of different levels of maturity apply to these children.

The above characteristics point to the importance of achievement. Success produces further involvement and effort and is the surest compensation we can offer. Possible weaknesses in learning have to be recognized. There is the likelihood of retarded perceptual development – visually in interpreting pictures, discriminating shapes, patterns and letters and in visuo-motor skills such as writing, drawing and manipulation – as a result of lack of pre-school experience. Likewise experience of language, stories, rhymes and conversation may have been insufficient to develop listening and auditory skills. More attention to these aspects of readiness for reading and writing is usually required. Once a start is made, it is important to ensure continuity. The disadvantaged child is less likely than children from average homes to have reading matter at home, to be read to or to be heard reading. His progress is more precarious so that continuity from class to class is all the more important. Since a proportion of these children are also the ones who move from school to school as parents are rehoused or move from one unsuitable accommodation to another, efficient liaison between schools would be a great advantage rather than the new teacher starting afresh. Disadvantaged children are liable to be among the 10 to 20 per cent of pupils who have barely made a satisfactory start in reading by the end of the infant school (Pringle et al., 1966) and a continuation of infant school methods is essential together with remedial teaching for the most retarded. A concentrated remedial attack at this point will not solve all the problems of learning and adjustment though it would alleviate many of them. A further opportunity for a fresh approach can be taken and is often successful at the beginning of the secondary school.

One of the most significant deficiencies for education is the disadvantaged child's retarded language. This often shows up clearly in infants' poor response to instructions in P.E., movement and their failure to grasp other communications in class. It is an important factor in their slow start in reading and also their failure to progress in higher reading skills such as comprehension and reading for information. It probably also contributes to the failure of some children to progress in secondary schools at the level expected for their general ability. Some of the issues about methods of improving language have been discussed in Chapter 6, but there is a need continuing through primary and secondary schools for English teaching which emphasizes oracy (Wilkinson, A. W. (1965), *Spoken English*, Educational Review Occasional Publications No. 2, University of Birmingham) rather than merely literacy and, inherent in that approach, emphasizes personal expression and experience.

Bernstein's hypothesis about social class differences in language has been very influential in this field. Middle-class or educated families use language to express meanings and feelings explicitly, to examine their experience, to explain and give reasons. Thus from an early age children's questions are answered; reasons for requests are given. Language is the important medium for communication as it is in school. This *elaborated* code draws upon a wide range of linguistic resources (vocabulary, tense, sentence structures) and the child comes to school not only well equipped with language but experienced in the uses of language for thinking, forming concepts and regulating his own behaviour. In the *restricted* code of lower-class families, language tends to be limited. Ideas and feelings are assumed and implied rather than explicitly stated and individually expressed. Questions are less likely to be answered; reasons for requests and commands less likely to be given. There is a restricted use of the resources of language, poor vocabulary, simple tenses, simple sentences, a greater use of gesture, facial expressions and common phrases which express vaguely and generally a tacitly assumed meaning.

This view of the problem suggests that the teacher's task is not only one of improving language skills but of extending the uses of language for the examination and imaginative assimilation of experience as well as for learning.

The need of these children for improved language, for oracy and literacy cannot be considered apart from their need for a general enrichment of curriculum. An important ingredient is enjoyment. They need to savour the happiness and satisfaction of creative activities in music, movement and creative work, often indeed finding achievement in these aspects. They, more than any children, need also the experience of visits with the opportunity of having things pointed out and talked about by adults. Since many children from poor homes have little experience except of their own neighbourhood, longer journeys can widen horizons. Many secondary schools have reported the benefits of expeditions or short stays in the country, the mountains, camping or residential weeks – benefits not only to the children themselves but also for the teachers' understanding and appraisal of pupils. Another need is that of feeling themselves to be part of the community. A first step is making them feel part of the school community and not hidden away and devalued in non-academic streams, and beyond this are many possibilities for service in the locality.

One of the features of a school with a high proportion of environmentally handicapped children is the amount of welfare and social work undertaken by the head and staff. The better they do this the more there is to do, since parents are more willing to seek help with problems, and tackling these problems inevitably entails more contact with social workers and other agencies. Trying to help a 'child in distress' and his family can be immensely time-consuming, yet who can tell what this may mean in human terms for a child's future? Undoubtedly, the appointment of teacher-social workers, counsellors or home liaison teachers can be of great value in undertaking a continuous responsibility for some of these problems and for making liaison with the social services department.

Many people have mixed feelings about the meaningfulness of the term compensatory education, and terms such as social disadvantage and cultural deprivation seem to include a value judgment. The NBCCC report *Living with Handicap* suggested the more neutral term, environmentally handicapped. Terms and labels are always a trouble but they can help to focus attention on particular needs. As suggested at the beginning of this section, teachers have always been concerned with those problems; they will not be too worried about terms so long as additional resources become available – nursery schools and classes; smaller classes; trained non-teaching helps; remedial resource materials and remedial teachers; additional resources of materials and books and equipment, essential for compensatory teaching; additional staff for social and welfare work; improved liaison and co-ordination of social work.

Further reading

BLOOM, B. G., DAVIES, A. AND HESS, R. (1965), *Compensatory Education for Cultural Deprivation*, New York: Holt, Rinehart & Winston.
CLEGG, A. AND MEGSON, B. (1968), *Children in Distress*, Harmondsworth: Penguin.
DEPARTMENT OF EDUCATION AND SCIENCE, Education Survey 5: *Parent-Teacher Relations in Primary Schools*, London: H.M.S.O.

INNER LONDON EDUCATION AUTHORITY (1968), *Home and School*, Inner London Education Authority.
JENSEN, A. R. (1967), 'The culturally disadvantaged: psychological and educational aspects', *Educational Research*, 10, 1, pp. 4-20.
MAYS, J. B. (1962), *Education and the Urban Child*, Liverpool University Press.
RIESMAN, F. (1962), *The Culturally Deprived Child*, New York: Harper & Row.
SCHOOLS COUNCIL PROJECT IN COMPENSATORY EDUCATION (1968), *Compensatory Education: an Introduction* (Occasional publications 1), University College, Swansea.
SCHOOLS COUNCIL WORKING PAPER 15 (1967), *Counselling in Schools*, London: H.M.S.O.
SCHOOLS COUNCIL WORKING PAPER 27 (1969), *Cross'd with Adversity*, Evans Methuen Educational.
WEBB, L. (1967), *Children with Special Needs in the Infant School*, Gerrards Cross: Colin Smythe.
WITTY, P. A. (ed.) (1967), *The Educationally Retarded and the Disadvantaged*, 66th yearbook, National Society for the Study of Education. Chicago University Press.

Delinquent children

The term delinquency covers a great variety of problems for which there are no simple explanations or remedies. Delinquent behaviour can be a by-product of a phase in adolescence associated with gang membership in certain localities; the result of poor personality and character development related to adverse home circumstances; a symptom of psychological disturbance – a cry for help; or a consequence of a combination of personal and environmental handicaps. The peak age is fourteen years; boys are ten times more troublesome than girls.

The majority of offenders are youngsters in whom troublesome behaviour can be seen as a response of their age group to various environmental circumstances – the temptation to steal to obtain easily such things as bicycles, transistors, etc.; having freedom and leisure as well as inadequate care and control from homes. There is also the lack of legitimate outlets for adolescent drives. The various fashions in dress and behaviour which have served as symbols for certain adolescent groups which tend towards delinquency are manifestations of an adolescent need for self- and group-identity. Willmott (1969) found two cycles of adolescent delinquency – an early one concerned with petty theft and a slightly later one around seventeen years involving motoring offences, hooliganism and violence. He regards this behaviour as transitory and that the boys settle down when they get married. Mays (1962) has argued that in some urban areas, delinquency is a social tradition; only a few youngsters are able to grow up in these areas without at some time committing illegal acts. It is not a symptom of maladjustment so much as one of adjustment to a sub-culture in conflict with the culture of the city. Clearly, schools have something to offer to provide alternative satisfactions and purposes for the adolescent.

This view is a corrective to the assumption that all delinquents are emotionally maladjusted. Nevertheless in groups of delinquent children, particularly in persistent offenders, there is a well-known pattern of adverse social background (child neglect, broken homes and other environmental stresses and inadequacies), and in others, not necessarily from poor homes, psychological factors affect the child's personality and general development. With these also the schools can contribute to prevention and remedy in co-operation with social workers and child guidance services.

Social factors in delinquency

There is no one cause of delinquency. Various kinds of explanation have been advanced and each helps to throw light on the origins of delinquent behaviour. One line of enquiry has consistently related delinquency to environmental conditions. Cyril Burt showed that half the juvenile delinquents in London came from poor homes in certain areas and many other investigations have shown that delinquency was concentrated in the slums. There has been an increase in delinquency rates on the outskirts of towns as populations are re-housed on new estates. While over-crowding, poor housing, lack of play space and things to do are obvious factors in inner urban areas, there are other factors to consider.

Among the factors implicated is low social class. In samples of delinquents, children of unskilled or semi-skilled workers occur in greater numbers than would be expected for the proportion of such families in the population, and children from upper working and middle classes are 'under-represented'. Douglas's (1968) longitudinal study obtained the following percentage delinquency rates for different social classes:

Upper middle class	2·7
Lower middle class	8·3
Upper manual working class	9·7
Lower manual working class	18·7

The delinquent boy from the better home is of course more likely to be dealt with by his parents or his school, and one of the aims of the new Children's Act is to try to increase the help given to the child and parents from poorer families. The child from the lower-working-class family is 'at risk' not only because of the area in which he lives but because of various adverse factors in his development. Bernstein's theory of a restricted language code in the lower-working-class family includes the idea that the child does not so easily internalize verbal prohibitions as codes of conduct. Parents probably have less influence on their children, are less able to direct their activities into suitable channels and to help with personal problems. Burt has stressed the importance of the mother's effectiveness, and recent research has increasingly focused on the role of the father – how far he serves as a model for the boy to identify with; the extent of his interest in the boy and readiness to do things with him.

Many factors in a poor social background militate against a successful response to school and many studies show that while delinquents are not as a group much below average in intelligence, a marked degree of backwardness is common. Anything schools can do to remedy basic educational deficiencies makes a positive contribution to the prevention of delinquency and, as Clegg (1968) and others have pointed out, the attitude of the head and staff towards the problem of vulnerable children has significance for allaying tendencies to delinquency. Schools drawing their pupils from the same or similar populations often show big differences in the occurrence of delinquency.

The school is important not only for promoting individual achievement but because it is perhaps the only organized social institution which many youngsters belong to. Some researchers, especially American ones, have explained delinquency as a conflict of cultures – the society's institutions (e.g. schools) and values are 'middle class' and the lower-working-class boy is handicapped culturally for achieving in this society. The delinquent sub-culture is a break with middle-class morality and legitimizes hostility and aggression against the source of frustration. Some delinquent behaviour (e.g. vandalism; the mess left in burgled homes) can be seen in the light of this theory. Willmott distinguished in his East London sample of adolescent delinquents a small number who did not get on well at school and disliked it. They went in for unskilled occupations; changed jobs frequently; did not get on with their parents or persons in authority. They felt rejected and their frustration was expressed in aggressive acts. The negative attitude to school of some youngsters prompts examination of several aspects of schools – organization, curricula and attitudes towards unsuccessful pupils – which could lead to ways of reducing their alienation from school and the values it stands for.

The factors in an adverse social background which are associated with troublesome behaviour have been pin-pointed by a number of investigations. A Nottingham survey showed that within areas with high delinquency rates certain streets stood out as having high rates and also that within these streets delinquency was more frequent in certain families. In these families, the children had a poor educational record, broken marriages and irregular sexual unions were more frequent, more than half were families of five or more. In general, the homes were squalid and uncared for and the care and discipline of the children was more lax and inconsistent; the mother received little help from the father.

Harriet Wilson (1962) concentrated on a group of families in direst circumstances, selecting for study families referred to welfare agencies on account of child neglect, shortage of clothing, inadequate meals and other adverse circumstances. These families had an average of seven children, income was low – often below a subsistence level – more than a third of the fathers had bad work records (often associated with mental or physical ill-health) and the majority of the children attended school irregularly. It was found that the rate of delinquency was eight times as high as in the city as a whole and twice as high as that in delinquency 'black spots'. Moreover, the ratio of boy to girl delinquents was 3 : 1 compared with the national average of 10 : 1. Wilson emphasized the extremely low material standards, the absence of parental supervision, lax or erratic handling of the children and the isolation of these families from any support from relations or neighbours, as well as the insufficiency of welfare and social help – without which the family, especially the mother, would be unlikely to overcome the combination of adversities.

Psychological factors

The examination of adverse environmental factors associated with delinquency does not explain the impulses and motivations which lead to persistent delinquency, nor why some children seem so vulnerable and others living in similar circumstances less so.

A basic explanation concerns the effect on personality development of disturbed family relationships. Bowlby (1946) in an early investigation compared forty-four children referred to a child guidance clinic for stealing with forty-four matched non-delinquent clinic children, and found that seventeen had experienced maternal separation for six months or longer during their first five years, compared with only two of the controls. Fourteen of them showed a poor ability to relate to others except at a superficial level. Much evidence has since accumulated about the effect of maternal deprivation, though its effects vary with the child, according to the duration of separation and the age it occurred. There are also the variations of maternal care – rejection, over-protection, anxiety and inconsistency – and the insecurity of instability and quarrelling in the family. As Stott (1966) has shown, disturbed relationships may result in a variety of reactions – e.g. attention-seeking alternating with hostility; hostility strongly in evidence and expressed towards the school, other children or authority. In some cases, there is a 'writing-off' of adults and a lack of concern for adult attachments and approval which may give rise to anti-social behaviour. Some children uncertain of adult acceptance seek compensation in acceptance by other children and dare-devil escapades can ensue.

A clear and very readable account of a psycho-analytic approach to delinquency is a book by Friedlander (1947) which traces some of the unconscious motivations which lead to some kinds of delinquent behaviour. There is a great variety of ways in which individuals react to circumstances and seek basic emotional satisfactions. The first four or five years of life are probably crucial for laying a foundation of personality and character development, the mother's care and handling of the child being of primary importance. Later in childhood, other environmental circumstances or inadequacies – leisure, companions, school, work – are influential in bringing out delinquent tendencies. But underlying all these there are probably also some constitutional factors – children differ from birth in their activity level, their amenability to control. Mild neurological impairments have been postulated in some cases. Stott describes an inconsequential pattern of behaviour – the child is restless, distractible, careless and slapdash; correction, punishment and approval have little effect; the child constantly needs petty correction.

Trasler (1963) has argued the need for a theory which explains why some children fail to learn socialized behaviour. He suggests that in normal development the child is conditioned to avoid prohibited behaviour (e.g. stealing) by the anxiety which becomes associated with it through training. This avoidance-conditioning needs to be consistent and depends upon exploiting some existing anxiety (e.g. fear of punishment or of losing parents' love and approval) to associate with the prohibited behaviour. Parents also need to be clear about the behaviour they are trying to mould and to be able to make clear to the child the behaviour he must avoid. It is easy to see that these conditions are not met or met only imperfectly in the family and in social situations which are common in the background of delinquent children. Differences in the 'trainability' of individual children (e.g. Stott's inconsequential children) could explain the difficult behaviour of some children from fairly normal backgrounds.

New legislation

The Children and Young Persons Act 1969 gives greater emphasis to preventive work. Social workers are given greater responsibility for providing help and support to parents of deprived and delinquent children, and for securing their agreement to the action proposed. Consultation between magistrates, police, social workers and teachers is encouraged with a view to avoiding court proceedings. The raising of the age of criminal responsibility by stages from ten to fourteen will mean that children below fourteen will be considered by the juvenile court only when it is a question of obtaining an order in care, and even after the age of fourteen the requirements of the Act are such as to encourage treatment of the problem by means other than court proceedings. Apart from social work help, intermediate treatment will be available where the need is for help and supervision in the home – attendance at evenings or weekends for training, treatment or recreation or some form of social service or adventure training. Instead of the present system of homes, hostels, approved schools, etc., there will be a single system of community homes under regional planning committees organized to provide flexibly for the variety of different needs for residential care. Much will depend on finding and training the additional social workers needed and on the development of co-ordination between the many people involved with delinquent children and their families.

Further reading

BOWLBY, J. (1946), *Forty-four Juvenile Thieves*, London: Baillière, Tindall & Cox.

DOUGLAS, J. W. B. (1968), *All Our Future*, London: Peter Davies.

FRIEDLANDER, K. (1947), *Psycho-analytic Approach to Juvenile Delinquency*, London: Routledge & Kegan Paul.

MAYS, J. B. (1962), *Education and the Urban Child*, Liverpool University Press.

STOTT, D. H. (1966), *Studies of Troublesome Children*, London: Tavistock Publications.

TRASLER, G. B. (1963), 'Theoretical problems in the explanation of delinquency behaviour', *Educational Research*, 6, 1, pp. 42-9.

WEST, D. J. (1967), *The Young Offender*, Harmondsworth: Penguin.

WILKINS, L. T. (1963), 'Juvenile Delinquency – a critical review of research and theory', *Educational Research*, 2, pp. 104-19.

WILLMOTT, M. (1969), *Adolescent Boys of East London*, Harmondsworth: Penguin.

WILSON, H. (1962), *Delinquency and Child Neglect*, London: Allen & Unwin.

Children of immigrants

Statistics of Education (D.E.S. 1967) indicates the diversity of countries in which 'immigrant' pupils or their parents were born (taking immigration after 1957 as the criterion).

Africa	5639	Spain	1289
Cyprus (Greek)	9826	West Indies	73605
Cyprus (Turkish)	4009	Other places within:	
India	33122	Central and	
Italy	10685	South America	601
Malta	988	Europe	5047
Pakistan	11862	Asia	3601
Poland	2878	Australasia	476
		North America	1097

The educational needs and problems of these children vary in many ways. It was estimated that about a quarter (41,816) had standards of written and spoken English so far below average that special language teaching was required. Many more, of course, require special consideration on account of language and other difficulties in school. Apart from this basic requirement for benefiting from schooling there is a variety of other important factors: (1) whether they were born or received a large part of their education in this country; (2) the difference between the English way of life and the cultural background of their country of origin. The influence of this is affected by the degree to which the family is or wishes to be assimilated. There are obvious possibilities of strain and conflict for children where the values of the culture of the home conflict with values of the school or those of the immediate environment. There is also the unsatisfactory state where the family has no stable point of reference either in its own culture or the new – a situation which can easily lead to behaviour disturbance and educational failure. Moreover, there are the additional variables – problems of housing and over-crowding, parents working too-long hours, lack of recreative and cultural opportunities in the neighbourhood.

Language teaching

First in importance for the teacher in the classroom is the problem of communication. If the child has little capacity to comprehend and express himself in English, his problem is not only the inability to benefit from teaching but also the inability to use communication as a means of feeling at home in the school environment, relating to the teacher and other children. It is one of several factors liable to create difficulties in behaviour and adjustment.

A variety of different methods of organization is in use. Some education authorities place children in classes with English children with no special linguistic or social preparation. While this may be defensible with young primary children, it is obviously unsuitable for older children who are likely to gravitate to lower streams. A more useful system is ordinary class placement supported by withdrawal for regular language lessons given by an experienced or trained teacher of English as a second language. In Birmingham a large team of peripatetic teachers visit a number of schools several times each week in a well-organized system. Another approach is the setting up of a special class within the school providing an intensive course in English with a view to normal class placement as soon as possible. Special centres which pupils attend on a part-time basis are organized in other areas. Some local education authorities with a rapidly increasing immigrant population have set up reception centres which pupils attend full time for language teaching and a general introductory course priory to placement in a school near their homes. Several authorities, in accordance with a recommendation of the Department of Education and Science, have dispersed immigrant pupils to other schools in order to avoid the educational and social opportunities in certain schools becoming limited by the need to concentrate on the language problem of a large number of immigrants. This requires adequate transport arrangements and the understanding and agreement of parents.

Whatever method of organization is used, considerable responsibility for language improvement remains with the class teacher. The language of children discharged from full-time centres is still likely to lag well behind that of other children in school. Those having part-time tuition benefit from co-operation between the class teacher and the language teacher, ensuring that the language patterns and vocabulary being taught are given further practice.

The class teacher can help most by creating an environment in which there are many opportunities for using language and encouraging the social participation of the child. Basic to this is an understanding of what is involved in learning a language – that it is not only a question of learning words but of acquiring the sentence patterns of the language both in respect of syntax and intonation and stress patterns. The teacher should use clear, unhurried speech rather than abbreviated, over-emphatic speech. Though the child may be limited in expression, he is acquiring language if he learns to comprehend language and understands the meaning of words through listening to stories and simple explanations. Many activities such as singing provide familiarity with language as well as enjoyment. As suggested in Chapter 6 it is also desirable to see language teaching as one of increasing the variety of purposes for which language can be used – for personal expression, enquiry, explanation and so on. It is obvious that while reading and writing can assist language growth, reading should have an adequate basis of language preparation and the two should keep roughly in step.

West Indian children present a different problem since, while they speak English, their mother tongue will often be one of the versions of Creole English spoken in the West Indies. Children recently arrived will be most affected in their comprehension and comprehensibility, though children born in this country may also experience some interference in reading and writing from the Creole dialect they speak at home.

Variations from Standard English in pronunciation are liable to affect spelling and phonic work in reading. Some of the commonest are th becoming d as in Di dag or t as in thief. Final d and t are liable to be omitted from words, and double tt, as in little and bottle, become lickle and bockle. In a useful article, Brazier (1970) summarizes some of the non-standard features which often result from the interference from Creole grammatical rules:

> The verb may not be inflected (I leave yesterday; the girl is play with the ball); or not inverted in a question (What their names are? How old he is?); or omitted (Im good for He is good). With nouns, plural and possessive s is omitted (Six boy; the cow tail). Sometimes *the mans* appears for *the men*.

It is a familiar situation to many teachers that children in areas of the country where the dialect is very different from Standard English have two (or more) languages – one for the playground and home and one for the classroom. In the classroom, their speech and language comes closer to the standard form used in school and it is equally important for their social relationships that they should return to dialect with their peer group or family. The West Indian child is no exception in showing this linguistic adaptability and the teacher's task is not to convey that his speech is wrong or sub-standard but to enable him to acquire facility in Standard English when required. Most of them do so relatively well in time though some differences may continue to elude some children.

The teacher needs to recognize that there is a problem and that some children are at a considerable disadvantage in the classroom. As with other children with language differences or retardation, the need is for ample oral expression and the opportunity of unobtrusive feedback of standard forms.

A more serious problem for many West Indian children is, in common with many indigenous children, a lack of adequate language experience in the pre-school years, for in spite of verbal fluency they may be limited in range of vocabulary and experience of using language for descriptive and explanatory purposes as required at school.

Cultural factors

The cultural background of immigrants exerts influences and pressures which inevitably affect their response to school. Children from India and Pakistan tend to come from 'extended families' in which grandparents, uncles and aunts are all members of the social unit and in which there is a strong emphasis on family ties and obligations and on the authority of older members. The roles of the sexes tend to be separate, the men spending their leisure time outside the home without their wives; the woman's sphere is mainly domestic. The father holds authority and takes decisions and usually, for example, is the one who brings the child to school for the first time and has any other contacts. Among Moslems mixing of the sexes beyond the age of puberty is forbidden and for girls there is the traditional dress which covers the legs. In Cypriot families, there is a similar structure of an extended family, firm paternal authority, a passive domestic role for the wife and strict behaviour for the children, especially for girls.

Such expectations for behaviour and discipline contrasting with the more relaxed teacher-pupil relationships in school and with the greater freedom and independence of native children, inevitably create some tensions and conflicts for the immigrant child. For adolescent girls in particular, the mixing of sexes, the very different social conventions of dress and behaviour create many problems.

An additional problem is caused by the immigrants' different expectations of school. Asian and Cypriot children who have attended school in their own country will have experience of a more authoritarian class atmosphere with emphasis on rote-learning, rather than child-centred methods of teaching and independent, meaningful methods of learning. While they are eager to learn, their conception of the task will be different from that of an immigrant child brought up in English primary schools. Parents' expectations are also affected, even to the extent in some cases of regarding activities other than basic work a waste of time. They are often educationally ambitious for their children, sometimes unrealistically so, but, at the same time, they are often unaware of how the home can help. There may be little or no awareness of the value of play materials and activities for the younger child.

The background of West Indian children presents some contrasts with these groups. The family structure is less firmly ordained by tradition and convention and in urban conditions there may be factors in home life which create insecurity in the child. The mother is often the dominant figure in the family and she traditionally goes out to work. In the West Indies she would leave her young children with the grandmother, but in England probably uses an official or unofficial baby-minder or gives older children a latch-key. Conceptions of child care differ from English ones. Standards of physical care are good but behaviour within the home may be more controlled. In the cramped circumstances in which some families have to live there may be little freedom for children to play and spread themselves psychologically. The ebullience of some West Indian children in school is often seen as a consequence. Where behaviour difficulties occur, punishment at home may aggravate the problem.

Such generalizations are hazardous. Wight and Norris (1970) pointed out that the generalizations teachers make about West Indian children are often inconsistent and conflict with each other. The fact is that, like any group, West Indian families and children vary widely. In his own work, Wight tried to assess the commonly held view that West Indian children tend to show emotional unsettlement more in awkward hostile behaviour than English children. Using assessments by teachers on the Bristol Social Adjustment Guides, he found no differences between West Indians born in Britain and those newly arrived but, compared with an English sample, there was a significantly higher occurrence of certain symptoms of emotional and behavioural difficulty – depression, symptoms of nervous and emotional strain, hostility towards adults, unconcerned behaviour – though differences between the two groups became much less marked in the older age groups. Wight's findings reflect the behaviour tendencies which make for troublesomeness in class but, as he suggests, they can be seen as part of a different response to the adult world. It is of interest that in a comparison of the attitudes of West Indian and English adolescents, Hill (1968) found that while the West Indians had less regard for parents and homes, they had a more favourable attitude towards their teachers and education.

A few West Indian children show severe maladjusted reactions to their circumstances and cause schools considerable concern. Wight reports that the centre for maladjusted junior children at Brixton found that the behaviour problems of West Indians subsided once means were found of coping with their learning difficulties. In many cases social work with the home has a similar effect.

Educational difficulties

In recent years, the number of immigrant children deemed to need special educational help in a special school has been increasing. Wight (1970) quotes an Inner London Education Authority report that in 1967 West Indian children made up a quarter of pupils in London ESN schools although they formed only 8 or 9 per cent of the ordinary school population. As noted in Chapter 3, poor educational progress leading to special school placement is often due to a combination of environmental factors in addition to lowish ability.

When immigrant children make poor progress in school, there may be many reasons. Language is an obvious source of failure; in the case of the West Indian there is the possibility of dialectal interference as well as possible limitations of linguistic experience in other ways. Cultural and social deprivations like those referred to in the last section may be involved; there is the possibility not only of cultural differences but of some distortion of cultural patterns in an English urban environment. In school, a tendency to rely on rote-learning, rather than meaningful discovery approaches used in English primary schools, may make for difficulties. Progress is also influenced by adjustment to the group and by self-acceptance, both influenced by community attitudes.

There is no evidence that immigrant children are less intelligent as a group than non-immigrant children. There is evidence that performance on the usual intelligence tests tends to be lower in pupils reared in non-technical or non-Western cultures. It is sometimes assumed that this is because of the language factor and that, if non-verbal tests were used, a fairer measure of ability would be obtained. The need for a culture-free test is often suggested but psychologists doubt whether tests could ever be completely free from the pervasive influences of culture. Different kinds of experience and motivation lead to different strengths and weaknesses not only in tests using language but also in pictorial, diagrammatic and performance materials.

Environmental influences on mental abilities were observed by Vernon (1965) in a comparison of schoolboys in the West Indies and English schoolboys on a variety of tests. The West Indian boys did only a little less well on average but they varied on different kinds of test. They performed better in educational tasks based on rote-learning than on meaningful material. They were noticeably poorer in practical and non-verbal tests of intelligence though they did reasonably well in a test requiring conceptual sorting of objects and in some, but not all, Piagetian tasks. Vernon considered that the uneven development of intellectual capacities could be related to various social and environmental factors.

Ferron (1965) concludes a careful survey of research on racial differences in intelligence by remarking that 'where circumstances are such as to ensure that white and coloured groups share a common way of life and have equal educational opportunities, differences are small or non-existent'. Teachers will agree on the basis of their experience that the longer and more complete the exposure of immigrant children to a full educational experience, the greater the chances of realizing their true potentiality. This implies good schooling, good school-home relations and also has implications for other aspects of life in the community.

Further Reading

BRAZIER, C. (1970), 'Teaching West Indian children', *Special Education*, 52, 2, pp. 6-10.

BURGIN, T. AND EDSON, P. (1967), *Spring Grove: The Education of Immigrant Children*, Oxford University Press.

DERRICK, J. (1966), *Teaching English to Immigrants*, London: Longmans.

English for Immigrants, Journal of the Association of Teachers of English to Pupils from Overseas.

MINISTRY OF EDUCATION Pamphlet No. 43 (1963), *English for Immigrants*, London: H.M.S.O.

NATIONAL COMMITTEE FOR COMMONWEALTH IMMIGRANTS (1968), *Practical Suggestions for Teachers of Immigrant Children*.

OAKLEY, R. (1968), *New Backgrounds*, Oxford University Press.

SCHOOLS COUNCIL (1969), *Teachers' Manual SCOPE; An introductory course for immigrant children*, Books for Schools Ltd. (Longmans).

SCHOOLS COUNCIL WORKING PAPER 13 (1967), *English for the Children of Immigrants*, London: H.M.S.O.

WIGHT, J. AND NORRIS, R. A. (1970), *Teaching of English to West Indian Children*, Schools Council Project, Report 2.

eight

Hearing impairment

The number of children receiving education in special schools and classes for hearing impaired children has increased from 3,800 in 1938 to 6,000 at the present time. This increase, which contrasts with the decline in the number of physically and visually handicapped children, does not result from an increase in hearing impairment but from improved methods of detection both in the pre-school and school years. The figures illustrate how easy it is for the hearing impaired child to 'get by' and be overlooked. In spite of the improved methods of ascertainment, there is still a considerable responsibility on teachers to look out for the signs of possible hearing loss and to seek special examination in any cases of doubt so that medical or educational treatment can be provided without delay. This is especially important with children of nursery and infant age, since early detection and treatment may prevent the handicap from worsening and will prevent additional educational, speech and emotional difficulties arising. It is particularly important to look for hearing loss in children who are educationally backward, or physically handicapped.

The detection of hearing impairments

Severe hearing impairment, congenital or acquired in early infancy, is one of the most serious disabilities since it impedes the development of language and normal communication, with obvious consequences for the child's education, and for his intellectual and personal development. Modern educational methods and modern individual and group hearing aids have contributed to a more hopeful outlook, particularly if the process of educating the child's hearing (there are few children without some residual hearing) and speech development starts early in infancy through the provision of suitable aids, auditory training and advice to parents. In order to ensure this, health services have in recent years intensified their efforts to detect hearing loss early, by following up children placed on the 'at risk' register, examining children with other handicaps, e.g. cerebral palsy and backwardness, especially in speech.

It is generally agreed that all babies should be screened for hearing loss between eight and ten months of age and that further facilities for screening should be available between then and school age. To ensure that children with an impairment are not missed, it is important that general practitioners, local health authority doctors and health visitors should be alert to the need for early detection. In some areas, considerable progress has been made towards a pre-school service in which, following screening, a team of people are able to provide expert examination and, equally important, parent guidance; the latter includes both guidance on how to help the child and dealing with the inevitable anxieties of the parents. Ideally the team consists of a doctor from infant welfare or school health with special interest and training in the assessment of hearing; an otologist (a doctor specializing in hearing); a teacher of the deaf and a health visitor with special training. Other medical specialists, speech therapists and educational psychologists should also be available. It is an advantage if the child can attend a nursery class either in a day special school or, as is increasingly happening in many places, a normal nursery school which either has a special unit or the frequent visits of a teacher of the deaf. In brief, by school age children with serious impairments should, ideally, have received appropriate attention. At school age, the first routine medical examination should include a screening test of hearing for all pupils, and teachers should also draw attention to any children whose hearing they have any reason to question.

Assessing hearing

Screening tests become possible at nine to ten months because at this age the normal baby shows by turning his head that he has learned to look for and locate quiet sounds, e.g. a high pitched rattle, a voice speaking or making sounds such as s at minimal intensity levels. From eighteen months onwards distraction tests are used and from three years tests which involve the child in carrying out repetitive activity such as putting pegs in a board in response to a sound stimulus. At school age a Sweep Frequency Test using an audiometer is

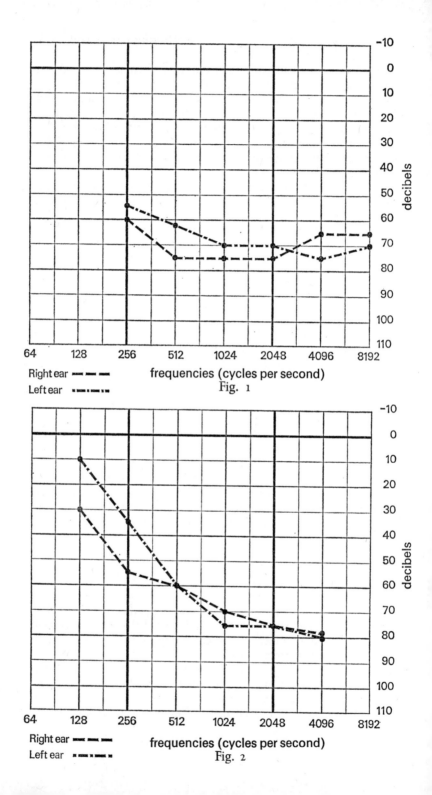

Right ear ▬ ▬ ▬
Left ear ▬·▬·▬·▬

frequencies (cycles per second)
Fig. 1

Right ear ▬ ▬ ▬
Left ear ▬·▬·▬·▬

frequencies (cycles per second)
Fig. 2

given. Pure tone audiometers provide a series of tones at different frequencies (or pitch) at 250, 500, 1,000, 1,500, 2,000 and 3,000 up to 8,000 cycles per second. The intensity of volume of sound can be varied and is measured in decibels from −10 to 100 or 110. On this scale, 0 is the point at which a normal young adult would just begin to hear. Quiet conversation at a distance of three feet would be around 60-70 decibels, shouting at 90 decibels; a sound at 120 decibels would be painful.

For a Sweep Frequency Test, sounds at 250, 500, 1,000, 2,000, 3,000 and 4,000 cycles are used with a set volume of 15 to 20 decibels. Each ear is tested separately. A child who fails one or two of these is referred for diagnostic examination in which testing is more thorough. At each frequency the volume is reduced until the child can no longer hear the tone and, contrariwise, the volume is increased until the point is reached when he just hears. The point at which he just hears or just fails to hear is the *threshold* and is established for each frequency over the whole range. The results are plotted on an audiogram. Fig. 1 shows the audiogram of a child with a flat loss over the range; Fig. 2 the audiogram of a child who hears low tones quite well but has little hearing for high tones. It will be seen, therefore, that the impairment varies according to the pattern of loss at different frequencies and different intensities, and also according to whether one or both ears are affected.

A further complication is that the audiometric result is not necessarily a close guide to the child's hearing for speech. How well he can make sense of words and sentences obviously depends upon his vocabulary and general language development as well as his intelligence and personality. To assess this, speech audiometry is used in which lists of carefully selected words are presented in such a way that the sound level is controlled. By this means, an estimate is obtained of the child's hearing for speech which is an important measure for assessing educational placement.

Another important factor is the cause of the deafness. There are two main kinds: *conductive* deafness is caused by a reduction of the intensity of sound reaching the auditory pathways in the inner ear. The outer ear may be blocked by wax or malformation (which may be operable); the eardrum may be damaged or the movement of the little bones in the middle ear may be obstructed as a result of infected adenoids or tonsils; the Eustachian tube connecting the nose and the ear may be blocked. Ear infections need prompt treatment to avoid the chronic middle ear infection (*otitis media*) since running ears used to be quite common and still need watching in disadvantaged families. Such conditions rarely cause more than a moderate loss (50-60 decibels) since there is also conduction of sound vibrations through the bones of the ear. There is usually the same amount of loss throughout the range of sounds.

The effect on a child's ability to function in school varies. The loss may be intermittent (for example, in catarrhal conditions which are very frequent, especially in large urban areas). How loud or near the teacher talks; the sound characteristics of the classroom; the child's intelligence and ability to adapt, all affect the degree of handicap.

A *perceptive* (or *sensory-neural*) impairment is the result of defects in the inner ear or auditory nerve and may be inherited, or due to damage or infection (such as meningitis). Some frequencies of sound, especially the high ones, may be affected more than others. Speech sounds contain a mixture of frequencies. Vowels are mainly low frequencies while consonants are composed mainly of high frequencies, especially sounds which enable the brain to distinguish similar consonants. The child not only has to learn to comprehend speech in which some sounds are scarcely represented, but also has to learn to discriminate other sounds on the basis of less information than the normal person receives. It is not surprising that many of these children show some articulation difficulties especially with *s, z, sh, sch, th, ch, p, b, t, f, v* and *h*. They may say 'tick' for 'stick', 'ace' for 'eight', 'tool' for 'stool'. So an infant-school child with poor articulation and, even more, one who makes odd noises, should always be referred for examination.

There is a third kind of hearing impairment in which there is damage or abnormality in the brain – *central* deafness. One variant of this is an inability to make sense of the sounds which are heard so that speech is not comprehended. It may be easy to demonstrate that such a child reacts to sounds (though in some cases a child may psychologically 'shut out' sound and appear deaf), or there may be conflicting reports about this. In some children, the failure is due to a speech and language disorder. There is, in fact, a puzzling group of children who need very specialized diagnostic study to disentangle the contribution of neurological, emotional and language disorders.

The hearing-impaired child in the ordinary school

What are the consequences for a child in ordinary school of a hearing impairment which is not severe enough to warrant special education? It is a well known fact that hearing impairment attracts less sympathy partly because it is not obvious; it may even be quite overlooked and allowances not made. It is difficult for the teacher to assess just how handicapped the child is and it is not uncommon for suspicions to be entertained that the child hears when he wants to. He is often thought to be naughty or awkward rather than deaf. More specifically he needs to be spoken to clearly rather than loudly; to sit so that he has a good view of the teacher's face and mouth and to be able to turn and watch other children's faces. It is important to ensure that he has really understood instructions. Any tendency to backwardness suggests the need for some extra help to ensure that gaps in understanding and learning are not allowed to accumulate.

A survey by Johnson (1962) in Cheshire provides information about the progress and difficulties of sixty-eight children aged five to fifteen years eleven months with hearing impairment greater than 30 decibels; three-quarters had an average loss of 50 decibels; 80 per cent of them had perceptive deafness, 63 per cent being high-frequency impairment. In spite of an average range of intelligence in the group there was a fair degree of educational retardation, especially in reading. The majority showed defective articulation, over a third to a marked degree, though their language development was within the normal range. Two-thirds were found to have some difficulty in comprehension of speech in school, and on speech audiometry it was shown that if they were not using a hearing aid and not lip-reading their scores dropped very markedly.

It was found that 57 per cent used their hearing aids regularly in school but only 17 per cent at home. It is notoriously difficult, as with spectacles, to ensure that children use the aids they have been supplied with. Hearing aids are so valuable that it is worth noting the reasons for their unwillingness. The main one is not wanting to draw attention to their deafness – not wanting to feel different. This is something that the experienced teacher will be able to help by her own attitude to the child and by influencing the attitude of other children. Some children had preferred to depend on lip-reading and other cues. Other reasons for aids not being used were the teachers' lack of knowledge about the need for their use, aids not being in working order and poor acoustic conditions in schools. Clearly, where there is a problem with an aid, help should be sought through the school health service – the increasing appointment of peripatetic teachers of the deaf should be of help here. The importance of this is underlined by the fact that the number of hearing aids supplied to schoolchildren had increased from 714 in 1957 to 6,006 in 1967.

Johnson's assessment of emotional and social adjustment of these children has implications for recognizing and helping these children in class. There were relatively few maladjusted children but a considerable number (38 per cent) showed some degree of emotional unsettlement – especially that of being unusually quiet, shy, timid, dreamy or reticent. Teachers reported: 'He lives in a world of his own,' 'We are baffled by him and cannot decide whether he is deaf or dull.' The understanding and sympathetic interest of teachers can do much to counteract these tendencies. Whereas the physically handicapped child in an ordinary school is liable to suffer from too much concern and protection, it seems that the hearing impaired child may suffer from too little understanding of his problem, partly because the teacher has difficulty in assessing how handicapped he really is. Some inkling of the child's difficulties can be gained by listening to a quiet lecturer from the back of a hall. Although one can just hear, the effort of attention makes it most difficult to maintain concentration. It is not surprising that children withdraw into their own daydreams or seek other satisfactions.

The organization of special education for hearing-impaired children

An important distinction in the education of the deaf is between the *profoundly deaf* child who has virtually no naturally acquired language and the *partially hearing* child who can acquire speech and language from hearing others' speech, but who would have too much difficulty in an ordinary class. The former requires education in a school for the deaf by special methods devised for such children, in particular for developing language by formal means, speech training, lip-reading and the use of amplifiers. The latter needs education in a unit in an ordinary school or in a school for partially hearing pupils where he can be helped to develop language and speech by the use of modern electronic equipment and by the skilled teaching of a teacher of the deaf.

In 1968 the number of partially hearing pupils slightly exceeded the number of deaf pupils – 3,611 compared with 3,225. In addition to twenty-one day schools and twenty-eight boarding schools for hearing impaired children, there are two schools (the Mary Hare Grammar School and Burwood Park) providing selective secondary education. There is one school for hearing impaired children with serious emotional handicaps and others for those with additional disabilities. A major development since 1947 has been the setting up of units for partially hearing pupils in ordinary schools – 215 classes in 1969. In addition there has been an increasing provision of peripatetic teachers of the deaf (sixty-six local education authorities were employing them in 1967). They assist in the diagnosis and assessment of hearing impairment, visit pre-school deaf children, give guidance to parents, individual teaching to children in ordinary schools and advice to class teachers.

The development of special classes for partially hearing children in ordinary schools is in accordance with the trend to seek ways of educating handicapped children with or alongside ordinary children, but has the more explicit purpose of putting partially hearing children into a normal language environment. In a special school, the environment is organized to promote the maximum use of hearing by good acoustic conditions and modern amplification equipment, and great attention is given to systematic teaching of language. But the pupils tend to be rather limited in opportunities for practising communication skills except among themselves and with their teachers. While teachers make much use of out-of-school contacts, incidental experiences and activities and topical events for motivating language work, it is not easy to produce a normal language environment. The special class for partially hearing pupils in an ordinary school should be able to provide greater opportunities for communication with ordinary children outside the classroom and for gradual or partial integration in the work of ordinary classes.

A survey of units for partially hearing children (Department of Education and Science 1967) provides not only a valuable assessment of this method of organizing the education of partially hearing children but also one of the few pointers to some of the issues which would be important in providing for other handicapped children in ordinary schools.

One of the first points to emerge is the need for careful and appropriate selection of pupils. Out of the 721 pupils in the survey, 12·5 per cent were thought not to be receiving the kind of education suited to their needs, either because they were too deaf or had marked additional handicaps, or, in a few cases, were not sufficiently hearing impaired to be in the unit. In some cases, a unit performing an assessment function was appropriate at younger ages but not later when poor progress had altered the prospects, especially in relation to capacity for academic work at the secondary stage.

It was suggested that the function of units should be clearly defined (and this would apply to other special classes for handicapped children). Children should be selected who function as partially hearing, who are likely to learn to communicate in a natural way more by listening than lip-reading, and by natural acquisition of language rather than by imposed patterns.

A second group of findings relates to organization: the difficulty of avoiding too wide an age range; of providing for progression through the age ranges and of transfer to the next stage; of providing guidance and leadership to teachers who are working in relative isolation from other teachers of the deaf; the difficulty of ensuring the most productive relationships with the staff of the ordinary school. The survey notes the possible danger that too much emphasis can be given to educational achievements which have value for the short-term goal of integration into the rest of the school to the relative neglect of the long-term goal of requirements for post-school adjustment. This is always a more explicit aim of special education.

How far was integration taking place? A very small number of pupils had been transferred to the main school. In eighteen schools a few pupils were placed in ordinary classes, returning to the unit for tutorial periods. A small number of pupils were working in ordinary classes for academic subjects in twenty schools and many were taking part in non-academic activities in forty-six schools. A number of factors were found to militate against integration : in some cases units were sited in schools where the age range of the unit did not match that of the main school; rigidity of organization, over-crowding, large classes and frequent staff changes in the school made successful placement in ordinary classes difficult. Differences in school hours between unit and school and the distance travelling from home to children in the unit were other factors noted.

These observations have been considered at some length not to detract from the advantages of this method of organization but to illustrate the complexity of factors which have to be considered in seeking the desirable goal of integrating handicapped children into ordinary schools.

Further light on these difficulties was shed by a survey of severely deaf children who had been transferred from special schools or units to ordinary schools (Ministry of Education, 1963). The progress of thirty-three children who had been transferred to ordinary schools was assessed. The evidence indicated that severely deaf children are likely to make satisfactory educational progress in ordinary schools only when a variety of conditions occur together : considerable help and support from the home; good abilities, personal qualities and determination in the child and helpful conditions in the school. Even so, the strain of keeping up educationally and trying to take a full part in school life was considerable and often not fully realized by staff or parents. Teachers did not always realize that, though the deaf child had reasonable communication abilities, he might be more limited in vocabulary, general knowledge and experience, or that the conditions in the classroom for listening and lip-reading could easily become difficult for the deaf child – noise, teacher moving about, discussion too fast, etc. In adolescence, children tended to become more isolated, withdrawing from contacts at school and home.

The personal and educational development of hearing-impaired children

The education of the deaf child ideally begins with the earliest possible detection of his disability, followed by guidance to parents on what steps can be taken in babyhood and early childhood to compensate for the disability and to promote the best all-round development. How the child learns to react to his environment, to relate to his mother and family and to educate what hearing he has is of great importance to the later development of abilities, personality and readiness for acquiring language and speech. The frequent help and advice of a teacher of the deaf is therefore essential.

The family need to be aware of some of the consequences of impaired hearing so that they can understand the child's needs. Hearing provides a continuous scanning of the environment to detect changes which are then attended to visually. The hearing child thus has warning of things which are going to happen, is assured of mother's continued presence even though she is unseen, and is also stimulated to pay attention to the environment. The deaf infant compensates to some extent by being more visually alert to his environment and more aware of vibrations, but he is obviously more likely to be isolated and to miss happenings which hearing children would quickly be aware of. The mother can ensure that as far as possible he can see what she is doing and that he is made aware of things going on around him. Mother-child relationships which normally make use of speech have to rely more on physical contact, gesture and facial expressions. The deaf child needs to be encouraged to participate in family life as fully as possible, and later to have other social experience with people and children and to grow in independence.

Few children are without some hearing and quite young babies are given hearing aids and helped to be aware of sound, to learn the meaning of sounds in the environment, to become more aware of the sounds of speech and their own voices. Research and experience confirm that this is an important aspect of readiness for the later benefiting from more systematic teaching of speech and language.

These important developments will be carried further by attendance at a nursery class in a deaf school or unit for partially hearing children or in a normal nursery school. If the latter, the help of a teacher of the deaf is needed and some local education authorities have arranged for a teacher of the deaf to be on the staff or attached to a nursery school. In thinly populated areas, the only alternative to being at home is sending the child to a boarding nursery for the deaf or partially hearing, and this has obvious disadvantages.

One of the benefits of good pre-school experience and training is that it provides a basis for assessing whether the child should be educated as a partially hearing or a deaf child. The former can learn to communicate more by hearing than by lip-reading and can acquire language more through the experience of language in the environment. The deaf child must learn to rely more on lip-reading assisted by his hearing for amplified sound; language has to be built up systematically since he will have very little, or insufficient, experience of language. Likewise he will have to be taught to speak whereas the partially hearing child will need only some correction of speech sounds heard imperfectly. It follows that the partially hearing child can usually benefit from the experience of language in an ordinary environment and his education is more like that of other children. The deaf child in his learning is more dependent on communication with the teacher. Since reading is a skill superimposed on other language skills, he is likely to be later than normal children in being able to use reading for widening knowledge and understanding – although he is likely to start reading earlier as an additional means of acquiring language.

The way ahead for the deaf child is an arduous one and the skills required of his teacher are among the most demanding of any kind of special teaching. The central aim is to develop language first as a means of thinking and learning and secondly as a means of communication. Even though achievements in communication may be less than desired, it is an important achievement if the child has developed an inner language which assists the development of thinking. Without it, his educational progress would be limited. Reading, written expression and the ability to profit from more academic work can only be as good as language attainment permits.

Different methods of education have been advocated and practised – indeed the subject is one of the most debated in special education. *Oral Methods* aim to develop language and communication through lip-reading, teaching speech, exploiting residual hearing by amplified sound and utilizing reading and writing. In some countries and at certain periods in most countries, teaching has relied on manual methods which include *finger spelling* and *signs*. *Combined methods* use oral methods simultaneously with varying amounts of manual communication.

Finger spelling consists of spelling out individual words letter by letter on the fingers, each letter being represented by a conventional sign. Most British teachers of the deaf are reluctant to use it lest it reduces the child's incentive to acquire and practise speech and lip-reading. In combined methods, finger spelling may be used to make clear a word difficult to distinguish on the lips or to introduce a new or difficult word, or as an additional means of communication for children who can acquire language but have difficulty with lip-reading and speech. Russian educators have reported their use of finger spelling together with oral methods with pre-school children. They claim accelerated progress in language and that children drop finger spelling as they improve. *Signing* can mean a variety of more or less natural gestures which are common in deaf children, or systems of formalized movements, much used, for example, as a means of communication in the adult deaf. At first glance, it might appear that signing is an obvious means of easy communication, but it does not permit communication with hearing people and, more importantly, it has serious inadequacies for acquiring language. Signs do not follow normal word sequences, symbols are lacking for certain parts of speech and verbs are used less frequently and in an uninflected form. Particular signs may serve for a variety of different meanings. Fry (1964) gives an example of how a nursery rhyme would be communicated by signs:

> Where you go to my pretty girl?
> I go milk   gentleman   she say
> Perhaps I go with you my pretty girl?
> Nobody ask you   gentleman   she say.

While signing obviously performs a valuable function for the adult deaf, it is no substitute for the language needed to underpin educational development. (The Paget system, a systematic sign language with normal grammatical structure, has been used experimentally in a number of places, including places with multiply handicapped children.)

The questions whether oral methods would benefit from supplementation by other methods, and at what age and with what kinds of pupils, are ones about which there is very little reliable information. It might be that additional means of communication would assist language development and make lip-reading, speech, reading and writing easier and quicker to acquire. On the other hand, they might interfere with progress. A report of a Committee of the Department of Education and Science (1968) provides a thorough discussion of the issue.

The teaching of language to children who have not heard language, or only very imperfectly, presents immense problems. While most of us without training might succeed in teaching a few words referring to observable objects, we should run into difficulties as the level of abstraction increased (fruits, honest, old, big) and as words were used for different meanings and contexts. Structure words such as prepositions, conjunctions, auxiliary verbs (are, is, will be, would be) and determiners (every, other, this, that) present obvious difficulties. Then there are the change of tense (he is going; he has gone; he went) and the rules for word order in sentences. Various techniques are used to help with some of the grammatical difficulties. The Fitzgerald Key uses guiding words and symbols such as *whose? who?* or *what?* for filling in the subject; a symbol indicating the place for a verb; and *what* or *whom* for filling in the object: and provision is made for guiding more complex patterns. Pictorial material and actions supply other needs. As in other kinds of language teaching, there is the question of balance between systematic (or formal) methods and incidental (or informal) methods which draw upon recent experience and topical interest through discussion. How far can one go towards teaching language in ways comparable to the way the normal infant learns it? Many teachers aim to go a long way in this direction, at the same time always keeping in mind the particular language elements being taught at a particular stage.

In addition to the language, there is the problem of teaching lip-reading. Many fine discriminations are required for distinguishing the shape of the lips, their position and the gap between them, and the use of the teeth and tongue for certain sounds. Some sounds are made at the back of the mouth, not on the lips, and some words are indistinguishable. So the context must be used to fill in the gaps, and how well the child can do this depends on adequate vocabulary and language patterns as well as knowing the subject being talked about. Clearly, the attentional, perceptual and thinking processes involved in lip-reading depend on a great number of abilities in the child; his motivation for the demanding task depends on personality and home background.

In acquiring *speech production*, the function of hearing in providing feedback and correction has to be supplied by other means – observing lip movements in a mirror, feeling with the hand the vibrations of various speech organs. In addition to correct sounds, there are the problems of teaching the correct intonation, rhythm and volume.

What effect does hearing impairment have upon the development of the child's abilities and personality? Since language is so closely involved in the different kinds of thinking and behaviour we term intelligence, it might be expected that the deaf would suffer considerable intellectual retardation. The question has been the subject of many investigations which are discussed by Myklebust (1964) and Lewis (1968). As a generalization, the findings are that on most kinds of non-verbal intelligence tests using concrete materials and patterns, deaf children perform about as well as normal hearing children. On verbal tests, scores are related to the degree of hearing and language impairment, the age of onset of deafness and also the kind of mental task – the more it calls for abstraction, symbolization and language experience the more intellectual performance is affected. But Lewis (1968) comes to the interesting conclusion that 'with little or no use of language they are as successful as hearing children over a wide range of cognitive tasks'. At the same time it is also true that 'over a wide range of cognitive tasks the achievements of deaf children are impaired by the inadequacy of language'.

The personal development of deaf children is, of course, likely to be affected by home and other environmental factors in a similar way to other children with handicaps. There are also the more particular consequences of hearing impairment. Myklebust (1964) considers that a sensory disability requires a different way of organizing experience, and this has consequence for the person's whole development. Thus, certain traits which have been observed, such as poorer self-awareness and self-concepts, a tendency to perseverate and to be rigid rather than flexible, have implications for education at home and school. Limitation of language can have many consequences for emotional development. Poor communication limits socal experience through which so many personal qualities and adjustments are made. Language also contributes to the development of ideas about the self, about one's feeling's, self-control, understanding human relationships and moral concepts. This is yet another facet of the complex task of educating hearing impaired children.

Further reading

BLOOM, F. (1963), *Our Deaf Children*, London: Heinemann.

DALE, D. M. C. (1967), *Deaf Children at Home and School*, University of London Press.

DEPARTMENT OF EDUCATION AND SCIENCE (1967), *Units for Partially Hearing-Children*, Education Survey No. 1, London: H.M.S.O.

——(1969), *Peripatetic Teachers of the Deaf*, Education Survey No. 6, London: H.M.S.O

——(1968), *The Education of Deaf Children*, London: H.M.S.O.

EWING, A. W. G. AND E. C. (1964), *Teaching Deaf Children to Talk*, Manchester University Press.

EWING, I. R. AND A. W. G. (1958), *New Opportunities for Deaf Children*, University of London Press.

JOHNSON, J. C. (1962), *Educating Hearing-Impaired Children in Ordinary Schools*, Manchester University Press.

LEWIS, M. M. (1968), *Language and Personality in Deaf Children*, National Foundation for Educational Research.

MINISTRY OF EDUCATION (1963), *Report on a survey of deaf children who have been transferred from special schools or units to ordinary schools*, London: H.M.S.O.

MYKLEBUST, H. R. (1964), *The Psychology of Deafness*, New York: Grune & Stratton.

WATSON, J. (1966), *The Education of Hearing-Handicapped Children*, University of London Press.

nine

Visual handicaps

Defects of vision are the most frequent physical defects (apart from dental disease) discovered in routine medical examination of school children. Fortunately the number of blind children is small (about 1,200 in special schools in England and Wales in 1968) but a larger number of children have visual defects sufficient to require education in special schools for partially sighted children. There were about 2,000 children receiving or waiting for this form of education in 1968, but this certainly does not include all the children who would benefit. While more than four out of every 10,000 children find a place in a school for partially sighted children in the London area, in other areas only two or three children per 10,000 are so provided for. Even in areas where there is good provision for partially sighted children, it is not uncommon for pupils to be referred quite late in their school careers. They have often been struggling in ordinary classes until their backwardness resulted in belated recognition of their special need.

The fact that the majority of visual defects are not severe enough to require very special treatment does not mean that they are insignificant. Like mild degrees of hearing loss, clumsiness and ill health, they play their part with other adverse factors in affecting a child's learning, his attitudes to school and even to life in general. It is essential, therefore, that teachers should be alert to the possibility of undetected visual defects, especially in areas where parents are less likely to be observant and concerned about such an apparently trivial weakness.

Teachers of handicapped children should be especially alert to signs of visual difficulty, since these can easily be confused with the common signs of backwardness – poor concentration, poor writing and copying, visual errors in reading. Moreover, a visual difficulty is likely to have greater effect on slow learners than on more able children. Whenever there is neurological impairment – cerebral palsy, epilepsy – there is increased chance of visual defect: 60 per cent of cerebral palsied children are found to have visual defects. In children with hearing impairment, defective sight can be a serious handicap since it may affect the capacity to learn lip-reading.

Assessing vision

Teachers often assume that routine visual testing ensures the detection of defects, but this assumption is not completely true since absences and other sources of unreliability in routine tests may result in children being overlooked. There are still some local education authorities which do not test children in their first year at school. Moreover, it is important to have several tests during the ten years or so of school since errors of refraction may develop rapidly. Clearly, where testing is less frequent and when children may have missed examination, the teacher's responsibility is all the greater. What is more, the Snellen chart assesses the distance vision which is not necessarily closely related to the near vision which is so important in education.

Snellen charts consist of rows of letters or, for non-readers, capital letter Es rotated in different positions. Each row of letters has a figure at the side indicating the distance in metres at which that row can be seen by a normal eye. The figures such as 6/6, 6/9, 6/12, etc., occurring on medical record cards represent a comparison between the distance at which a row of letters can be seen by the eye being tested (top figure) and the distance at which that same row can be seen by a normal eye (bottom figure). Thus, if at 6 metres the eye being tested can see what a normal eye can see at 6 metres, the vision is normal and expressed as 6/6. If, however, at 6 metres the eye can see only a much larger row of letters which the normal eye can see at 24 metres, it is expressed as 6/24. This would probably indicate that the eye had difficulty reading ordinary newspaper print. The scale runs from 6/6 to 6/60; for vision poorer than this, the eye can be tested at 3 metres. Thus 3/60 means that the eye can see at 3 metres what the normal one could at 60 metres.

Some children unable to discriminate at a distance have near vision which is adequate for reading print. This can be tested by using different sizes of type, and the efficiency of near vision is recorded according to the smallest size of type that the eye can read: N5, N6, N8. N12, etc., where N stands for near vision and the figure for the size of type-size which can be read.

The process of detecting visual defects starts, of course, well before school age. Severe visual defects are normally, but not invariably, noted at an early age and if, as a result of ophthalmic examination, the child is registered as blind, routine procedures follow for providing appropriate help.

Lesser degrees of defect also need to be looked for, since loss of visual acuity may result in retarded visual perception and manipulative difficulties and may have effects on posture and general development. The young child may not be able to describe what is wrong; he probably does not know that he is having difficulties since he has nothing with which to compare his blurred impressions or double images. As noted earlier, paediatricians and health services are making great efforts to detect physical, sensory and other disabilities early, for example, by screening children who were considered on certain criteria to have been born 'at risk'. Sheridan (1969) has developed various procedures for examining the visual competence even of babies and young children by observing the child's visual performance when balls, dolls and toys are moved in their line of vision.

It is clearly important that teachers in all schools should be aware of the signs of visual difficulty, even in children who wear spectacles, and not only in the younger age groups since difficulties may develop at later ages. A variety of signs have been suggested which should lead a teacher to seek further visual examination – it is better to over-refer children than to fail to refer a child who needs treatment. There are signs associated with *visual behaviour*: covering or shielding one eye habitually when reading; thrusting the head forward or frowning when looking at objects; looking with head held sideways; holding reading material at an unusual angle or distance. There are signs indicative of *visual fatigue*: rubbing eyes; pressing a finger in one corner of an eye; excessive blinking, complaints of dizziness; headaches or nausea; tiring quickly or being unwilling to concentrate on visual tasks. There are many signs of *perceptual difficulty* which may or may not be associated with a sensory inefficiency: skipping letters, words or lines in reading; difficulty with details in charts, maps or diagrams; difficulty in copying, writing and other visuo-motor tasks; inability to acquire simple games skills resulting in lack of acceptance and withdrawal. In the majority of these perceptual and motor disabilities, visual defect is not a factor, but the possibility that it may be has to be kept in mind.

Defects of vision

The commonest visual defects are due to errors of refraction, that is, in focusing the light coming through the cornea and lens onto the retina. In *far-sightedness (hypermetropia)* distant objects can be seen with less strain on the muscles of lens accommodation than can near ones. The eye is too short from front to back so that the focus is behind the retina. There is difficulty in appreciating detail at close range and the eye tires in the process of trying to focus. A convex lens is used to correct the error.

In *short sight (myopia)* the eyeball is too long from front to back so that the light is focused in front of the retina which the child corrects by reading close to the page. Greater efforts are needed to see at a distance and there will be difficulty in seeing blackboards and displays unless the child is brought nearer. A concave lens is used to spread out the rays of light and focus them further back in the eye. This condition develops quite frequently in affected children from ten to twelve years of age, and is one of the reasons why frequent eye tests and observant teachers are needed.

In *astigmatism* there is an irregular curvature of the cornea or lens so that light rays do not focus at the same point on the retina. Part of the image may be blurred and may cause misreading of letters and words. The irregularity may also make for difficulty in reading off lines of print vertically or horizontally, e.g. log tables. The correction is a cylindrical lens.

Defects occurring in the *field of vision* can easily go unnoticed. In *hemianopia*, half the visual field is lacking and there may be a tendency for the child to turn his head sideways in order to look ahead; or he may miss out one side in drawing or writing from a copy. In other cases there can be blind spots (*scotoma*) somewhere in the field of vision.

Disorders in the movements of the eyes are of several kinds. A common one is *squint* (strabismus) in which one eye turns inwards or outwards and the eyes do not focus together. Double vision may occur and in time vision in the weak eye may be suppressed so that the condition of 'lazy eye' or amblyopia is caused. In other words the weak eye is providing only some peripheral vision and is not joining with the other in central vision so that binocular vision is lacking. Although this is not a great handicap except for some loss of depth perception, it would obviously be a disadvantage should the good eye be damaged. It is important, therefore, that tendencies for eyes not to move together should be observed and referred for ophthalmic examination. Treatment by glasses, orthoptic exercises or surgery may be needed. In *nystagmus*, the eyes oscillate continuously or jerkily. Vision may be quite good and school learning apparently little affected. But, as with other disorders of eye movement which occur more frequently in handicapped children than with normal children, a small defect added to others can have a cumulative effect.

A variety of diseases and abnormalities cause visual defect sufficient to require special schooling. Only a few will be mentioned here. A number of conditions may interfere with the passage of light through the cornea and the lens onto the retina. The cornea may be scarred (as in keratitis) or the lens may be congenitally opaque (as in cataract). The latter accounts for about 30 per cent of the partially sighted and 20 per cent of the blind. An operation (needling) to make openings in the lens is often successful in alleviating the condition. The passage of light may also be impeded by difficulties in the circulation of fluid in the eye (glaucoma).

The retina, a delicate structure, is liable to a variety of conditions. In high myopia, there is the possibility of its being detached as a result of an accident or sudden movement. Anxiety about this possibility led ophthalmologists at one time to prescribe severe restriction on physical activities in partially sighted schools – a nice example of how a disability can become even more of a handicap – but the present practice is one of caution rather than restriction. An example of how medical advance can have unfortunate by-products is the dramatic story of retrolental fibroplasia. This cause of blindness was not known until 1938; its nature was known by 1942 but its cause was not discovered until the 1950s – an excess of oxygen given to premature babies causing changes in the retina – and by 1955, it had been considerably reduced. A recent survey of blind schools showed 38·4 per cent of children born blind between 1951 and 1955, and only 10 per cent between 1955 and 1960, suffering from this condition.

A number of other diseases affect the retina. In some, there is a loss of vision at the central part of the retina (the macula) by which the eye sees fine detail. There may, however, be no loss of peripheral vision and, in such cases, the individual is not handicapped in getting about and ordinary glasses are not usually helpful – two of the signs which are ordinarily associated with visual handicap. Telescopic lenses or low vision aids (magnifying glasses or lenses in frames) can sometimes improve vision for detail (e.g. reading) by enlarging the image in the eye. In albinism, lack of pigment in body cells results in intense reaction to light and requires the use of tinted glasses.

Another cause of defect is atrophy or damage in the optic nerve – due either to inherited conditions, infection (such as meningitis), tumour or pressure on the nerves (as in hydrocephalus). This accounts for impairment in 12 per cent of partially sighted and 20 per cent of the blind in schools.

Educating partially sighted children

What degree of visual handicap is likely to require special educational help? The answer to this question depends on the findings of an ophthalmic examination which will assess the visual impairment and also the prognosis. But it is also a question for teachers and psychologists, since the degree of *educational* handicap depends on many factors other than the degree of visual defect.

In terms of Snellen ratings, vision of 6/24 or worse in the better eye using spectacles is a strong indication of the need for special educational help. A rating of 6/18 or worse indicates that the child should be considered for special help, and final judgment depends on many other factors. With this degree of defect, the partially sighted child will be able to read and do other school tasks involving near vision, but it is necessary to assess whether his distant vision or his field of vision allows him to profit fully from blackboard work, wall diagrams and demonstrations by the teacher, if any of these are important in the kind of schooling being given. If near vision is good enough for reading ordinary print (e.g. in primary reading books), will he be handicapped later by the use of smaller and less legible print in dictionaries or mathematics books? The kind of school building and its lighting may also have to be considered. If the child's field of vision is very limited, will this affect his participation in the general activity of a modern primary classroom? Such considerations must also be related to the child's ability and the kind of academic work expected of him; it may be that he can manage in an ordinary school at first, but less well later on. Level of intelligence also affects the child's capacity to adapt – the bright child may find ways of coping which the dull child may not. It is important, however, to ask whether the brighter child is simply managing to keep up (and at what cost to himself) or whether much better progress could be expected of him under more suitable conditions. The presence of other disabilities (such as physical handicap, epilepsy, emotional disturbance), the child's personality and the degree of home support and interest are other factors to be taken into assessment. Inevitably, too, it is necessary to balance the advantages of special education against the possible disadvantages of lengthy travelling or residential placement. In general, the aim can be to provide efficiently for a child with a not-too-severe defect in ordinary school, but it is important for the child's progress, happiness and future that his need for special help should be kept under review.

The organization of provision

The small number of ascertained partially sighted children makes it difficult to organize their special education. In large urban areas, there are enough children to warrant special schools for the partially sighted. In London there are four schools and in Birmingham two. In smaller towns, a special class or several special classes catering for infants, juniors and secondary children may be set up. At present, however, in England and Wales there are only eight classes in ordinary schools, seven in schools for the physically handicapped and two in schools for the delicate. In other cases the local education authority relies on being able to place children in one of seven residential schools for partially sighted children, one of which provides selective secondary education.

The organization of partially sighted education illustrates many of the problems of special schools and classes discussed in Chapter 1. The special school is able to provide continuous special education from five to sixteen (and, one hopes, from pre-school ages where desirable). It offers greater likelihood of continuity of staffing and depth of knowledge and experience of the needs of partially sighted children. It also provides easily for an educational progression through the age group. There are, however, the possible disadvantages of segregation and, owing to the small size of many schools, some probable limitations on the breadth of activities and curriculum which can be offered. This is perhaps less true of larger residential schools and in day schools part-time attendance at normal secondary schools for older pupils can widen opportunities. Special classes offer greater opportunities for integration into a normal school and for mixing with other children but, as noted earlier, a special class does not guarantee integration. Classes for the partially sighted in the past have sometimes been unsatisfactory, partly because there may be a lack of the intimate knowledge of the needs of partially sighted children which a special school has, and partly because of the wide age ranges of pupils. As was suggested earlier, special classes attached to ordinary schools have much to commend them ideologically, but it is not a simple matter to organize them well.

The small numbers are even more of a problem in the education of blind children, and necessitates residential schooling. A possibility for the future is combined schools or units for visually handicapped children in which, of course, the educational needs of the blind and the partially sighted would need to be separately catered for. This would be to reverse the process which occurred in 1945 when the blind and the partially sighted were deliberately separated in order to provide a distinctive education for each and particularly for the partially sighted. One advantage of such a development would be that deterioration or improvement of vision would not mean a change of schools. It could be that both groups would benefit from having special educational facilities provided nearer their homes.

The educational and personal needs of partially sighted children

One of the most important advantages of a special school or class for partially sighted children is that it provides an environment in which their difficulties are understood, accepted and allowed for, so that children are less likely to experience the insecurity and sense of strain which would be an additional burden for children already handicapped by defective vision, by slower abilities in learning and by parental anxieties and over-protection. They need eventually, of course, to be able to adapt satisfactorily to the normal requirements of working and living, but are more likely to do so if they have a good foundation of educational progress and harmonious personality growth on which to build. A special school facilitates the regular and frequent visits of the ophthalmologist. Not the least advantage of this is that the teacher and the doctor can discuss the child's vision in relation to the child's education rather than having a purely ophthalmological assessment at the clinic.

It is easy for the teacher in ordinary school to assume that the problem is mainly one of seeing print. It is equally one of being able to see sufficiently well to move and act appropriately in one's environment. Apart from the obvious problems of seeing blackboards, displays and the many different kinds of apparatus in modern schools, there is the use of vision in communication. Much verbal communication is augmented by expressions and gestures and it is easy for the partially sighted child to misinterpret or fail to receive the communication. It is easy, too, for the partially sighted child (like the partially hearing) to be treated with impatience. Being unable to participate in many of the more active pursuits of other children may lead to a measure of social isolation. In the partially sighted school, the effect of these factors is minimized.

In addition, of course, conditions in the special school are adapted and apparatus is available to suit the partially sighted child. Particular attention is given to lighting. An illuminated ceiling provides a high level of light needed for pupils with marked refractive errors and cataracts, but without the glare which would affect the light-sensitive albino children. There are raisable desks to prevent continual stooping over near vision tasks. (Continual attention to good posture is needed with the visually handicapped.)

Large-print books are needed by many children and some progress has been made in the provision of these. But there are many kinds of printed matter which need to be enlarged, particularly at a time when academic opportunities and expectations are being expanded – hymn and song books, mathematical tables, maps, geometrical and other diagrams, knitting patterns, recipes, music manuscripts.

Audio-visual aids have much to offer. Good projectors and television are ways of providing visual experiences which would otherwise be limited; tape-recorders and other audio-visual aids are additional means of communication.

In a large school, it may be possible to provide adequately for full secondary education including work towards academic qualifications but, where this is not possible within the school, attendance at a local secondary school part-time or full-time is increasingly being arranged, supervision by the special school or class teachers being continued. There is, as with other handicaps, a need for after-care, further education and, with a proportion of pupils, for higher education.

Blind children

Just as there is no clear-cut division between normal vision and partial sight, so is there a broad border zone between partial sight and blindness. The most critical factor is whether the child can or will be able to read ordinary or large print or will need to be taught braille. The Scottish report on ascertainment of visual handicap suggests that a child with visual acuity of 6/60 should normally not be regarded as blind; it puts most emphasis on the ability to see ordinary or large print, so that if a child can read N18 with the help, where appropriate, of spectacles or low vision aids, it is normally appropriate to try him in a school for the partially sighted. As with the partially sighted children, many other factors have to be taken into account – the child's intelligence, personality, the presence of other handicaps, and the immediate prognosis for the visual deficit. In Fine's survey of schools for the visually handicapped (DES, 1968), sixty-three of 817 blind children had been transferred from partially sighted schools; thirty-six children in partially sighted schools had previously attended blind schools. These facts illustrate what is not always realized by visitors to blind schools – that blindness shades off from the rather more than half who have no vision, or only some perception of light, through to those on the borderline in whom it is difficult to say whether they should be considered educationally blind or partially sighted.

The educational and personal needs of blind children

The significance of blindness for a child's development depends on many variable factors. In general, a normal blind child who does not suffer from additional disabilities, who is well cared for by parents and is helped to compensate for his sensory loss, is able to develop very much as other children do. Compared with the communication and learning problems presented by profound deafness, blindness itself does not present such severe obstacles to progress. But, as with the deaf, there is a great need for early and continuing assistance, information and guidance to parents through pre-school services.

As we have seen, additional disabilities are frequent complications and another important factor is age of onset of blindness. A child who is totally blind at birth or becomes so before the age of five is different from one who goes blind after five, since the latter has been able to build up basic concepts and an awareness of himself and his environment through visual experience. He also retains some visual imagery. There are also different emotional and educational problems for the child who becomes blind later. For example, the child losing his sight gradually may be unwilling to face up to his disability and is sometimes difficult to teach braille. The amount of residual vision is also a factor not only educationally but in other ways – the child may feel frustration and physical and emotional strain from wanting to make greater use of his remaining vision.

Lack of vision narrows the child's experience to that which can be explored by touch, hearing, movement, taste and smell. Many things such as colour, or distant or very large objects which cannot be experienced by touch, will never be comprehended normally. Very small or delicate objects may be difficult to comprehend and large objects (e.g. cars) must be apprehended by integrating successive experiences of touch. Other important ideas such as number, shape and size have to depend on tactile experiences. A variety of sensory clues which are normally subordinate to vision assume much greater importance and value for making sense of, and moving around in, the environment – perceptions of movement, temperature, texture, sound and smell. An important task, therefore, is ensuring that the blind child is helped to experience and learn through these sensory channels, and that he has sufficient real experience to support the language which he readily acquires through hearing. It is a common enough experience in any branch of education for children to be talking and learning about things of which they have limited experience and understanding and this could happen in extreme form in blind children with the danger of using 'empty' words and language forms. The danger of 'verbalism' is one which teachers of the blind are alert to avoid.

Lack of vision has consequences which are probably even more fundamental for the child's intellectual and personality development – influencing the way the child learns to respond to his environment. The seeing child is continually open to visual stimulation which prompts him to active enquiry and exploration. Touch does not provide this continual stimulation and, though hearing may alert the child to certain aspects of his environment, the meaning of sounds is less easily learnt when listening is not supported by looking. So the young blind child needs to be encouraged and helped to explore his environment. Without this help he may be inactive – many blind babies, for example, do not crawl, lacking the visual stimuli which help to provoke it. If left to himself too much, the child may have recourse to internal stimulation – rocking, eye-poking, odd finger movements – or may be rather passive, falling seriously behind in the development of fine co-ordinations and larger movements. Experiences of being hurt by obstacles is an additional inhibiting factor.

While the seeing child acquires and practises many skills by imitation and assimilates observed actions and events in symbolic play, the blind child receives less information to evoke these important activities. The inability to guide manipulation and large physical movements by vision is another limitation which can affect a wide range of skills from self-help in feeding and dressing to constructive and creative play.

Emotionally, the blind child is, like any child with a disability, vulnerable to unsuitable parental attitudes and anxieties. As he grows older, he has to adjust to inappropriate attitudes in the community as well as his own problems of adjustment as he meets the usual developmental tasks of adolescence and young adulthood. Fine's survey (DES, 1968) reported a high incidence of emotional disturbance. Apart from the doubtful adequacy of the method of assessment used, it is to be noted that an unexpectedly high incidence of disturbance has also been found in samples of normal children (Chapter 3). The question deserves a thorough study.

Many factors affect the social development of blind children. There is the obvious need to ensure social experience with other blind or sighted children and there is the less obvious fact that much social interaction and insight depends on visual cues – observing the reactions of others to one's behaviour or remarks, understanding situations as they occur in play and group activity. And as we have seen, lacking visual stimulation the child may become somewhat withdrawn and egocentric rather than developing sociability and a sense of Self through experience of the environment.

The education of blind children truly begins at birth or as soon as the defect is discovered. Not only do the parents need support, advice and information which helps to avoid fruitless and unproductive anxieties; it is also important that the child's awareness of his environment (which depends so much on vision in the sensori-motor developments of the early years) should be developed in other ways. Perhaps even more important, the relationship with mother and father on which later social and emotional growth is based needs consideration. The seeing baby responds to the mother's facial expressions and gestures; hearing alerts him to her actions and her presence, and vision enables him to see what she is doing and to respond more readily. This important interaction cannot be left to chance. Visiting help is available to families, and the Royal National Institute for the Blind runs a parents' unit where a mother may stay with her baby for a few days having advice and practical help from people experienced with young blind children (Toomer, 1967).

During the pre-school years, attendance at a normal nursery school may be appropriate and beneficial. The RNIB also runs residential nursery schools for blind children (Sunshine homes) which tend to be used for blind children with additional disabilities or difficulties in home circumstances.

At school age, it is desirable for a blind child to attend a school for the blind. Though his broad educational needs are the same as those of ordinary children and though he might manage in some respects in an ordinary school, it is unlikely that he could receive the special attention he needs to ensure his optimum intellectual and educational progress. There is also the crucial question of teaching him to read and write braille. Owing to the small number of blind children, it would be difficult to gather enough children together for a day school, so all the schools are residential. They encourage links with home by enabling children to go home at weekends and links with normal schools by arranging in some cases for some pupils to attend ordinary schools. In the USA a number of ways are used to educate blind children in ordinary schools. Peripatetic teachers may be used to give advice and services to visually handicapped pupils and their teachers. Alternatively, a resource room and resource teacher operating in one school provide help, materials and advice on a regular and full-time basis for eight to twelve children who are taught in ordinary classes but who go to the resource teacher for special help and materials. While consideration has been given to this by teachers of the blind in this country, the very small number of blind children in any one locality and the variety of problems and needs they display would make it difficult to organize satisfactorily.

In 1967, there were only 1,153 children in schools for the blind. This means that for the whole country age groups are rarely more than 80 to 100. Moreover, there is a great variety of needs. Fine's survey of children in blind schools shows that about 20 per cent have a physical handicap, 9 per cent a hearing impairment, 10 per cent a speech and language difficulty and 7·7 per cent have epilepsy. While 18 per cent are above average in intelligence and 59 per cent average, 23 per cent are of low intelligence.

These figures illustrate the variety and complexity of needs which have to be catered for in one small group of handicapped children.

There are nine schools for junior and secondary age children and schools providing selective secondary education for boys and girls respectively. One college provides further education and vocational training, and two centres provide assessment and training when an adolescent's future and vocation is uncertain. Two schools, Rushton Hall for juniors and Condover Hall for seniors, cater for visually handicapped children with additional handicaps – low intelligence, physical, sensory or emotional handicaps. Pathways at Condover Hall is a unit for children who have both a hearing and visual impairment. There may be any combination of moderate to severe impairment in both senses requiring skilled teaching by teachers of the blind and the deaf.

The transfer of responsibility of the subnormal to education will bring another sizeable group into the concern of education. There are about 600 severely subnormal blind children, about half of whom are in hospitals for the subnormal; some at home and attending training centres.

Defective colour vision

Defective colour vision is more frequent than is often realized. It occurs in 8 per cent of males and only 0·4 per cent of females and is determined by a recessive gene. It is not usually associated with other visual defects and is not susceptible to treatment though the affected individual learns to adapt to some extent by associating colour names and discriminations with the hues he actually sees.

Complete congenital colour blindness is very rare and since parents and children may get the wrong impression from the words, it is better to use the term 'a defect of colour vision' followed by some explanation of which colours are affected. The most common deficiency is in red-green vision but there are several variants. The important thing is that there will be uncertainty about discriminating, matching and naming certain colours as they occur in different kinds of material and under different lighting conditions. A common situation is likely to be uncertainty about distinguishing the red and green wires in an electric flex. Close to, red and green traffic lights may present no problem but discriminating the colour in single lights at a distance, such as railway signals or navigation lights at sea, presents difficulty.

The disability is not much of a handicap in everyday affairs. In shopping, the individual can judge what colour of shirt, socks or curtain material he likes but may become confused if the assistant asks whether it is the brown, grey, or green he is going to have. The disability is mainly of consequence in relation to vocational choices. A boy with colour vision defect going into the electrical industry which requires sorting of wires by colour coding, or into rail, sea or air transport would be a danger, and it is essential, therefore, that tests of colour vision should be given as part of vocational guidance. But it would be an advantage if colour vision could be tested earlier than this in secondary schools. Practical work in chemistry can be impeded by uncertainty in identifying the colour of salts, solutions and flames. In botany, no more than embarrassment may be caused from at first thinking that purple flowers such as Campion or Herb Robert are blue until the pupil learns to detect the red element. In science subjects generally, there is likely to be some difficulty in following charts, diagrams and graphs which use coloured lines or codes, or in blackboard work using colour as an important distinguishing feature. It is unlikely that a child with defective colour vision would get as far as selective art education, but he might well be a good draughtsman having compensated by an emphasis on reproducing form rather than colour. According to *The Health of the School Child* (1966), 115 out of 148 local education authorities now undertake routine testing as part of vocational guidance procedures and nineteen arrange for testing of special cases according to career choice of pupils in grammar and technical schools. Testing is usually done by the Isihara Colour Plates. These consist of coloured dots which are so designed that the person with normal colour vision is able to read off a number for each plate. The person with colour defective vision can read some numbers but not others and, according to the pattern of failure, an indication of the type of defect is obtained.

The problem of the child with a defect of colour vision in the primary school merits examination. Coloured number apparatus and colour coding of letters in reading are widely used quite apart from the less critical uses of colour in art, matching cards and colour coding of library and reading books. An incidence of 8 per cent suggests that a class of twenty boys is very likely to have one child and, by chance, several more with a colour deficiency. Using Stern or Cuisenaire apparatus a child would not be unduly hampered. He would be slower to discriminate rods by colour but he would quickly learn to use the more important cue of length. His main difficulty would occur when the teacher asks him to select a named colour, and in other activities dependent on confident colour naming. In other words, the main purpose of colour – quick sorting and retrieval of rods – would be a source of uncertainty. The main benefits of structural apparatus – representing number relationships – would not be affected. The use of colour in reading is more questionable. *Words in Colour* makes use of a wide range of colours for letters according to their sound. The child with a colour defect would be quite confident of some and very uncertain of others. This uncertainty and confusion would be best avoided in such a critical task as reading. Since *Colour Story Reading* uses both colour and shape in its code the confusing effects might not be so great. However, with the child who has a colour defect it would be better to use other methods of teaching phonic generalizations.

Waddington (1965) has described a simple task she applied to 8,755 children aged five to eleven which consisted of asking children to copy with crayon patterns cut out in coloured paper with a matt surface. This task identified all but 8 per cent of children who were found to have a defect when given the Isihara test and these were mostly older children who had learnt to adapt. It is significant that none of the teachers of the children tested knew of any child's defect; this is partly due to children's success in covering up the deficiency, and also partly due to the teacher's failure to observe or realize the significance of children's hesitations about colour.

It would seem desirable that the disability should be detected and known to teachers, but it should be stressed that this should not lead to treating the child as a special case or object of curiosity: for example, testing him out with such questions as, 'What colour is this?' 'Which one is green?' It should be treated in a matter-of-fact way without undue emphasis. Otherwise it would be better to leave the matter alone, allowing the child to make his own adjustments just as generations of boys have been doing with only a vague awareness of their difficulty.

Further reading

ASHCROFT, S. C. (1963), 'Blind and partially seeing children', in *Exceptional Children in the Schools*, Lloyd Dunn (ed.), New York: Holt, Rinehart & Winston.

DEPARTMENT OF EDUCATION AND SCIENCE (1968), *Blind and Partially Sighted Children*, Education Survey 4, London: H.M.S.O.

HATHAWAY, W. (1959), *Education and Health of the Partially Seeing Child*, New York: Columbia University Press.

KELL, J. (1967), chapter in *What is Special Education?*, Proceedings of 1966 International Conference Association for Special Education.

—— (1965), 'Children who see in part', *Special Education*, 54, 4, pp. 26-9.

LANSDOWN, R. (1969), 'What the research doesn't know', *Special Education*, 58, 4, pp. 20-4.

LOWENFELD, B. (1964), *Our Blind Children*, Springfield: Thomas.

LUNT, L. (1965), *If You Make a Noise I Can't See*, London: Gollancz.

MARSHALL, G. H. (1969), 'Detecting visual disfunction', *Special Education*, 58, 3, pp. 21-2.

SCOTTISH EDUCATION DEPARTMENT (1968), *Ascertainment of Children with Visual Handicaps*, London: H.M.S.O.

SMITH, V. H. AND JAMES, F. E. (1968), *Eyes and Education*, London: Heinemann.

WADDINGTON, M. (1965), 'Colour blindness in children', *Educational Research* 7, 3, pp. 236-40.

ten

Physical handicaps

Teachers making their first visit to a special school for physically handicapped children usually find their attention focusing on the variety of physical conditions from which children suffer. Likewise teachers about to receive a fairly severely handicapped child into an ordinary school are likely to think first, perhaps rather apprehensively, of all the problems of coping with the physical handicap. The physical disability must not, of course, be under-estimated and the teacher needs to understand its nature, consequences and treatment, but for the teacher, physical handicap has to be seen as an educational and psychological handicap rather than a mainly medical or physical one. Those who work with physically handicapped children soon find they can view the physical disability in proportion and, as in any teaching task, the main preoccupation of the teacher is recognizing and providing for the variety of children's characteristics and needs.

The presence of physical disability does, of course, demand continued thought and ingenuity to ensure that the child is provided with as normal an experience and education as possible, and is helped not only to cope with any limitations imposed by his disability, but is also provided with the best opportunities for fully realizing his potentialities. One of the advantages of a special school is that it has the staffing, organization and experience for supervising the provision and use of a variety of apparatus such as walking aids, wheelchairs and special seating. It also provides physiotherapy, speech therapy and medical care with the least interruption of the child's schooling and with the opportunity for close co-operation between medical and teaching aspects. Though these differences from ordinary schools are among those most likely to be noticed, the essence of the special teacher's task is less easily observed and defined.

The teacher has to assess how far physical disability affects the child's learning. With some children, physical weakness and ill health affect attention, the duration of effort and the pace of learning. Absence and periods in hospital may mean that important learning has been missed. Disability may have restricted the opportunities for learning through incidental experiences, for acquiring and trying out new mental and physical skills, for exploring the immediate environment and for becoming aware of the wider social one. With some children, involvement of the hands or other physical disabilities directly affect the performance of learning tasks, and in some cases special apparatus needs to be made or provided. In general, however, it is surprising how normal the activities and work of the classroom can be. Many of the special teaching requirements arise from secondary handicaps – speech and communication difficulties; low intelligence; difficulties in perception, thinking and learning; emotional and social immaturities. These are all factors increasingly complicating the learning and teaching of children who need to be educated in a special school.

The teacher also has to consider how disability has affected the child's development as a person. The physically handicapped child is often called upon to display effort and persistence and to tolerate circumstances which we would consider made excessive demands on an ordinary child. It is often a matter of surprise to visitors that a child without arms has learnt efficiently to use his feet, but it is perhaps harder to appreciate the long, continued effort which many cerebral palsied children make in learning to walk or to talk clearly. The way the child reacts to his limitations and difficulties is partly dependent upon his personal qualities. One meets physically handicapped children whose equable temperament and cheerful disposition seem to make it easy for them to accept and minimize their difficulties. Others, no more severely disabled, seem to have characteristics and traits which magnify the effects of their disability. Much depends, as we shall see later, on the home. The cohesiveness of the family, parental attitudes towards the child and his disability, the setting up of reasonable expectations and hopeful but not unrealistic goals are all important influences. The extent to which the child has learnt to make relationships with adults and other children, to acquire a reasonable and appropriate degree of independence and self-reliance and to develop adequate self-concepts are other important aspects affecting the child's response to education.

It is also important to see physical handicap on a time scale. If the disability is a congenital one, development may have been impeded or distorted from the beginning by family reactions and by lack of environmental or social experience, whereas the child handicapped later in childhood has several years of normal development behind him. The child handicapped from birth, however, has had to adapt gradually to his situation. The child handicapped by accident or disease later in childhood has the advantage of a foundation of normal experience in the earlier years, though the shock of sudden illness may in a different way be disturbing and difficult to adjust to. For the congenitally handicapped the shock may come later when he realizes that the goal he was working towards is a mirage – that in spite of his achievements and progress he is still limited vocationally or socially by his disability. Moreover, though the disability remains the same, the handicap may change with age according to the extent that it hinders the achievement of the main developmental tasks of growing up. In some ways it is not as difficult to provide the child with the experiences and opportunities he needs for his development at younger ages as it is to provide for the healthy growth of personality and social competence in adolescence since the tasks of adolescence involve independence and the exploration of a wider environment.

Educational provision

About 20,000 pupils are provided for in schools for the physically handicapped, delicate and epileptic children, in hospital schools and by home tuition. Also about 300 physically handicapped children are in thirty-five special classes in ordinary schools and 141 delicate children are in twelve special classes.

Schools for the physically handicapped generally cater for a variety of disabilities, though there are some schools, mainly run by voluntary organizations, which cater for particular handicaps. The age range is typically from five to sixteen, but more schools are having nursery classes which facilitate an early start to treatment and liaison with the home, and which give a valuable preparation through play and social experience for later schooling. The ability range is also wide: schools need to provide for able pupils who will benefit from academic work leading to secondary courses either within the school or by part- or full-time attendance at local secondary schools, or by going away to a selective boarding school. Schools also have to develop suitable approaches for slow learners and for pupils with special learning disabilities.

An important feature of a school for physically handicapped children is that many adults work together as a team. Beside teachers, staff may include a nurse, physiotherapist, occupational therapist, speech therapist, helpers to bring children from their classes for treatment and, in a residential school, child care staff. Each contributes to the life and work of the school and to understanding and educating children. The *physiotherapist* is concerned with systematic training of movement and posture so that children learn to use muscles in the best and most useful way. This is a long process for many children requiring daily treatment sessions. For example, many cerebral palsied children learn over many years to go through the normal stages of holding head erect, sitting up, rolling over, crawling, standing and walking. Various methods of educating the child's movements and his awareness of movement have been advocated (Cotton & Parnwell, 1967). Some schools have an *occupational therapist* who is mainly concerned with the development of self-help skills and basic motor patterns required for education. Devices and apparatus of various kinds need to be adapted to the child; the child needs training in their use and the teaching staff need to know what the child can be expected to do with them (Rockey and Garnham, 1968). A *speech therapist* is a very necessary member of the team, especially for children with cerebral palsy and those with retarded development.

Regular visits by school medical officers and medical consultants ensure that children's physical condition and progress are kept under review and medical, surgical and other treatment provided. Meeting thus at the school, consultants are able to make their contribution in an educational context rather than purely as a medical matter – some indeed become very interested in the wider issues of educational treatment.

Schools for delicate children were established as open-air schools at the beginning of the century to remedy malnutrition, respiratory complaints and sub-standard health of children suffering from bad social conditions in urban areas. Plenty of fresh air, additional meals, rest and medical care were features of the régime, but in recent years improvements in social conditions and medical treatment have considerably reduced the number of debilitated children and the need for this special régime. These schools have therefore been able to take other children in need of a period of special education – the mildly physically handicapped and those who are educationally backward for social and emotional reasons. Some schools, in fact, have always provided for a mixture of handicaps – physically handicapped, delicate and partially sighted – and some now include classes for autistic and speech handicapped children.

Hospital schools are run by local education authorities in a wide variety of hospitals and cater for children who are in hospital for a relatively short time as well as those whose treatment necessitates a longer stay.

Home tuition is provided for a variety of reasons, severe physical handicaps or multiple handicaps being frequent ones. The work of home teachers has been well described by Seabrook (1966).

The changing pattern of handicap

The necessity for looking at physical handicaps in terms of their very varied psychological and educational consequences is greater than ever before as a result of changes in the kinds of physical handicaps requiring special schooling. In 1938, there were about 33,000 children in special and hospital schools. In 1968, this number had fallen to about 20,000. This was due to a general improvement in child health and welfare and especially to advances in medical treatment which have virtually eliminated some causes of physical handicap. In pre-war days, tuberculosis of bones and joints crippled quite large numbers of children, but in 1967 there were only thirty-one pupils in special schools in England and Wales with this disease. Poliomyelitis, which used to be the second most frequent cause of handicap, has been almost eliminated as a result of vaccination. Weak heart due to rheumatic fever is another disease which has been drastically reduced, and though the number of children with congenital heart disease remains about the same, more of them have been able to attend ordinary schools as a result of improved surgical and medical treatment. A number of other conditions affecting small numbers of children continue to occur at about the same rate (e.g. haemophilia, Perthes' disease, muscular dystrophy), though in some cases improvements in medical care and general management have eased the problems.

The big change is that the commonest handicaps are now congenital ones. The largest group is cerebral palsy in which the motor disability is frequently complicated by additional disabilities – visual, hearing and speech impairments, low intelligence and specific deficits in perception and thinking. The most frequent abnormality occuring in new-born babies is spina bifida, and until recently many children died early in life or were too handicapped for schooling. Improved medical care and surgery in the first few hours after birth have resulted in an increasing number of these children surviving and reaching school age. These children often have additional disabilities (e.g. hydrocephalus) as well as presenting other problems of care in school.

The education of physically handicapped children has thus become a more complex task. It is less a matter of adapting education to normally developing children who have a physical disability, and more a matter of providing an education designed to remedy and minimize the long-term effects on development, learning and adjustment of conditions which have not only been affecting the child's development from birth but which are also liable to have additional effects on the child's capacities for learning in school.

The nature of physical disabilities

Physical disabilities can be considered in the following groups (1) muscular or neuromuscular impairments; (2) skeletal defects; (3) a variety of conditions affecting the child's health, vitality and normal activity. The conditions are described in greater detail in books listed at the end of the chapter.

MUSCULAR AND NEUROMUSCULAR CONDITIONS

Muscular dystrophy is a term covering several forms of an inherited disease in which the muscles degenerate and the child becomes gradually weaker. Beginning with difficulty in walking and climbing stairs, the child subsequently has difficulty in pushing himself up into a standing position; eventually he needs a wheel-chair. The majority of sufferers die of a respiratory disease early in life though good management increases the life span. The educational requirements are to maintain the child's participation and interest as long as possible. Zeiger and Orgel (1969) describe the group characteristics of these children as immature, easily irritated and frustrated, withdrawn, apathetic and lethargic. They tend to be given compensatory fantasies of motion, movement and activity. There is unfortunately little in the way of specific educational implications and in spite of a fair amount of research no medical treatment has yet been found.

Poliomyelitis is a disease in which nerve cells in the spinal chord are inflamed by a virus infection. Recovery can be complete or paralysis of certain muscles may ensue depending on the degree of damage to motor nerve cells. The range of disability is wide and the majority of children are able to return to ordinary schools. Fortunately, the disease is now controlled by immunization and in 1968 there were only 442 post-polio cases in special schools.

Spina bifida includes a number of conditions in which the child is born with incomplete development of some of the bones of the spinal column, so that the normal covering and protection of the nerve of the spinal cord is lacking. There is a swelling usually towards the lower end of the spine. In the most serious condition, spina bifida with myelomeningocele, the cord protrudes into this swelling and is also imperfectly formed. Depending on the nerves affected, there may be loss of sensation and movement in the lower part of the body including loss of sphincter control. A further complication in 70 per cent of cases is hydrocephalus, an enlargement of the head, which is due to interference with the circulation and absorption of cerebrospinal fluid (the fluid which surrounds the brain and spinal cord).

The build-up of fluid causes the skull to enlarge and may cause damage to brain function.

Until a few years ago, the majority of children died fairly soon after birth as a result of infection (e.g. meningitis) or hydrocephalus. The 20 per cent who survived were mostly mild cases with very little defect, but some severe cases were badly paralysed and often mentally retarded or blind. In recent years, however, the spine has been closed by surgery in the first few hours or days of life, reducing the risk of infection. The hydrocephalus can be controlled by inserting a tube into the brain cavity and taken beneath the skin to a vein in the neck so that the fluid drains into the blood and is dealt with in the normal way. A Spitz-Holter valve placed in the tube prevents flow back As a result of these measures, the survival rate has increased to about 40 per cent and a marked increase in the number of children of school age has occurred. Local education authorities have been asked to assess the need in their area for special school places. In addition to provision in schools for physically handicapped children, there are two schools for children with spina bifida and another is planned. Estimates of the amount and kind of need are tentative owing to regional and other variations, but an estimate in London (Spain, 1969) suggests that, of those at present surviving to school age, 60 per cent require special education and about 10 per cent are severely retarded and multiply handicapped.

Regular medical care is needed during the early years, in particular because of the frequency of abnormalities in the urinary system resulting from the absence of normal bladder control. Special care is needed to help the parents and child to manage the problem of incontinence. Physiotherapy is required to assist the development of mobility and to avoid orthopaedic complications. Since many children have limited sensations in the lower half of the body, care is needed to avoid burns, scalds and pressure sores from sitting or from calipers. Educationally, it is important to ensure the optimum academic progress, to develop good self-concepts and generally assist the process of adjustment to the disability.

Cerebral palsy   The term 'spastic' is a familiar one to most people, but this is only one, though the most common, of a group of conditions in which there are varying degrees of paralysis, weakness, or inco-ordination as a result of injury or defect in the motor areas of the brain. The physical disability ranges from a slight lack of control (many such children are in ordinary schools) to complete physical helplessness.

The majority of cases of cerebral palsy fall into three groups. *Spasticity*, which accounts for 70 to 80 per cent of cerebral palsy, is characterized by stiff contracted muscles; the carrying out of a movement is inhibited by the automatic contraction of the antagonistic muscle because the normal cerebral inhibition of the stretch reflex has been lost. The defect varies in severity and also in the muscles involved. In monoplegia, one limb is affected; in hemiplegia, one side of the body; in triplegia, three limbs (usually two legs and one arm); in paraplegia, both legs. In quadriplegia or tetraplegia all four limbs are affected. Educationally, involvement of hands, defective speech and low intelligence are of significance. In *athetosis*, which occurs in about 10 to 20 per cent of cases, there are involuntary and uncontrollable movements so that, for example, the child makes many random movements as he strives to reach for something, and in walking there may be writhing or squirming movements together with facial grimaces. The uncontrolled movements tend to increase when the child makes an effort or is emotionally tense. The degree of disability may be severe enough to interfere completely with movements, or may appear only as a degree of restlessness.

Ataxia affects balance and muscle co-ordination so that the child is unsteady in his movements, may fall easily and walks with a slow, cautious step. This condition occurs in about 5 per cent of the cases. A small number of children suffer from *tremor, rigidity* or *atony* (the muscles are floppy and limp).

The degree of motor handicap varies from severe to mild. *Severely* handicapped have very limited control of arms, legs and hands and therefore have a limited degree of independence. Speech may be limited as well. *Moderately* handicapped children are those who can walk, though unsteadily, and have some difficulty with hand control and some interference with speech. Moderate and severe cases need the therapies and special teaching available at a special school for physically handicapped children. In *mild* cases, the disability may be apparent only as clumsiness or slight inco-ordination. Children with mild handicaps are likely to be in ordinary schools where they need some extra care on account of slowness, difficulty with certain tasks and the possibility of associated speech or learning difficulties. Marlow (1968) followed up mildly handicapped children who went to ordinary schools after attending a nursery unit. Progress was disappointing in a number of cases owing to insufficient individual attention. A further follow-up indicated that children with mild or moderate handicaps who were transferred at age eleven or over settled more easily.

Additional handicaps　The neurological damage affecting movement is likely to have other effects on brain functions so that limited intelligence, epilepsy, defects of speech, hearing and vision are common and indeed may have greater significance for the child's education and post-war school adjustment than his motor handicap.

There have been many investigations of the intelligence of cerebral palsied children and the findings are that about one-quarter are of average or above average intelligence, another quarter are backward or below average, one-quarter are moderately mentally retarded (IQs 50-70) and one-quarter are severely retarded (IQs below 50). These figures indicate the wide range of educational provisions needed and also the extent to which special help for the mentally retarded is a major need.

In general the more severe the motor handicap the lower the intelligence, but this is not invariably so. Some heavily handicapped children are quite intelligent and the Spastics Society has made special provisions for their secondary schooling and further education.

About 50 to 70 per cent of cerebral palsied children have speech difficulties resulting from some paralysis of the speech organs or from hearing impairment or aphasia. It is important, therefore, that speech therapy be available.

Defects of vision, particularly strabismus and nystagmus, occur in about 25 to 30 per cent and hearing impairment in about 20 per cent. Athetosis following jaundice is frequently accompanied by hearing loss. Such children may be placed in a deaf school if the physical disability is moderate, or in one of the special schools which has a unit for hearing impaired children. Convulsions occur in about 25 to 40 per cent of cases.

In addition to these physical and sensory deficiencies it is common to find cerebral palsied children showing specific difficulties in perception and thinking processes; for example, their ability to match or recognize or to copy shapes and patterns is sometimes very much poorer than would be expected for their general level of mental development. Occasionally a spastic child shows a marked inability to copy a diamond. Having drawn one side he cannot find which way to make the next side so that the angle ends up with a little ear or the whole copy as a square. There seems to be difficulty in managing the spatial relationships involved particularly in co-ordinating what is seen and what is done in motor movements – there is a visuo-motor difficulty. Such children are sometimes able to learn to read quite well but have difficulty in forming letters and keeping the right spaces between letters and words. Some of these children have marked difficulty in mathematics, perhaps because their perceptual difficulties hinder the appreciation of sizes and amounts in concrete number experiences. Though the 'spatial inabilities' of some cerebral palsied children have attracted most attention (a useful discussion of these is provided by Abercrombie (1964)), they have other difficulties in perception, attention and thinking processes as described in Chapter 5. Research results show that these specific difficulties occur more frequently in spastics and in hemiplegics. These difficulties occur in some degree sufficiently often to indicate the need for careful assessment of children with a view to providing remedial activities and to giving special help in the educational tasks which are most affected. Accounts by teachers who have done so are Dick (1969); Tyson (1963); Brereton and Sattler (1967).

SKELETAL DEFORMITIES

A number of deformities are congenital, such as *talipes* (clubfoot), in which one or both feet turn down and inwards, or congenital *dislocation of the hip*, in which the head of the thigh is displaced from the hip socket. Both conditions are looked for in early babyhood and treated. If dislocation is not treated early, it may require long and tedious treatment. Curvature of the spine (*scoliosis*) may be congenital or the result of infection or other factors. Infections of bones and joints in *tuberculosis* and *osteo-myelitis* are now less serious and frequent as a result of modern medical treatment. In *Perthes' disease* (osteo-chondritis of the hip) the head of the femur is affected. Immediate bed rest is required and when the child comes out of hospital the hip has to be protected from weight bearing for many months or longer while the bone is being restored. In this and several other conditions, there may be educational consequences from restriction of movement and periods of hospital treatment (though hospital teachers aim to continue education). The sudden discovery of disease, hospitalization and restriction of activity can be a setback emotionally.

Some children have brittle bones which easily fracture. In some the skeleton does not grow properly, as in the dwarf condition *achondroplasia*, in which the limbs are short though the trunk is almost normal.

There have always been a number of children born without certain limbs or with partly formed ones. Between 1958 and 1961 there was a sudden increase in limb deficient children which proved to be the result of the effects of the sedative thalidomide on the developing baby in the early months of pregnancy. About 250 'thalidomide' children, as they came to be known, were born, often with fairly severe limb deficiencies including lack of both arms. A great deal of research and experiment has been put into the development of limbs powered by gas or even by using the minute electrical impulses given off by muscles just before a contraction which can be used where some of the limb is present. Various gadgets have been developed to make it more possible for children with congenital limb deficiencies to be as independent as possible.

More than half of these children are in ordinary primary schools; this is possible so long as there is available any special help that may be needed and advice and guidance on the use of aids. Much depends on the nature of the child's disability, his personality, home circumstances, and the attitude of schools. The special schooling and care of more severely handicapped children has been described in articles by Bruce and Stevenson (1965). A study of the progress of thalidomide children in Scotland by Pringle and Fiddes (1970) shows a normal spread of ability, achievement and emotional adjustment.

A few children require special school placement on account of disabilities following accidents, e.g. head injuries from road accidents and disfiguring burns. The latter are often emotionally disturbed by their experience and their disfigurement. Benians (1970) studied 105 children admitted to Guy's Hospital burns unit, thirty-seven being of school age. The social backgrounds of the children showed an over-representation of immigrant families, broken homes, low socio-economic class and families with five or more children. Of the twenty-three boys, thirteen showed clear indications that they had been seriously disturbed before being burned (insecure, emotionally immature and socially isolated), and in eleven of them the burn was sustained while engaged in experimental activity with petrol or electricity outside the home. Seven of the fourteen girls also showed a variety of disturbed behaviour before being burned. All of the children with extensive burns showed disturbance in the unit, a withdrawn state giving way to rebelliousness and frequent examples of feelings of anxiety, self-blame and misinterpretation of the treatment. Follow-up within a year of discharge showed about three-quarters displaying some signs of disturbance, particularly increased dependence between parent and child resulting from the separation experience and the parent's need to indulge and compensate the child.

CONDITIONS AFFECTING CHILDREN'S VITALITY AND ACTIVITY

A great variety of conditions affect children's performance in school either directly as a result of lowered vitality and restricted activity, or indirectly as a result of absences from school. There may be a need for medical and nursing surveillance at least for a time. Where there is a special educational or medical need, children may be provided for in day or residential schools for physically handicapped or for delicate children. For a number of conditions there are schools catering for one kind of disability, e.g. epileptic children and asthmatic children.

CARDIAC CONDITIONS

There has been a considerable reduction in the number of children suffering from rheumatic fever which often results in damaged hearts and requires extended periods of bed rest and restrictions on activity. The incidence of children with congenital heart disease remains, however, about the same, although advances in heart surgery and medical care have enabled more of these children to spend much or all of their school life in ordinary schools.

Respiratory complaints used to be a common cause of placement in an open-air school. In bronchiectasis, there is dilatation and congestion of the bronchi requiring treatment by hygienic living conditions, avoidance of respiratory infections and other treatment, such as postural drainage, to relieve the condition. Improved medical treatment and better social conditions have considerably reduced the number of children needing special education.

Asthma has not shown a comparable reduction because it is basically an allergic condition of the respiratory system in which there are recurrent attacks of wheezing and paroxysms of difficult breathing. A variety of factors are associated with it – heredity, respiratory infections and various irritants such as dust and feathers to which the child is allergic; emotional disturbance often plays a part. Whether special schooling is advisable depends on a consideration of many factors, particularly the extent of interference with school progress. A period in a day special school for delicate children may help both medically and educationally. In more severe cases a period in a residential school often reduces or avoids attacks, improving the possibility of general progress.

Children with severe *haemophilia* are liable to haemorrhages into joints, muscles, soft tissues and internal organs as a result of knocks or falls which would have no more consequence than a slight bruise for normal children. Apart from being painful this internal bleeding may cause permanent limitation of movement. Prompt treatment with plasma to bring about coagulation is required if these consequences are to be avoided and if time away from schooling is not to occur. In one survey it was found that many boys had lost more than a quarter of their schooling, some as much as half of each term. Since their disability precludes manual employment, it is most important that they should achieve as well as possible educationally by ensuring continuity of education and making up for absences. The problem is well discussed in an article by Britten and others (1966).

Epilepsy. Many teachers have not seen a child having a fit, yet various epileptic conditions are much commoner than is generally realized. A recent report, *People with Epilepsy* (Department of Health and Social Security 1969), concludes from the evidence of recent studies that the prevalence rate is about 8 per 1,000, which would mean about 60,000 school children. Probably little more than half of these are known to School Health Services. The vast majority are in ordinary schools, some in various special schools, and about 650 in six special schools for epileptic children.

Epileptic seizures are synchronous discharges of cell activity spreading through the brain. It is not known why some people are more liable to these seizures. Some affected children have seizures only under certain conditions – feverish illness or emotional upset. Children with brain damage are more liable to them. Fortunately, modern developments in anti-convulsant drugs have made it possible to control seizures so that many epileptic children do not have fits or only infrequently.

In a major fit, *grand mal*, there is loss of consciousness with contraction of the muscles and lack of breathing for a minute or two. The child falls and there is violent twitching and body movements which gradually subside leaving the child limp and sleepy. During the attack there may be incontinence and vomiting. There is not much to be done except to ensure that the child does not hurt himself against hard objects and to loosen tight clothing. After the seizure, sleep is usually required. Some children have warning of the fit in the form of auditory, visual or olfactory sensations or twitching of a muscle.

The discharge is sometimes confined to one part of the brain (a focal fit) and the symptoms may be limited to jerking of certain muscles or hallucinatory sensations without the child falling or losing consciousness. In temporal lobe epilepsy, the child may show confused behaviour, have sensations, or make movements of which he is unaware – walking about the room in a daze, moving hands aimlessly and even more complex automatic behaviour.

One frequent kind of seizure might even be overlooked unless the teacher is aware of it. In *petit mal* there is only a momentary cessation of consciousness; a sudden immobility, a halt in the middle of speaking, a faraway look in the eyes – this might be confused with inattention or day-dreaming. There may be a brief eye-blink or rhythmic movements of the eye-lids. Usually the child does not fall.

The educational handicap is often minimal as can be gauged by the fact that the vast majority of epileptic children are in ordinary schools – their condition sometimes even unknown to their teachers. Anti-convulsant drugs have contributed greatly to minimizing the effects of epilepsy and there has been a considerable decline even in the small number of children requiring forms of special education, though the number attending special schools for epileptic children appears to have remained constant.

The majority of children who still have fits tend not to have them in school and, in any case, are able to engage normally in most activities – except that some, such as swimming, if allowed at all, must obviously be carefully supervised. The general view is that seizures are less likely to occur if children are active and interested and that over-protection and restriction is likely to have adverse effects on the child's attitudes and personality. Where there is any uncertainty about activities, the school health service should obviously be consulted.

The distribution of intelligence in epileptic children approximates to normal, apart from a larger number in the low intelligence groups owing to the association of epilepsy and brain damage. Educational response and progress may be slowed by the effects of sedation, and in some cases, as in petit mal, variable attention and difficulties in concentration must be recognized and allowed for. Hutt (1969) and others have shown that periodic interference with mental activity may occur even though a convulsion has not taken place.

Emotional and behavioural characteristics also follow a normal pattern except that, as with any disability, unwise attitudes and care may result in some emotional unsettlement. The child's own attitude is also a factor. An accepting and unworried attitude by the teacher is helpful and will be communicated to other children so that the child is not hampered socially.

A small number of children with epilepsy are liable to be irritable, restless or aggressive. Behaviour disorders of this kind occur in temporal lobe epilepsy. In the extreme cases, there are symptoms of an underlying brain damage and are often aggravated by additional social and educational problems.

For children whose seizures are not effectively controlled or who have additional handicaps – maladjustment, serious educational backwardness or difficult family circumstances – there are six boarding special schools providing places for about 700 children all told. These aim to sort out the medical, psychological and educational problems so that children can return home, though a proportion continue to school-leaving age.

Epilepsy is a common additional disability in other special schools. Seizures were reported by Ingram in 25 per cent of cerebral palsied children, mostly in spastics and equally in those with mild or severe disabilities. Fine's survey found epilepsy in 5 to 8 per cent of the visually handicapped. In subnormal children, epilepsy becomes more frequent the more severe the mental handicap, though according to Illingworth it is rare in mongol children.

Emotional needs of physically handicapped children

It is often assumed that physically handicapped children are liable to be handicapped in personality and emotional development because of their many difficulties and because of the additional and unfamiliar problems created for the family. One form of this assumption is a traditional 'folklore' view which tends to associate certain personality characteristics with particular handicaps – a notion which is unfortunately perpetuated by, and unconsciously absorbed from, stories and literature. Thus there has been the myth of the epileptic personality. While there is a proportion of epileptic children, especially among those with temporal lobe epilepsy, who do display difficult behaviour, it is generally accepted that there is no particular personality pattern in epileptic children. Unsatisfactory personality development and behaviour, when it occurs, is due to unwise, restrictive, over-anxious methods of management, and, perhaps most of all, it is a reaction to the negative attitudes of fear and uneasiness which the condition arouses in other people.

The urge to make generalizations from experience is a strong one and up to a point is useful since it facilitates attention to aspects which should be noted. Taken too far, generalizations can lead to overlooking the exceptions and the differences between children arising from both their individual make-up and their particular environmental circumstances. But there are certainly characteristics which occur frequently enough in some handicaps to encourage the tendency. It is often noted, for example, that hydrocephalic children tend to be talkative, sociable and uninhibited, e.g. making socially inappropriate remarks through lack of judgment. It is probable that some of these characteristics are related to a degree of brain damage, for these and their other perceptual and conceptual difficulties are found in other brain damaged children. It is also possible that their sociability and their parroting of verbally mature remarks are related to their frequent contact with adults and to their inadequate opportunities for participation with other children. But it is important to remember that all hydrocephalic children do not show these characteristics.

A view was expressed by Phelps in 1948 that spastic and athetoid children showed different kinds of personality traits – the spastics being more fearful and emotionally inhibited; athetoids being not fearful, more sociable and showing stronger emotional reactions. A number of studies have failed to substantiate these impressions. Block (1954) found no difference between the two groups, but did claim that cerebral palsied children showed fairly strong emotional reactions, especially in perceiving their parents as rejecting or ambivalent, in feeling frustrated in their need for independence and for acceptance on equal terms with others. Miller (1958) compared cerebral palsied children and normal children who had been referred to a child guidance clinic, and found that the emotional difficulties of both groups were very similar; so much so that, if the case data were compared without reference to the physical handicaps, it would have been impossible to pick out the handicapped children. Interestingly enough, Miller found that the severely handicapped had less serious adjustment problems than the slightly handicapped. This seemed to be related to the difficulty of parents in accepting and recognizing the mild handicap with the result that too much was expected of the child. The parents of the severely handicapped were more accepting of the handicap and their worries tended to be realistic ones about the child's future. This finding has relevance to the criteria for placing a child in an ordinary school; as is suggested elsewhere, it is not only the degree of disability but the child's personality and the parents' attitudes and expectations which have to be taken into account.

Wright (1960), whose book made a careful examination of the effect of disability on psychological development, found 'no substantial indication that persons with impaired physique differ as a group in their *general or overall development*'. She also concluded that there was no clear evidence of an association of particular types of disability with particular personality patterns. This is not to say, of course, that in individual cases factors associated with the disability do not play an important part in poor adjustment and personality development. One has only to read some of the biographies of handicapped individuals to get an insight into the particular problems of the handicapped person. The fact that these accounts are written mostly by rather exceptional people (in the sense that they were able to write about it) does not invalidate the insights they provide. One thing which emerges from these (and which would be corroborated by teachers' observations of children) is that it is not the disability that determines the child's adjustment but his attitude to it. To some extent this is affected by the attitude of people in the environment, but the developing attitudes, values, drives and motivations of the individual are of primary importance. This is sometimes shown clearly when a child with a marked disability as well as unfavourable environmental circumstances nevertheless does better than similar children placed more favourably. In brief, it is not only the physical disability which has to be assessed : one has to assess what sort of person it is who has the disability.

There are many concepts which are helpful in thinking about personal development and what can be done in schools to promote it. An obvious question is how far disability has affected the satisfaction of basic emotional needs. The need for security and affection is often met very adequately; the majority of parents are very much concerned and have a genuine affection for their child. Obvious or concealed rejection occurs in only a small minority of cases and one wonders how far even this small number could be reduced by better support, counselling, information and practical help in the early formative period. Kendall and Callman report in their survey of handicapped children and their families in the West Midlands (Carnegie, 1964) that, of 221 children studied, only seven were openly and obviously rejected, and in twenty-four cases there was a marked tendency to rejection. The effects vary according to the child – ranging from withdrawal and depression to attention-seeking and aggressive behaviour – and also according to many other factors such as the presence of substitute mothering from grandmother, aunt or friend. There is also the more subtle rejection when the parents do not recognize and accept the handicap. Sometimes the child is liable to interpret situations as rejection because of his 'failures' or parental anxiety. Certainly the consistent and accepting attitude of the school can do much to alleviate these feelings and reactions.

Secondly, there is the need to be accepted by, and be a part of, social groups, first within the family and later within wider social relationships. For all children, the family provides the most important emotional experiences and the effect of these are likely to be intensified in the handicapped child who is more limited in his range of emotional and social experience. Siblings' rivalries are a normal part of family life; Gibbs (1958) records having been impressed by the violent reactions of some handicapped children to being overtaken by younger siblings in certain developments and achievements. She also points out the possibility of the child becoming not a *part* of family life but its *pivot*. A point which applies to schools as well as homes is that children have a need not only for receiving but also for giving. It is easy in the family and in the community generally to think first of what we can provide for the handicapped child, but it is an important human need to be in the position at times of being the giver.

The need for a playmate, friend and later for participation in group play and activities is one through which normal children learn a great deal about how to relate to other people and how to win acceptance. In the give-and-take of social play children learn how to evaluate themselves, to put up with rebuffs, quarrels, failures and to enjoy innumerable successes and satisfactions. Many handicapped children are lonely children, for adult contacts do not fulfil the same purposes. The provision of pre-school experience is to be considered not as a luxury but as an essential if later personal development is to be surely founded. Once children attend school this social need is partly met, but there is still the problem that the child may have no contacts with children in his immediate neighbourhood. At adolescence there is a great need for social experience with normal and other handicapped youngsters. Many special schools provide social and recreational opportunities for past pupils.

Another important set of needs are those for achievement, recognition and self-expression. To be able to do the normal things and to do some things better than other people is important for a child's self-esteem. Hence the pleasure which all children, whether handicapped or not, take in new accomplishments. Most children are able to balance failures in some things by their successes in others and this can be true of handicapped children. However, for some children (for example, cerebral palsied children with severe difficulties in movement and speech) it may be hard to find such achievements, and those they have may have required a long, sustained effort. Clearly an important issue for teachers and parents is how to promote and maintain good self-concepts. One aspect is the child's need for recognition from other children and adults. With the normal child there are countless occasions when recognition and praise can genuinely be given. For very handicapped children, the occasions are often fewer and the achievements are often smaller steps forward. There is also the problem of avoiding too-high expectations with consequent feelings of inadequacy and failure, and, on the other hand, of giving praise and recognition when there it little to warrant it. With some children this is necessary, but others are not taken in. In any case it is difficult to develop positive yet realistic self-concepts in handicapped children as is illustrated by a proportion of children who reach the end of school life with unrealistic ideas about what they can do in the future.

Another aspect of these self-needs is the need for self-expression, not as a diffuse emotional expression (as it is sometimes taken to mean) but as the exercise of personal capacities, the outward expression of thoughts, fantasies and feelings in speech, art, music and constructive and dramatic play. Most handicapped children, denied certain channels of expression, can use others, but, as Gibbs points out, children with multiple handicaps may be very limited in the means of self-expression; possibly some of their restlessness and other behaviour characteristics are a reflection of this. It is certainly a need which schools can do much to provide for.

The contribution of the family

The child's development, his self-concepts and his attitude to his handicap are obviously very much influenced by his experience within the family. The view is expressed elsewhere that more needs to be done to provide counselling, information and practical advice from the beginning so that the inevitable adjustments to a handicapped child in the family can be made with the least strain and unproductive anxiety.

The view that parents of handicapped children display strong emotional reactions to their predicament is frequently stated. There is perhaps a danger of over-generalization with insufficient attention to the wide individual differences and the many factors which are involved. Boles (1959) compared mothers of cerebral palsied children with those of a control group of normal children. While the former certainly showed anxiety, feelings of guilt, rejection and unrealistic aspirations for the child's future, it was also found that the parents of non-handicapped children showed very similar tendencies. Differences were found, however, between the two groups in the extent of over-protection of the child and the greater frequency of marital conflict.

Over-protection is, however, difficult to evaluate. Handicapped children need more help, care and dependence; at what point does this become over-protection? Furthermore, it is necessary to distinguish between over-protection which is a 'natural expression of love and over-protection which is excessive, smothering and somewhat pathological'. Wright (1959) in an article on 'Taking a new look at over-protection and dependence' points out that dependence and independence are not opposites; that as well as learning to be independent, people also need to learn how to be dependent, for example, being able to rely on others, to ask for and accept help. Yet the emphasis in education tends to be on independence. She remarks correctly that while we would not be surprised to see a chapter heading 'Growing towards Independence' we would be rather surprised to find the heading 'Growing towards Dependence'. The fact that a proportion of handicapped young people are not going to achieve the goal of independence on which the community and they themselves set much store prompts support for Wright's plea for reconsideration of the dependency-independency balance and how it can be achieved. She also warns against the over-generalization that over-protection is always negative. In fact, studies of normal child rearing and of handicapped children indicate that where over-protection is accompanied by genuine warmth and is not a reaction to anxiety or rejection, the child's personality traits tend to be favourable ones. This is the kind of over-protectiveness which usually responds fairly readily to realistic suggestions for promoting the next step in independence, especially if actual techniques are explained and practical situations discussed.

The finding of more frequent marital conflict was attributed by Boles to the effort required for dealing with a handicapped child, the child becoming the centre of family life and putting a strain on other relationships. An interesting light on this is provided by a study of thirty pairs of twins, one of each pair being cerebral palsied (Shere, 1956). The parents were found to have better understanding for the cerebral palsied twin and to have fewer difficulties in the relationship. The normal twin was expected to be more responsible and independent than his age and capability would warrant. In this study, there was evidence that the parents did not realize that the normal twin might feel unfairly treated and somewhat rejected. The Carnegie Report of surveys in three areas of Britain into the problems of handicapped children and their families provides much data about this. Kendall and Calmann reporting on the West Midland survey suggest that 'there is a different kind of balance in the family with a handicapped child, a restructuring of attitudes and roles which has implications for all members of the family. In a number of cases we were particularly concerned about the extent to which the handicapped child's brothers and sisters were being deprived of their parents' time and emotional resources'. They were also struck by the crucial importance of the father's role. His active concern and help contributed greatly to the effectiveness of what was done. They considered that out of 221 children studied only seven were openly and obviously rejected by the mother and in twenty-four cases there was a tendency to rejection. On the other hand, their report gives many examples of how parents adapt sensibly and positively to their situation. The need for more information, for guidance about management and for someone with whom parents can discuss their problems was very clear in all three surveys.

In a more recent study in the East Midlands, Hewett (1970) interviewed 180 mothers of cerebral palsied children (aged one to eight years) and obtained information about their problems and their methods of caring for the handicapped child. Comparisons were made with the results of studies in the same area of mothers of normal four-year-olds (Newson, J., and Newson, E., 1968). The general impression from the enquiry was that patterns of mothering tended to be very like those shown towards the normal children in the same family and towards normal children generally, and, where differences in family interaction and activity occurred, they tended to be realistically oriented to the degree and kind of handicap. Nevertheless there are many examples in the report of the extra effort psychologically (and no doubt physically) that mothers make in order to do this. There were only eleven cases where mothers were worried by the behaviour of a sibling, and in half these cases there was some disruption of normal family pattern – father dead or absent, or marital discord. The main problems of the mothers were:

(1) Inadequacies in communication with medical and social workers, so that many parents were not receiving adequate explanation of their child's condition or of ways of dealing with the problems arising from it.

(2) Lack of co-ordination of support from the social services.

(3) Inadequacies of educational provision, especially for nursery age children and for the mentally handicapped cerebral palsied child.

Further reading

ABERCROMBIE, M. L. J. (1964), *Perceptual and Visuo-motor Disorders in Cerebral Palsy*, London: Heinemann.

ASSOCIATION FOR SPECIAL EDUCATION (1965), 'Children in Hospital', Conference Report 1965.

CARNEGIE UNITED KINGDOM TRUST (1964), *Handicapped Children and their Families*, Dunfermline: Carnegie United Kingdom Trust.

DEPARTMENT OF EDUCATION AND SCIENCE, *The Health of the School Child* (1960-1; 1962-3; 1964-5; 1966-8), London: H.M.S.O.

DUNSDON, M. I. (1960) 'Cerebral palsy', *Educational Research*, 3, pp. 37-50.

FAIRFIELD, L. (1954), *Epilepsy*, London: Duckworth.

FIELD, A. (1963), 'The education of children who are incontinent because of spina bifida', *Special Education*, 52, 3, pp. 12-16.

FRANKLIN, W. A. (1960), *The Care of Invalid and Crippled Children*, Oxford University Press.

HEWETT, S. (1970), *The Family and the Handicapped Child*, London: Allen & Unwin.

HUNT, P. (1966), *Stigma – the experience of disability*, London: Geoffrey Chapman.

ILLINGWORTH, R. S. (ed.) (1958), *Recent Advances in Cerebral Palsy*, London: Churchill.

INGRAM, T. S. *et al.* (1964), *Living with Cerebral Palsy*, London: Heinemann.

LORING, J. (ed.) (1965), *Teaching the Cerebral Palsied Child*, London: Spastics Society and Heinemann.

NATIONAL UNION OF TEACHERS (1963), *The Day School for Delicate Children*, National Union of Teachers.

NOBLE, E. (1967), *Play and the Sick Child*, London: Faber & Faber.

SWINYARD, C. A. (1966), *The Child with Spina Bifida*, Association for the Aid of Crippled Children, New York.

WRIGHT, B. A. (1960), *Physical Disability – a psychological approach*, New York: Harper & Row.

eleven

Multiply handicapped children

It has been necessary to point out at many places in this book that children with one major disability are liable to have other disabilities of greater or less consequence. Backward children in special schools and classes are likely to show a greater frequency of minor health deficiencies, speech difficulties, mild sensory or motor impairments as well as emotional difficulties and environmental handicaps. The occurrence of defects of speech, hearing and vision, epilepsy and specific learning disorders is quite considerable in cerebral palsy. Minimal cerebral dysfunctions are possible sources of learning and behaviour difficulties in all groups of children with special needs. It is important, therefore, that preoccupation with the major disability should not lead to neglect of additional ones. This emphasizes the need for teachers to have a broad knowledge of disabilities and to have an understanding of the approaches needed for such common additional problems as low intelligence, maladjustment, speech and language problems, learning disorders and environmental handicaps.

The needs arising from dual or multiple handicaps are sometimes so equally demanding that it is difficult to decide the best school placement – whether a physically handicapped child with a hearing impairment should go to a school for hearing impaired or for physically handicapped children; whether a maladjusted child with low ability and attainment should go to an ESN school or a school for maladjusted children. Decision in these cases depends on which educational need is greater, on the schools available and the kind of help they can give. A number of special schools are able to provide a special class for children with additional problems; many schools (especially for the delicate) are accustomed to providing for a wide range of disabilities.

There are also schools provided specially for children with additional disabilities – for blind children with physical disabilities, low intelligence, epilepsy or maladjustment; for subnormal, maladjusted or physically handicapped deaf children. Several schools for cerebral palsied children include units for those with hearing impairments and others provide for cerebral palsied children with low intelligence. Most of these are boarding schools and there is a case for more day schools or units for multi-handicapped children, able to provide for the variety of treatment and welfare needs and the thorough assessment needed as a basis for education. The idea has also been canvassed of general special schools to include a range of disabilities. This would be especially useful in rural areas with younger age groups, possibly reducing the need for boarding education. But it would not be easy to ensure effective teaching for all the different needs.

Some children with multi-handicaps present problems calling for very specialized provision. Deaf-blind children suffer from a combination of disabilities preventing them from benefiting from normal approaches in the teaching of the deaf or the blind. Their educability depends on the degree of impairment in each sense, the age of onset of deafness and blindness and their mental ability. While some make little progress, others learn to communicate to some degree by using the manual alphabet, signs and the facial vibrations of speech; a few have even reached open employment. Other severe multiple handicaps are combinations of severe subnormality with blindness, deafness or physical handicap. Considerably more attention is likely to be given to their problems in the future – thorough assessment and a period of teaching often indicates unsuspected potentiality or promotes a higher level of personal-social functioning. The Spastics Society has recently opened a school, Meldreth, for severely subnormal cerebral palsied children which aims to provide educational, social and therapeutic work in a stimulating and well staffed environment. The need is also apparent for more opportunities for sheltered employment and services for welfare and care after the end of the school period.

The number of children with multiple handicaps is increasing, largely because of the increased survival rate of children born with severe or multiple handicaps. We are also, of course, more aware of multiple disabilities which were formerly equated with subnormality or masked by the major handicap. This greater awareness of the multiple nature of many children's disabilities has contributed to suggestions that categories of handicap are unhelpful.. Up to a point, it is useful to group children as deaf, blind, physically handicapped, and so on, since there are obviously certain administrative and special educational requirements of each group. Categories, however, can restrict and narrow conceptions of special educational need, and at times can even be an impediment to administrative action, e.g. placement and organization of services. It has been suggested, therefore, that categories could be replaced by a broad concept of special educational need and it would be the function of the comprehensive assessment team to delineate individual children's needs in terms meaningful for their education and care. A functional classification like this would be particularly valuable for the severely multi-handicapped.

One kind of functional classification was proposed by Holt (1957), the child being assessed on nine characteristics: physique, upper limbs, locomotion, hearing, eyes, speech, toilet, intelligence and behaviour. The ratings are from Grade 1 (normal ability) to Grade 4 (complete absence of the ability). For example, Grade 4 under locomotion would indicate inability to walk even with help; Grade 3 for upper limb would indicate the need for complete supervision of feeding, washing and dressing. The complete assessment could be conveniently coded into letters and numbers representing the characteristics and their gradings. Something of this nature which carries information significant for education (upper limbs, hearing, eyes, speech, etc.) or for general care (physique, locomotion, toilet, behaviour) would seem a way out of the inadequacy of our traditional labels – about which many complain. Within schools, it would be an advantage to have a similar system which gave a profile of the individual child's abilities and disabilities in learning – something based on the observation and diagnostic assessment referred to in Chapter 2 – rather than categorizing a child as educationally subnormal or 'delicate'.

Further reading

BURLAND, R. (1969), 'Assessing progress at Meldreth', *Special Education*, 58, 2, pp. 14-16.
GARDNER, L. (1969), 'Planning for planned dependence', *Special Education*, 58, 1, pp. 27-30.
HOLT, K. S. (1957), 'A suggested medical classification of handicapped children', *Arch. Dis. Childh.*, 32, June.
KERSHAW, J. D. (1961), *Handicapped Children*, London: Heinemann.
ROYAL NATIONAL INSTITUTE FOR THE BLIND (1962), *Teaching Deaf/Blind Children*.
WOLF, J. M. AND ANDERSON, R. M. (1969), *The Multiply Handicapped Child*, Springfield: C. C. Thomas.

twelve

Post-school needs

No account of children with special educational needs would be complete without some reference to the transition from school to living and working in the community. All pupils need careful preparation for leaving school and careful job placement, but children with special needs require even greater care as well as services for continuing supervision and further education. A small proportion of pupils who cannot compete in open employment need sheltered employment and a few need provisions for their welfare at home.

The first requirement is preparation at school. In a true sense, all special teaching is a preparation for leaving since the more fully the aims of education have been achieved the better the pupil's capacity for functioning in the community and the wider his opportunities for training and employment. Education includes not only the optimum academic attainments but also the development of social competence, and a stable personality, the ability to get on with others, an understanding of the community and an ability to function in it. Research and experience indicate that within limits, level of intelligence and degree of disability are not all-important factors in adjustment to life and work. Character and personality, adaptability, attitudes towards work and reasonable self-appraisal are examples of favourable chacteristics. Preparation for leisure is important since handicapped pupils are less likely to have friends or to participate in the leisure pursuits of other young people.

Towards the end of the school period, increasing attention needs to be given to specific aspects of preparation. This includes information about various kinds of employment, visits to places of work, knowledge of working conditions and discussion about managing the affairs of daily living – money, transport, communication, social life and leisure. Many books and articles describe the variety of ways in which schools cater for this final preparation at a stage when pupils are likely to be most responsive to the information, skills and attitudes being developed (Tansley and Brennan, 1965).

During the last two years at school, or earlier, careers advisory officers can play an important part not only by seeing individual pupils and their parents but by assisting in the school's programme of preparation. In some areas, there are specialist officers for handicapped children and certain voluntary societies have their own employment departments. Successful assessment, placement, training and continued supervision calls for the co-ordination of advice and information from many sources – teachers, employers, parents, careers advisory officers, social workers.

Considerable thought is given by teachers to this transition to work and there is a strong feeling that further innovations and developments are required particularly in respect of children whose adjustment is likely to be precarious or whose severe or multiple handicaps reduce the chances of open employment. A survey by Matthew (1969) of leavers from an ESN school provides fairly typical results. Seventy-one per cent of the leavers were judged to show complete, partial or qualified success in employment; 23 per cent were partial and complete failures and 6 per cent were considered unsuitable for open employment on account of severe subnormality or other handicaps. Many schools feel that, especially for the 'probable failure' group, it would be an advantage to provide pupils with work experience which could be supervised and used as a more realistic basis for work preparation, for assessment and for remedying difficulties. Unfortunately, work experience is ruled out on legal grounds, and though some schools have gone some way towards simulating work conditions at school, it is not the same. In Chapter 3, mention was made of a pre-industrial training course for ESN pupils who had reached school leaving age but were not ready for employment. For the visually handicapped there are centres providing further education and vocational assessment and the Spastics Society has a variety of resources for further education, vocational assessment and training. Industrial Rehabilitation Units of the Department of Employment and Productivity are sometimes used for assessment of youngsters whose employment potential is uncertain. The Elfred Thomas report on the Handicapped School Leaver (1964) recommended that voluntary bodies and local authorities should be encouraged to establish centres at which the further education of handicapped young people is combined with an assessment of their suitability for training.

For many years, there has been a growing interest in further education for pupils with special needs, since this would provide a longer period for developing attainment, ability and personal maturity and would compensate pupils whose learning has been slow and hampered by disabilities. Staying longer at school is one solution. Part-time attendance at Colleges of Further Education has also been used in some places and this has the advantage of being a new experience, providing a wider range of studies and a supervised introduction to a more demanding environment – including integration with other young people. Some go on to full-time attendance at further education establishments and there is perhaps a case for special provision at some colleges. Children with the most severe multiple handicaps require separate provision. Apart from quite long established colleges for blind and physically handicapped young people, one was set up recently for physically handicapped at the instigation of the Department of Education and Science at Coventry.

The provision of social activities (e.g. youth clubs) also plays a part in the transition from school. Many special schools provide a club for their ex-pupils and this provides an after-care link as well as meeting a social need. In ESN schools, the club often provides further help with basic educational skills – pupils are sometimes more keen to remedy their academic weaknesses after a year or two at work. (Many towns arrange evening classes for poor or non-readers.) It is often found that ex-pupils of ESN schools begin to fade away from school clubs as they become adjusted to adult life, whereas clubs for hearing impaired and physically handicapped young people continue to meet a need which is less easily met in other ways.

A problem which is likely to grow with the increasing number of severely and multiply handicapped children is provision for those who cannot compete in open employment. The problem can be illustrated by a survey of fifty-four cerebral palsied school leavers in 1964. Twenty-one were in employment, six in niche employment and three in sheltered employment. In other words, only 50 per cent were in some form of employment. In addition to the severely subnormal, who in recent years have engaged in useful work in Senior Training Centres, there are children leaving special schools for the multiply handicapped and from ordinary special schools who need sheltered employment. There is also a need for social activities, further education and welfare on behalf of these young people and their families.

Arrangements for the follow-up and after-care of pupils with special needs have been a matter of concern to teachers for a very long time. To quote Matthew (1969) in his survey of ESN school leavers: 'I feel that the root of the problem lies in the abrupt withdrawal of support at 16 years … Many of the failures in my small sample school left school with every promise of a successful career. They met a bad patch, and had an interested agency or adult been there to help or advise, complete breakdown might have been avoided.' Many schools have provided their own after-care informally; some have given one member of staff responsibility for making liaison both with pupils and social agencies. Voluntary bodies provide after-care services for some handicapped young people. With the setting up of social services departments, it is hoped that a more co-ordinated and effective service will be developed.

Further reading

ASSOCIATION FOR SPECIAL EDUCATION (1968), 'The Child and the Outside World', 29th Biennial Conference report (Coventry).

BRITISH COUNCIL FOR THE REHABILITATION OF THE DISABLED (1964), *The Handicapped School Leaver*, Report of a Working Party, Tavistock House, London.

CHAPMAN, S. (1967), 'Assessing the School leaver', *Special Education*, 56, 3, pp. 12-15.

INGRAM, T. T. S. (1964), *Living with Cerebral Palsy*, London: Spastics Society and Heinemann.

JACKSON, R. N. (1968), 'Employment adjustment of educable mentally handicapped ex-pupils in Scotland', *American Journal of Mental Deficiency*, 72, 924-30.

MATTHEW, G. C. (1964), 'The social competence of the subnormal school leaver', *Journal of Mental Subnormality*, 10, pp. 83-8.

NATIONAL BUREAU FOR CO-OPERATION IN CHILD CARE (1970), *Living with Handicap*.

Appendix

Personal Attitudes, Skills and Knowledge	Social and Environmental Knowledge
GETTING ON WITH PEOPLE	
Personal appearance: cleanliness, manners, behaviour, humour.	Observation of people who work together in school, at work, in sport.
Communicating: listening, conversing, telephoning, writing letters.	Understanding people of different races, beliefs and backgrounds.
Friendships: making and keeping. Sharing possessions, responsibilities and interests.	
Understanding others' point of view.	
Entertaining visitors. Running a party.	Rules and conventions at work and in social life.
Routine and rules in class, school and work.	Law and order in society.
Moral concepts.	Justice.
BEING A CITIZEN	
Individual rights and responsibilities – in the family, in class, in school, at work, in the community.	Local study of 'our town or village'. Survey of local organizations. Churches. How people form and run organizations.
Class 'committees' to plan projects or events.	
Holding an election.	Government – local, national, international.
Stories of 'good citizens' in Religious Education and History.	Some current issues in local, national and international affairs.

Personal Attitudes, Skills and Knowledge	*Social and Environmental Knowledge*

INTERESTS AND LEISURE

Survey of interest and leisure pursuits in class or school. Study of knowledge, skills, equipment and costs for different interests. Qualities for successful club membership. Knowledge of (and skills in) indoor and outdoor games and activities.	Survey of opportunities for leisure and recreation in community: clubs, cinemas, theatres, societies, evening classes, etc.
Uses of reading: special reading skills; maps, charts, diagrams.	Bookshops and libraries. Daily and weekly papers.
Sources of information. Discussions: TV, radio, films, record preferences.	Local shops catering for hobbies and interests.
Using and caring for equipment: camera, record players, tape recorders, etc. Planning and costing holidays.	Survey of types of holiday. Sources of information.

HEALTH

The rules for healthy living. Working of the body. Personal care. Clothing and appearance. Physical and emotional developments and changes at adolescence. Attitudes to oneself and others. Knowing one's limitations and abilities. Relationships.	The family doctor. National Health Services. Public Health Dept. Hospital and clinics. Preventing diseases and ill health. What to do when ill.

Personal Attitudes, Skills and Knowledge	Social and Environmental Knowledge

SAFETY

Safety in the home: fire prevention, safety in toys, heating and other appliances. Safety in play, on the roads. Learning to swim. First aid.	Road safety: highway code, speed limits. Safety rules in places of work. Safety in leisure activities. Local services: fire, ambulance, Red Cross, etc.

THE FAMILY

The family. The respective contributions of mother and father. Helping in the family. Family relationships. Discipline and routine. Allowance for behaviour of younger members. What the family can teach. Courtship, marriage and birth. The needs of young children, their development and play. Events in the family.	How society helps the family. Allowances, welfare foods, etc., welfare clinics, helping families in need. Schools and social services. Telephoning the doctor. Talking to officials.

HOME MANAGEMENT

Making a home: furnishing, decorating; simple facts about heating, lighting, electricity, cooking, plumbing, walls and floors, safety. Planning a day's work in the home. Planning meals and shopping. Using and maintaining equipment. Modern fabrics and materials. Tools. Simple do-it-yourself jobs. Practical and creative work. Gardens.	Houses and homes in the neighbourhood. Costs of renting and buying. Shops in the neighbourhood. Shops selling different kinds of materials and household requirements.

Personal Attitudes, Skills and Knowledge	*Social and Environmental Knowledge*
SOCIAL ARITHMETIC	
Wages and jobs. Wage packet and deductions. Budgeting. Methods of saving. Wise buying and spending. H.P. Shopping – amounts and quantities. Time. Insurance. Costs of holiday and leisure pursuits.	Taxes. National Insurance. Rates. Allowances. National Assistance. Types of travel; timetables, lengths of journeys; costs. Banks. Types of communication and cost – post; telephone; telegram; cable. Radio, TV, newspapers.
EMPLOYMENT	
Choosing a job – security, conditions, pay, hours, companionship, prospects. Educational and personal qualities required by jobs. Training and qualifications. Application and interviews. Working life, etc. Qualities of a good worker.	Work-places in neighbour-hood. Working conditions; people at work – foreman, personnel manager, etc. Trade Unions. Y.E.O. Disablement register.

Reprinted by permission from *The Spastic School Child and the Outside World*, Spastics Society and Heinemann.

Bibliography

ABERCROMBIE, M. L. J. (1964), *Perceptual and Visuo-motor Disorders in Cerebral Palsy* (Little Club series No. 11), Spastics Society.

ANDREWS, G. AND HARRIS, M. M. (1964), *The Syndrome of Stuttering*, London: Heinemann Medical.

BALLANTYNE, A. (1966), 'A suggested classification of the causes of dyslexia', *Word Blind Bulletin*, 1, 5, pp. 5-14.

BARRASS, M. (1968), 'The physiotherapist in school', *Special Education*, 57, 2, pp. 6-9.

BARRON, A. (1969), 'The psychotherapist in school', *Special Education*, 58, 1, pp. 23-6.

BARRY, H. (1961), *The Young Aphasic Child, Evaluation and Training*, Washington: Alexander Graham Bell Association for the Deaf.

BELL, P. (1970), *Basic Teaching for Slow Learners*, London: Muller.

BENDER, L. (1938), *A visual-motor gestalt test and its clinical use*, Research Monogram No. 3, American Orthopsychiatric Association No. 3.

BENIANS, R. C. (1970), 'Children with burns', *Maternal and Child Care*, 6, 57, Feb.

BEREITER, C. AND ENGLEMANN, S. (1966), *Teaching Disadvantaged Children in the Pre-School*, Englewood Cliffs, N. J: Prentice-Hall.

BERNSTEIN, B. (1961), 'Social structure, language and learning', *Educational Research*, 3, 3, pp. 163-76.

BIRCH, H. G. (ed.) (1964), *Brain Damage in Children*, New York: Williams & Wilkins.

BLANK, M. AND SOLOMON, F. (1968), 'A tutorial language program to develop abstract thinking in socially disadvantaged children', *Child Development*, 39, 379-89.

BLOCK, W. E. (1954), 'Personality of the brain-injured child', *Exceptional Children*, 24, 94-100.

BOLES, G. (1959), 'Personality factors in mothers of cerebral palsied children', *Genetic Psychology Monographs*, 59, 159-218.

BOWLBY, J. (1946), *Forty-four Juvenile Thieves, their characters and home life*, London: Baillière.

BOWLEY, A. (1969), 'Reading difficulty with minor cerebral dysfunction', *Developmental Medicine and Child Neurology*, 11, 493-501.

BRAZIER, C. (1970), 'Teaching West Indian children', *Special Education*, 59, 2, pp. 6-10.

BRENNAN, W. K. AND HERBERT, D. M. (1969), 'A survey of assessment – diagnostic units in Britain', *Educational Research*, 12, 1, pp. 13-21.

BRENNER, N. W. *et al.* (1967), 'Visuo-motor disability in school children', *British Medical Journal*, 4, pp. 259-62.

BRERETON, LE GAY B. AND SATTLER, J. (1967), *Cerebral Palsy: basic abilities*, Mosman: Spastics Centre, N.S.W.

BRITTEN, M. I. *et al.* (1966), 'The haemophilic boy in school', *British Medical Journal*, 2, pp. 224-8.

BRUCE, M. (1965), 'Thalidomide children at Chailey', *Special Education*, 54, 4, pp. 7-9.

BURDEN, R. (1969), 'A truly comprehensive education', *Special Education*, 58, 4, pp. 11-15.

BURLAND, R. (1969), 'Assessing progress at Meldreth', *Special Education*, 58, 2, pp. 14-16.

CARNEGIE UNITED KINGDOM TRUST (1964), *Handicapped Children and Their Families*, Dunfermline: Carnegie U.K. Trust.

CENTRAL ADVISORY COUNCIL FOR EDUCATION (England) (1967), *Children and their Primary Schools* (Plowden Report), London: H.M.S.O.

CHAZAN, M. (1964), 'The incidence and nature of maladjustment among children in schools for the educationally subnormal', *British Journal of Educational Psychology*, 34, pp. 292-304.

CLARKE, A. D. B. (1970), 'Stretching their learning skills', *Spec. Educ.*, 59, 1, pp. 21-5.

CLARKE, A. D. B. AND A. M. (1954), 'Cognitive changes in the feeble minded', *Brit. J. Psychol.*, 45, 173-79.

CLARK, G. D. (1965) (in Weston), P. T. B. (ed.), *Some Approaches to Teaching Autistic Children*, Oxford, Pergamon.

CLEGG, A. AND MEGSON, B. (1968), *Children in Distress*, Harmondsworth: Penguin.

COHEN, R. S., LAVIETES, R., REENS, R. AND RINDSBERG, B. (1964), 'An inquiry into variations of teacher-child communication' in Knoblock, P., *Educational Programming for Disturbed Children: the Decade Ahead*, Division of Special Education, Syracuse, N.Y.

COTTON, E. AND PARNWELL, M. (1967), 'From Hungary: the Peto Method', *Spec. Educ.*, 56, 4, pp. 7-11.

CRAFT, M., RAYNOR, J. AND COHEN, L. (eds.) (1967), *Linking Home and School*, London: Longmans.

CREAK, M. *et al.* (1961), 'Schizophrenic syndrome in children', *Brit. Med. J.*, 2, pp. 889-90.

CRITCHLEY, M. (1964), Developmental Dyslexia, London : Heinemann.
CRUICKSHANK, W. M. et. al. (1961), A Teaching Method for Brain-injured and Hyperactive Children, Syracuse, N.Y : Syracuse University Press.
DAVIS, RUSSELL D. (1967), 'Failure to have learnt', Spec. Educ., 56, 1, 6-8.
DE HIRSCH AND JANSKY, J. J. (1966), 'Early prediction of reading, writing and spelling ability', British Journal of Disorders of Communication, 1, 2, pp. 99-108.
DEPARTMENT OF EDUCATION AND SCIENCE (1964), Slow Learners at School, Education Pamphlet 46, London : H.M.S.O.
——(1967), Units for Partially Hearing Children, Education Survey No. 1, London : H.M.S.O.
——(1968), Blind and Partially Sighted Children, Education Survey No. 4, London : H.M.S.O.
——(1968), The Education of Deaf Children, London : H.M.S.O.
DEPARTMENT OF HEALTH AND SOCIAL SECURITY (Welsh Office) (1969), People with Epilepsy, London : H.M.S.O.
DICK, A. (1969), 'Training Children at Westerlea', Spec. Educ., 58, 1, pp. 15-17.
DOUGLAS, J. W. B. (1964), Home and School, London : McGibbon & Kee.
——(1968), All Our Future, London : Peter Davies.
DUNN, LLOYD AND SMITH, O. (1967), The Peabody Language Development Kits, Minneapolis : American Guidance Services.
ELGAR, S. AND WING, L. (1969), Teaching Autistic Children, London : College of Special Education.
ERIKSON, E. H. (1965), Childhood and Society, Harmondsworth : Penguin.
FERRON, O. M. (1965), 'The test performance of coloured children', Educ. Res., VIII, 1, 42-57.
FIELD, A. (1963), 'The education of children who are incontinent because of spina bifida', Spec. Educ., 52, 3, pp. 12-16.
FRANCIS-WILLIAMS, J. (1970), Children with Specific Learning Difficulties, Oxford : Pergamon.
FRANKEL, M. G., HAPP, F. W. AND SMITH, M. P. (1966), Functional Teaching of the Mentally Retarded, Springfield, Illinois : C. C. Thomas.
FRASER, E. (1959), Home Environment and the School, University of London Press.
FRIEDLANDER, K. (1947), A Psycho-analytic Approach to Juvenile Delinquency, London : Routledge & Kegan Paul.
FROSTIG, M. (1964), The Frostig Development Test of Visual Perception, Palo Alto, California : Consulting Psychologist Press.
——(1968), 'Testing as a basis for educational therapy', in Loring,

J. (ed.), *Assessment of the Cerebral Palsied Child for Education*, Spastics Society.

FROSTIG, M. AND HORNE, D. (1967), *The Frostig Programme for the Development of Visual Perception*, Chicago: Follett.

FRY, C. (1964), 'Language problems of the deaf', in Renfrew, C., and Murphy, K., *The Child Who Does Not Talk*, London: Heinemann Medical.

FURNEAUX, B. (1969), *The Special Child*, Harmondsworth: Penguin.

GARDNER, L. (1969), 'Planning for planned dependence', *Spec. Educ.*, 58, 1, pp. 27-30.

GESELL, A. (1954), *The First Five Years of Life*, London: Methuen.

GIBBS, N. (1958), in Illingworth, R. S., *Recent Advance in Cerebral Palsy*, London: Churchill.

GOLDSTEIN, H. AND SIEGLE, D. (1958), *The Illinois Curriculum Guide*, Urbana: Interstate Publishing Co.

GORDON, M. AND WILSON, M. (1969), 'Helping the inadequate – a flexible approach', *Remedial Education*, 4, 2, pp. 76-8.

GORDON, N. (1969), 'Helping the clumsy child in school', *Spec. Educ.*, 58, pp. 19-20.

GRAY, S. W., KLAUS, R. A., MILLER, J. O. AND FORRESTER, B. T. (1966), *Before First Grade*, New York: Teachers College Press.

GUNZBURG, H. C. (1963), *Progress Assessment Charts*, National Association for Mental Health.

HALLIDAY, M. A. K. (1969), 'Relevant models of language', *Educational Review*, 22, 1, pp. 26-37.

HARE, E. H. *et al.* (1966), 'Spina Bifida Cystica and Family Stress', *Brit. Med. J.*, 11, 757-7.

HARING, N. G. AND PHILLIPS, E. L. (1962), *Educating Emotionally Disturbed Children*, New York: McGraw-Hill.

HERBERT, D. AND CLACK, M. (1970), 'Meeting parents on home ground', *Spec. Educ.*, 59, 1, pp. 18-20.

HEWETT, F. (1964), 'A hierarchy of educational tasks for children with learning disorders', *Except. Children*, 34, 4, 207-14.

HEWETT, S. (1970), *The Family and the Handicapped Child*, London: Allen & Unwin.

HILL, D. (1968), 'The attitudes of West Indian and English adolescents', unpublished M.Ed. Thesis, Univ. of Manchester.

HUTT, S. J. (1967), 'Children with epilepsy' in *What is Special Education?*, Association for Special Education International Conference, 1966.

INGRAM, T. T. S. (1960), 'Paediatric aspects of specific developmental dysphasia, dyslexia and dysgraphia', *Cerebral Palsy Bulletin*, 2, pp. 254-76.

——(1964), 'Late and Poor Talkers' in Renfrew, C., and Murphy, K., *The Child Who Does Not Talk*, London: Heinemann.

JENSEN, A. R. (1967), 'The culturally disadvantaged', *Educ. Res.*, 10, 1, pp. 4-20.

JERROLD, M. A. AND FOX, R. (1968), 'Pre-jobs for the boys', *Spec. Educ.*, 57, 2, pp. 15-17.

JOHNSON, D. J. AND MYKLEBUST, H. R. (1967), *Learning Disabilities*, New York: Grune & Stratton.

JOHNSON, J. C. (1962), *Educating Hearing-impaired Children in Ordiary Schools*, Manchester University Press.

KAHN, J. (1967), 'Reluctantly to School', *Spec. Educ.*, 54, 4, pp. 27-30.

KEPHART, N. C. (1960), *The Slow Learner in the Classroom*, Columbus, Ohio: Merrill.

KIRK, S. A. AND JOHNSON, O. (1951), *Educating the Retarded Child*, London: Harrap.

——(1959), *The Early Education of the Mentally Retarded*, Urbana: University of Illinois Press.

——(1966), *The Diagnosis and Remediation of Psycho-linguistic Disabilities*, Urbana, Illinois: University of Illinois Press.

LANGDON, J. N. (1968), 'A matter for concern', *New Beacon*, 52, 619, pp. 282-6.

LANSDOWN, R. (1970), *Day Schools for Maladjusted Children*, Association of Workers with Maladjusted Children.

LEA, J. (1968), 'Language and receptive aphasia', *Spec. Educ.*, 57, 2, pp. 21-5.

LEWIS, M. M. (1968), *Language and Personality in Deaf Children*, National Foundation for Educational Research.

LOVELL, K. (1961), *The growth of Basic Mathematical and Scientific Concepts in Children*, University of London Press.

LURIA, A. R. (1961), *The Role of Speech in the Regulation of Normal and Abnormal Behaviour*, Oxford: Pergamon.

MCCARTHY, J. J. AND KIRK, S. A. (1961), *Illinois Test of Psycholinguistic Abilities*, Urbana, Illinois: Illinois University Press.

MCGINNIS, M. (1963), *Aphasic Children*, Washington: Alexander Graham Bell Association.

MARLOW, E., THOMAS, M. AND INNES, A. (1968), 'Spastics in ordinary schools', *Spec. Educ.*, 57, 1, pp. 8-13.

MARSHALL, A. (1967), *The Abilities and Attainments of Children Leaving Junior Training Centres*, N.A.M.H.

MARTIN, E. (1969), 'Children and examinations', *Spec. Educ.*, 58, 4, pp. 25-30.

MATTHEW, G. C. (1969), 'The post school adaptation of educationally subnormal boys', Association for Special Education Conference Report, 1968.

MAYS, J. B. (1962), *Education and the Urban Child*, Liverpool University Press.

MILLER, E. A. (1958), 'Cerebral palsied children and their parents', *Except Children*, 24, pp. 298-302.

MINISTRY OF EDUCATION (1946), *Special Educational Treatment*, Pamphlet No. 5, London: H.M.S.O.

——(1955), *Report of the Committee on Maladjusted Children*, London: H.M.S.O.

MITTLER, P. J. (1968), *Aspects of Autism*, British Psychological Society.

——(1969), 'The Need to end uncertainty', *Spec. Educ.*, 58, 4, pp. 6-11.

——(ed.) (1970), *The Psychological Assessment of Mental and Physical Handicaps*, London: Methuen.

MORGANSTERN, M. *et al.* (1966), *Practical Training for the Severely Handicapped Child*, London: Heinemann Medical.

MORLEY, M. E. (1965), *The Development and Disorders of Speech in Childhood*, Edinburgh: Livingstone.

MOTT, B. AND SMITH, B. (1968), 'Programmes for specific needs', *Spec. Educ.*, 53, 3, pp. 27-30.

MYKLEBUST, H. R. (1964), 2nd edition, *The Psychology of Deafness*, London: Grune & Stratton.

NATIONAL BUREAU FOR CO-OPERATION IN CHILD CARE (1970), *Living with Handicap*, N.B.C.C.C.

NEWSON, J. AND E. (1968), *Four-Year-Olds in an Urban Community*, London: Allen & Unwin.

NICHOLLS, R. H. (1963), 'Programming Piaget in practice', *Teaching Arithmetic*, 1, pp. 24-26.

O'CONNOR, N. AND HERMELIN, B. (1963), *Speech and Thought in Severe Subnormality*, Oxford: Pergamon.

O'GORMAN, G. (ed.) (1969), *Mental Subnormality*, London: Butterworth.

OLIVER, J. N. AND KEOGH, J. R. (1967), 'Helping the physically awkward', *Spec. Educ.*, 56, 1, pp. 22-5.

PALMER, M. (1962), 'Educational problems of the aphasic child', *Spec. Educ.*, 51, pp. 13-19.

PETER, L. J. (1965), *Prescriptive Teaching*, New York: McGraw-Hill.

PRINGLE, M. L. K. AND FIDDES, D. O. (1970), *The Challenge of Thalidomide*, London: Longmans.

PRINGLE, M. L. K., BUTLER, N. R. AND DAVIE, R. (1966), *11,000 Seven-Year-Olds*, London: Longmans.

PRITCHARD, D. (1963), *Education and the Handicapped 1760-1960*, London: Routledge & Kegan Paul.

REDL, F. (1957), *The Aggressive Child*, Chicago: The Free Press.

RENFREW, C. E. AND MURPHY, K. (1964), *The Child Who Does Not Talk*, London: Heinemann.

RENFREW, C. E. (1959), 'Speech Problems of Backward Children', *Speech Pathology and Therapy*, April.

ROCKEY, J. AND GARNHAM, H. (1968), 'Occupational therapists in school', *Spec. Educ.*, 53, 3, pp. 15-17.

RUTTER, M. *et al.* (1966), 'Severe reading retardation : its relationship to maladjustment, epilepsy and neurological disorders', in *What is Special Education?*, Association of Special Education.

RUTTER, M. (1967), 'Schooling and the "autistic" child', *Spec. Educ.*, 56, 2, pp. 19-24.

——(1967), 'A children's behaviour questionnaire for completion by teachers', *Journal of Child Psychology and Psychiatry*, 8, pp. 1-11.

——(1970), 'Autism : concepts and consequences', *Spec. Educ.*, 59, 2, pp. 20-4; and 59, 3, pp. 6-10.

SAMPSON, O. C. (1964), 'The conversational style of a group of severely subnormal children', *Journal of Mental Subnormality*, 10, 19, pp. 89-100.

——(1968a), 'Language for the subnormal', *Spec. Educ.*, 57, 1, pp. 15-20.

——(1968b), 'A real need for re-scrutiny', *Spec. Educ.*, 58, pp. 6-9.

——(1969), 'Remedial education services', *Rem. Educ.*, 4, pp. 3-8, 61-5.

SCHOOLS COUNCIL (1967), *Society and the Young School Leaver*, Working Paper 11, London : H.M.S.O.

——(1968), *Community Service and the Curriculum*, Working Paper 17, London : H.M.S.O.

——(1970), *Cross'd with Adversity*, Working Paper 27, London : Evans Methuen Educational.

SEABROOK, J. (1966), 'Children receiving home tuition', in *What is Special Education?*, Assoc. Spec. Educ.

SHERBORNE, V. (1969), 'Movement education for Brian', *Spec. Educ.*, 58, 4, pp. 15-18.

SHERE, M. O. (1956), 'Socio-economic factors in families of the twin with cerebral palsy', *Except. Children*, 22, 5, pp. 197-9.

SHERIDAN, M. D. (1960), *The Developmental Progress of Infants and Young Children*, London : H.M.S.O.

——(1960), *The Stycar Vision Test*, N.F.E.R.

——(1969), 'Vision screening procedures for very young children', in Gardiner, P. *et al.*, *Aspects of Developmental and Paediatric Ophthalmology*, London : Heinemann Medical.

SHIELDS, R. (1962), *A Cure for Delinquents*, London : Heinemann.

SLOANE, H. N. AND MACAULEY (1968), *Operant Procedures in Remedial Speech and Language Training*, Boston : Houghton Mifflin.

SPAIN, B. (1969), 'Estimating the future school population of spina bifida children within London', *Bulletin of the Research and Intelligence Unit*, Greater London Council.

STOTT, D. H. (1966), *Studies of Troublesome Children*, London : Tavistock Publications.

——(1963), *Bristol Social Adjustment Guides*, University of London Press.

STRAUSS, A. A. AND LEHTINEN, C. A. (1947), *The Psychopathology of the Brain-Injured Child*, New York : Grune & Stratton.

TANSLEY, A. E. (1967), *Reading and Remedial Reading*, London : Routledge & Kegan Paul.

TANSLEY, A. E. AND BRENNAN, W. K. (1965), *The School Leavers' Handbook*, Leeds : E. J. Arnold.

TAYLOR, P. (1970), *Curriculum Planning for Compensatory Education: a suggested procedure*, Schools Council.

THOMAS, D. J. (1965), 'Modification in behaviour', *Spec. Educ.*, 54, 4, pp. 9-13.

THOMAS, E. (1964), *The Handicapped School Leaver*, British Council for the Rehabilitation of the Disabled.

TIZARD, J. (1964), *Community Services for the Mentally Handicapped*, Oxford University Press.

TIZARD, J. AND GRAD, J. C. (1961), *The Mentally Handicapped and their Families*, Oxford University Press.

TOOMER, J. (1967), 'The needs of young blind children and their parents', *The Teacher of the Blind*, 55, pp. 112-17.

TRASLER, G. B. (1963), 'Theoretical problems in the explanation of delinquency behaviour', *Educ. Res.*, 5, 1, pp. 42-9.

TYSON, M. (1963), 'A pilot study of remedial visuo-motor training', *Spec. Educ.*, 52, 4, pp. 22-5.

VERNON, P. E. (1965), 'Environmental handicaps and intellectual development', *Brit. J. Educ. Psychol.*, 35, 2, pp. 117-26.

WADDINGTON, M. (1965), 'Colour blindness in young children', *Educ. Res.*, 7, 3, pp. 236-40.

WEBB, L. (1967), *Children with Special Needs in the Infant School*, Gerrards Cross, Colin Smythe.

WEDELL, K. (1968), 'Perceptual-motor difficulties', *Spec. Educ.*, 57, pp. 25-30.

WEPMAN, J. (1958), *Auditory Discrimination Test*, Chicago : Language Research Association.

WIGHT, J. (1970), 'Testing West Indian children', *Times Educational Supplement*, 30 January.

WIGHT, J. AND NORRIS, R. A. (1970), *Teaching of English to West Indian Children*, Schools Council Report, 2.

WILLIAMS, K. (1969), 'The role of a remedial department in a comprehensive school', *Remed. Educ.*, 4, 2, pp. 69-72.

WILLIAMS, P. AND GRUBER, E. (1967), *Response to Special Schooling*, London : Longmans.

WILLMOTT, M. (1969), *Adolescent Boys of East London*, Harmondsworth: Penguin.

WILSON, H. (1962), *Delinquency and Child Neglect*, London: Allen & Unwin.

WOODWARD, M. (1967), 'Plans and strategies in young children', *Bulletin of the British Psychological Society*, 20, 66.

WOODWARD, M. AND STERN, D. J. (1963), 'Developmental patterns of severely subnormal children', *Brit. J. Educ. Psychol.*, 33, pp. 10-21.

WRIGHT, B. A. (1960), *Physical Disability – a psychological approach*, New York: Harper & Row.

——(1959), 'A new look at overprotection and dependency', *Except. Children*, 26, 3, pp. 115-25.

YULE, W. AND RUTTER, M. (1968), 'Educational aspects of childhood maladjustment: some epidemiological findings', *Brit. J. Educ. Psychol.*, 38, pp. 7-9.

ZEIGER, R. A. AND ORGEL, M. (1969), 'A contrast in educational needs', *Spec. Educ.*, 58, 2, pp. 24-6.

Index